First Tie Your Camel,
Then Trust in God

First Tie Your Camel, Then Trust in God

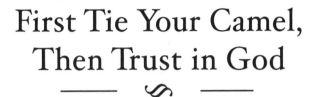

An American Feminist in the Arab World

Chivvis Moore

NORTH LOOP BOOKS

MINNEAPOLIS

North Loop Books
322 First Avenue N, 5th floor
Minneapolis, MN 55401
612.455.2294
www.NorthLoopBooks.com

ISBN-13: 978-1-63413-953-3
LCCN: 2016903910

Distributed by Itasca Books

Cover Design by Biz Cook
Typeset by Mary Ross

Printed in the United States of America

"*First Tie Your Camel, Then Trust in God* is an at times delightful and at times distressing narrative full of insight, humor, wisdom, lament and challenge. Chivvis helps us explore the ways human beings can at once be strangers and allies, students and teachers, guests and guides."
—Pastor Jim Hopkins, Lakeshore Avenue Baptist Church, Oakland, CA

"Chivvis Moore has written an insightful and refreshingly modest and respectful account of her 16-year sojourn in Arab lands, principally in Egypt and Palestine. There she experienced the effects of the Israeli occupation on her own life, and served as witness to its impact upon Palestinian friends, colleagues and neighbors. Her account is as fair and accurate as it is detailed, not dispassionate but tempered always by the human and humane aspects of her experience. Anyone who wishes to better understand Arab culture as well as the experience of the Israeli occupation of Palestine should read this account of Moore's sojourn and acceptance into a culture very foreign to, and misunderstood by the majority of Westerners."
—Marcia Freedman, Former Member of Knesset and Founding President, Brit Tzedek v'Shalom (The Jewish Alliance for Justice and Peace)

"Reading this book was like being able to pass through one of the arched doorways into another world."
—Terry Greenblatt, Advisor, Middle East Children's Alliance

"Chivvis Moore takes us on a striking journey, one that is fascinating, eye-opening, and ultimately heart-breaking—initially as a fresh-eyed newcomer working in a 1970s community in Cairo that most Americans have never seen—to life in occupied Palestine, before and after the 2nd intifada. Living in the latter for eleven years, though always an outsider, Chivvis leads from the heart—earning hard-won bonds of respect from Palestinian neighbors, students, colleagues. Honest, unassuming, and vulnerable, she asks the hard questions."
—*Penny Rosenwasser, author of* **Hope into Practice: Jewish Women Choosing Justice Despite Our Fears**

"I have been reading your beautiful, sad, and deeply moving story, learning a lot of disturbing history about something I thought I knew about but never saw in such depth or personal detail. This is an important memoir that needs to be read and can have a powerful impact. It's timely, original, and written with a painful authenticity. It evokes tears and also some laughter, with a great sense of compassion and empathy. I suspect I'll carry your story in my head and heart henceforward, as so many events of the world today continue."
—*Alan Rinzler, former editor, Simon & Schuster*

"I cried all the way through reading *First Tie Your Camel, Then Trust in God*. The tone, the genuine and honest description of reactions and feelings about the experiences enabled me to truly understand for the first why, as a Palestinian living in the West Bank, I always feel so upset and physically ill."
—*Muna Giacaman, Instructor, Department of Languages and Translation, Birzeit University, Birzeit, West Bank*

To the people of Egypt, Syria, and Palestine

Contents

AUTHOR'S NOTE ON TRANSLITERATION

Arabic words are rendered in English as closely as possible to the way they sound in Arabic.

For instance, the name of the renowned Kurdish leader who retook Jerusalem from the European Crusaders, although sometimes written with an "l," as in Salah al Din and other variations, is rendered in this text as Salah ad-Din. Sufi Street is rendered *"Shari'a as-Sufiyya"* rather than as *"Shari'a al-Sufiyya."*

Exceptions are phrases or names commonly written with the "l," as in Nawal El Sadawi.

The Arabic article "al" is written with an "a" rather than an "e," as in "Al Qal'a" except when mostly seen with an "e," as in "Nawal El Sadawi" and "El Gama'a." The article is capitalized when it begins a proper name. It is attached to the noun with a hyphen when this is common usage.

INTRODUCTION

One evening in early May 1992, a group of friends sat about in a little living room in a ground-floor apartment in an Arab and Turkish neighborhood in Paris. These women were not of Turkish or Arab origin; and most had come from families so long in France that their origins were not, that evening, considered worthy of comment. All were middle-aged. They had gathered to say good-bye to a foreigner, who in a few days would be leaving France for Syria on a one-way ticket, with no plans to return. I was that visitor, from the United States of America.

My destination being Syria, conversation turned naturally to the Middle East. The first question was: of the Arab countries, why had I chosen to go to Syria? The reason, I told them, was that I wanted to live in a country as close to the "heart" of the Arab world as possible. I wanted to live in a country as purely Arab, in cultural and political terms, and as free of Western influence as I could find. These criteria eliminated Lebanon, where I'd heard the

Lebanese might begin a sentence in English, switch midway to Arabic, and finish in French. Nor would it be Tunisia, where the Frenchwomen who had visited there assured me "everyone" spoke French. Of the other Arab countries, I selected those that had fewest ties to the West and had generated a rich and varied civilization going back the farthest in time. Iraq was out; the United States had invaded it the year before. The remaining country, as far as I knew, was Syria. From there, I would go on to Palestine.

The next question, predictably, was: why was I choosing to live in *any* Arab country? A visit—fine, the women said. A short visit, a vacation, or a tour to learn a bit. But, they asked, how could I, a staunch feminist like themselves, stomach living in a culture that abused women so badly, where women were so degraded and repressed. How could I stand the thought of living where women had to suffer so?

The original question—why an Arab country?—did not surprise me, for many people today wonder why a Western woman would travel alone to live for years in the Arab world. I was taken aback, rather, because the question carried a measure of disapproval, possibly even disgust. The implication was that, in going to live in an Arab country, I was "slumming," certainly "politically incorrect." To me it seemed that whether I went or not—and whatever the situation I found—it was as it was. Why, I wondered, in their eyes was it more reprehensible to move closer to Arab women than to stay away?

Today, all these years later, the questions still being put to me are yet more fraught. The main question is the same:

why would I want to live in an Arab country? But now, after the attacks of 9/11 and the US-led "war on terror," there are additional questions. Don't Arabs hate the United States? Don't they resent our freedom? Don't they all want to kill us? Aren't I afraid? Surely a woman traveling alone can't want to live in a Muslim country—considered by definition a misogynist society. And as for Palestine, how could I want to be in a place of bombs and violence and flying stones?

I understand why people ask these questions. I see the same news they watch each evening on television. I read the newspapers they read.

That evening in Paris, I did my best to answer. I had lived in the Middle East before. In 1978, I had gone, as ignorant as anyone could be, to Egypt, and had lived a year in Cairo. I had met and known Egyptian men and women, lived in a Muslim culture, and had loved being there. The experience had changed my life, and I was returning, more than a decade later, to try to understand what exactly had attracted me so—whether it had been Egypt, or Arab culture, or Islam.

To the Frenchwomen of that evening long ago, to other Europeans, and to my fellow US citizens, this book is my effort to answer these questions and others I have been asked. This book is not a travelogue; it, in part, is an attempt to come to terms with the meaning of evil—and its opposite—in the world outside and within myself.

This book is also the story of the ways my inner self was touched by people in two countries, in two different times. The first part describes a year in a Cairo community of thirty-five years ago, where I worked with a master carpenter and was welcomed into his family and into the family of a young architectural student I'd met by chance one day in California. I describe how it felt to enter that world, knowing nothing of it, and what I found in the broad and narrow streets of several different neighborhoods in the city. I show what I loved, what I didn't love, what I resisted, what I took for my own.

The second part of the book is the story of what happened when I lived in the West Bank, from 1997 until I returned to the US in July 2008, after sixteen years in the Middle East. I show what I saw and heard in the West Bank and Gaza, how I was transformed, what I learned.

Although massive amounts of US government funds are devoted to the Middle East, and the US military and giant US-based corporations are deeply involved in these countries, whenever I talk to people in the United States, I find that almost no one knows what life is like in an Arab, predominantly Muslim, society. This book is an effort, however inadequate, to pay a debt to the Middle Eastern peoples who have welcomed me, and to show my own people, through my own story, something of what life in those countries looks like. Much of what I found suggests why much of the world now considers the US government arrogant to other nations and, in many of its trade, political, and military policies, dismissive of countries poorer than ours.

PROLOGUE

Jenin Refugee Camp,
West Bank, Palestine, April 2002

I had come alone, on my own, walking over the hills from my home in Al-Bireh, near the West Bank town of Ramallah, where I'd been teaching English to Palestinians at Birzeit University since 1997.

I had hitchhiked as far as I could, then come on foot on roads closed to cars. I was heading for Jenin Refugee Camp, where Israeli soldiers had bombed and shelled and burned the homes of Palestinian refugees beginning April 3. I was hoping to help deliver bread, baby milk, medicine, whatever people needed; and I wanted to get people to the hospital. There had been rumors of a massacre—hundreds of fighters and civilians—and we'd heard soldiers were not allowing ambulances to take the wounded to hospitals.

Wearing a volunteer medic's tunic, I walked through villages under curfew, and arrived in the camp before

UN vehicles or Red Crescent ambulances were able to get inside. At first, as I walked up through the rubble-strewn hills, which were utterly still and quiet, I saw no one except for a few Israeli soldiers. The camp residents had not been allowed out of their homes for almost three weeks. But several times in the first hour, probably thinking I was a journalist, women flitted furtively from doorways, led me into shattered houses ripped apart and burned by missiles shot from Israeli planes, and showed me charred statues, human remains twisted grotesquely by the heat.

When at last the camp residents were allowed by the Israeli army to leave their homes, amid the awful din of bulldozers digging among the ruins to locate bodies, alive or dead, I walked with young Palestinians wearing vests like mine, who picked up body parts—small ones—a finger here, a toe there, sometimes snatching them from the beaks of chickens, which, like the population, had gone unfed during the weeks of bombing.

Still, even in the midst of grief and loss, humor flashed alongside compassion, especially among the children, many of them homeless now. Gradually, as the days passed, some of them began to play. And so, as I wandered about amid the destruction and debris, searching for someone to help me carry food and water, a mountain of children waved and called to me from the highest point in the shattered landscape, with their posters and Palestinian flags. I waved back and called hello. Then, after a second's scrutiny for strength and height, I called to them again.

"Want to come with me to get water?" I shouted across the distance, as no self-respecting Palestinian adult would do.

"Yes!" came the cry, and the multicolored mountain unformed itself and began squirming erratically toward me. We headed toward one of the two places where I'd been told water could be found—down the hill, outside the camp, in a building in the town of Jenin, where the UN had stored water and powdered baby milk until it could distribute them. For the time being, no vehicles were allowed on the roads, so whatever was to be brought, had to be fetched by hand. The problem was, I couldn't describe to the children where we were going, since I wasn't sure myself. I knew, as our little band headed down the dirt roads under the hot April sun, that finding the place would be a matter of luck. So when the children asked, *"Wayne al maya?* Where's the water?"* instead of answering, I echoed the question in a kind of chant.

"Wayne al maya?"

In the same rhythm, one of the children called out, *"Wayne al bisqueet?"* Bisqueet being a generic term for any sort of packaged cookie, we added that to the chant, and shouted the refrain as we trudged along the dirt roads into the town.

"Wayne al maya? Wayne al bisqueet?" the children sang. As I moved through the camp, and until the day I left weeks later, I'd hear some little voice cry, *"Wayne al maya? Wayne al bisqueet?"*

PART ONE: EGYPT

A man dies when he stops building his house.
Arabic proverb

1 : Coffee and Tea

Books are known to open doors, but I could not have imagined, when I read *Architecture for the Poor* in 1978, that it would open a door through which I would walk so immediately and with such lasting effect. The cover of the paperback showed a series of rounded arches, looking as if they had been molded and smoothed by hand, stretching farther than you could see, in stunning shadows of black and white. Down the side of some great enclosure, light streaming in from outside, walked a man, clad in a long, straight robe, his hands clasped behind his back. That photograph gave me my first glimpse into a world that was to influence the direction of my life from that day on. That world was the world of Arabs and Islam, which, given the way the region has historically been perceived by the West, might seem an unlikely choice for a 1970s feminist tradeswoman.

In the book, an Egyptian architect named Hassan Fathy described his dream of building homes for poor Egyptian peasants, without having to use modern steel or concrete.

Builders in Luxor, south of Cairo, the architect wrote, were already learning from the masons of Nubia, in Upper Egypt, how to build the arched doorways and domed roofs typical of Arab and Islamic architecture by placing mud bricks in a particular way, without having to use under-pinnings of wood. Hassan Fathy had already designed and built a small village in Luxor. The houses were lovely, styled with graceful domes and arches, and they were inexpen-sive, made of the desert floor. To shade the windows, a carpenter—a woodworker, really—turned a length of wood on a lathe, transforming it into intricate jewel-like shapes, which were then separated one from the other and strung, interlocking, within wooden frames.

The result was a kind of wooden latticework that covered the window opening. The lattice simultaneously blocked the desert sun and gave privacy to those inside the house. At the same time, it allowed in cooling winds, and so acted both as air conditioning and as refrigeration for the earthen pitchers of water set at the window's edge. Wooden doors were crafted in designs I had never seen before, made of pieces of wood joined together in intricate geometric forms.

The vision was that these homes would be designed by architects, masons, and carpenters in consultation with the families who would live in them, in what Hassan Fathy called an "ongoing seminar." The mud brick, in addition to being cheap and readily available, served as excellent insulating material, ensuring that the houses would be cool in summer, warm in winter. Each dwelling was lovely, in traditional Arabic and Islamic style. My image of Egyptian art had up to then consisted of pyramids and the paintings in Pharaonic tombs; I had known nothing of Islamic architecture. I had never seen anything so beautiful.

All of this appealed to me. It was the late 1970s, and I was working in the San Francisco Bay Area with a group of other women carpenters. But our women's collective mostly contracted to build or remodel houses for clients with lots of money. I wanted to learn a way to build beautiful housing for people without financial resources.

The seed of that desire was doubtless planted long before my lifetime. I could go as far back as the Irish uprising of 1916 and my family's collective memory of famine and oppression. The seed was nurtured, no doubt, by my having lived in Brazil for three years when I was a child, where I walked to school in the shadow of the impoverished favelas on the hills outside Rio de Janeiro. I was also touched, like many other US citizens of my generation, with the tendency to assume that not only did we over-privileged Americans have a responsibility to try to "change the world" and make it fairer for those without privilege, but also that whatever we chose to do would be useful.

In any case, the thought of moving somewhere new was not daunting. First with my family, then on my own, I'd never lived anywhere for more than a few years at a time. My father, unable during the Depression to find a job in journalism, his chosen profession, worked for an advertising agency in various US cities and in Brazil, selling Ford trucks, Kodak cameras, and Johnson & Johnson baby products. He was a restless man, and my mother was excited to travel and live in new places.

By the 1970s I had found my way from St. Louis, Missouri, where I was born, to Rio de Janeiro and São Paulo in Brazil, to the East Coast of the United States, next to Kentucky, then Arizona, and, finally, on to California. The little I knew about Middle Eastern history and politics came from one excellent high school teacher. I knew still less of Arab culture or Islam. Nor had I participated in any major way in what would turn out to be two of the most important social movements of our generation. I had allowed myself to be dissuaded from involvement in the Freedom Rides and voter registration drive in the civil rights struggle of African Americans in the southern United States by my parents' pleas for my physical safety. And later, I had remained the middle-of-the-road liberal Democrat my parents had brought me up to be, solid in my belief in the integrity of the US government as it waged the Vietnam War.

᜕

But I had inherited my father's restlessness and both my parents' love of travel. And so I was ready, one evening in 1978, when I stopped by the house of a neighbor and architect friend, Jean, to meet the young Egyptian who had given her the book she'd lent me. His name was Halim, and he was a graduate student in the philosophy of architecture at the University of California, Berkeley. He knew Hassan

Fathy, who had written the book.

"What if I wrote to Hassan Fathy?" I asked the tall Egyptian who stood before me in my friend's light-filled, unfinished wooden house in the Berkeley flatlands. He was impressive, intimidating even, in his height, his beardedness, his solid build. He was the first Egyptian I had ever met. "What if I wrote to him, and asked him if I could come and be of use to the project in some way, and learn?"

"He doesn't answer letters," Halim answered. Taken aback, I just looked at him. He repeated: "He doesn't answer letters."

"I'm going to Greece this summer," I invented on the spot, knowing suddenly this would be true. "What if I just went to Egypt, while I was there, and asked him myself?"

"He'd say yes," answered Halim, again without the slightest hesitation, and for the only time that night, his face, his great, bearded, full face, twinkled and shone. "He'd serve you coffee and tea."

I believed him. The next morning, I woke early, wondering: what is an Egyptian morning? And thinking of the stories of Isabelle Eberhardt, who traveled North Africa on horseback, dressed as a man, and seeing hard pebbles in a sandy sea.

2: Arrival

From that time on, I existed as if in an altered state. I never doubted the decision I had taken so precipitously. Not long before, and soon after I got my contractor's license, I had managed to get my heart broken by the woman I loved. The dubious prospect of committing myself to the major undertaking of launching a business, combined with a sense of my own inability to commit myself in matters of the heart, converged to make this seem like a fortuitous time to exit the scene. All my thoughts and actions ran to an unknown future. Exhilarated, excited, I prepared to go.

Two and a half months after meeting Halim, having crossed Europe by train and the Mediterranean aboard the Russian ship *Bashkiria*, I stepped ashore in Alexandria, the Mediterranean city at the northernmost tip of the African continent and Egypt's second largest city.

I had three hundred dollars in my pocket, to last until I could find a job. From other passengers, I had already gleaned some information about Egypt and about Arab culture. An Egyptian woman taught me to say the Arabic expression "Respect yourself!" if I were harassed on the street by a man. An Egyptian who had been visiting his wife in Germany told me, when I asked, what a single Western woman ought not to do in Egypt: "Don't speak to men on the street, except to ask directions. Don't be out alone after 9 p.m. in winter and 10 p.m. in summer. And don't change money on the black market." A Russian passenger living in Cairo told me that I would be able to support myself in Egypt teaching English, that English teachers would be needed more now that Egypt was turning away from her old Cold War ally, the Soviet Union, and toward the United States of America.

I didn't know it at the time, but that circumstance meant that I was coming to Egypt at the end of one era and on the cusp of another. The year was 1978, just before the historic signing of the peace accord between Menachem Begin, prime minister of Israel, and Egyptian President Anwar El-Sadat, on the White House lawn with US President Jimmy Carter. While European countries were happy about the agreement, Arab countries, I was told, were not.

With the death of Gamal Abdel Nasser in 1970, Egypt's promotion of regional solidarity and socialism, including nationalization of the Suez Canal, and leadership of the movement of nonaligned nations in the developing world, came to an end. Egypt had recently suffered a humiliating defeat at the hands of Israel in the Six-Day War in 1967, and another in the October War of 1973. Nasser's successor, President Sadat, would be assassinated in 1981, two years after I'd left Egypt. President Hosni Mubarak, who came after him, would expand Sadat's neoliberal policies, reducing the role of government in the economy, enlarging the private sector, and welcoming foreign investment. In the process, he would bring Egypt into the sphere of influence of the United States and certain US-dominated multinational economic institutions, such as the World Bank and the International Monetary Fund (IMF).

My visit to Egypt came, then, as the light was fading from Egypt's early years as an independent nation, but before it had been eclipsed by the increasing inequality and poverty that would result from policies connected to government corruption and alliance with US-dominated global capitalism (Maher 2011). The Egypt I visited in 1978 was more hopeful, less cynical, than the Egypt to which I would return some twenty-five years later. This fact, in addition to my own general ignorance of political and economic realities, no doubt made my early experience a brighter one than it would have been had it taken place much later.

∽

The morning I stepped off the boat and onto the North African shore, my first impression was of sun so stark that I squinted in the brilliance reflected off buildings of bright white stone. The second impression, just as strong, was of people's kindness.

On a sun-drenched Alexandria street whirling with glittering vehicles that caught and recast the light as the cars spun by, a white-uniformed policeman waved white-gloved hands in a high-walled booth inside a circle of traffic. Wading toward him through the swath of cars, I took out the miniature phrase book Jean had given me, circled the sentence "Where is the railroad station?" and reached up to hand him the book. He took it in one hand and read, but as he lifted his other arm to gesture, pages fluttered out of the paper binding and scattered down into his little booth. Traffic handled itself as he vanished to pick them up, then pointed me in the right direction.

A few blocks on, a young man guided me to a bus, amid the whirl of honking cars, bright light, the smell of dust and, most remarkable, everywhere more people than I had ever seen together at one time. I was passed, hand to hand, bus to train, all the way from Alexandria to Ramses Station in Cairo.

High on a pedestrian walkway near the train station, I must have looked as lost as I felt, for a man stopped and spoke to me. After politely asking if he could help me, and learning where I was from, he asked, "Do you know Ralph Nader?"

"I've certainly heard of him," I said, whereupon he introduced himself as one of Ralph Nader's Lebanese cousins, then escorted me the short distance to the Everest Hotel, which I had been looking for, and which, it turned out, he owned.

The next morning, stepping out into the busy Cairo street, I could not identify the proper bus to take. Which number should I try to read—the one on the front of the bus? the one on the back? the one on the side of the bus nearest the front, or the one on the side of the bus by the rear door? All the numbers were different and all, naturally, in Arabic. What had I expected? I burst into tears.

Instantly, I found myself surrounded by a little crowd—merely to window-shop in Cairo can result in a pileup of people equal to the size of a respectable demonstration in a medium-size US city—none of whose members spoke English. One woman pointed at her own cheeks and shook her head: I must not cry! From this little crisis I was extracted by the sympathetic Coptic owner of a coffin shop who sat me down among the coffins and gave me soda in a green bottle. Someone else hopped on a bus with me, accompanied me to downtown Cairo, and delivered me safely at the hostel I had marked on my map.

By the end of that first day in Cairo, I was hot, exhausted, and overwhelmed. I had never seen a city so enormous or so packed with people. Cairo's sounds were deafening to someone who had been living in the suburban United States: hawkers cried their wares, music competed in tone and rhythm as it blasted from various speakers, and cars honked, as if compulsively, with each of the minute shifts in speed and direction drivers made constantly to avoid smashing into other cars. I was hungry and had no idea what I might eat. I settled on a piece of bread and a hard-boiled egg bought from two sellers in the street. I was delighted to have arrived, but where was I? I dropped onto my bunk in the women's dormitory and did what I usually did when the world was too much: I slept.

∽

The following morning, ready once more for adventure, I set out on my own for the address in Giza that Halim had given me. Giza, some twelve miles southwest of central Cairo, on the west bank of the Nile River, is one of four cities that form greater Cairo, and is most famous for its sphinx and three great pyramids. In retrospect I doubt that Halim, who in Berkeley had generously given me his family's address, would have imagined that I would go there within twenty-four hours of arriving in Cairo, and saddle them with myself and my request. He probably assumed that after I was settled, with somewhere to live and my life in some sort of order, I might pay them a polite visit, bearing some small gift, as an Egyptian would. Nor had I stopped to think what an unusual offer this was. Did I know anyone who, upon meeting a stranger in a foreign country, would direct the stranger to his or his family's home? At the time, however, the thought of going anywhere other than directly to Halim's family did not even occur to me. The morning after I arrived in Cairo, I set out to find their apartment, this time determined to take a bus on my own, without having to be handed in and out like some precious but insensate piece of cargo.

Buses in Cairo thirty-five years ago were the cheapest means of travel and by far the most crowded. To see one of these creatures lumbering up the street, assorted extremities sprouting out of doors and windows and a mound of humans riding perilously on top, called to mind, however incongruously, a many-limbed Hindu deity. Sometimes a passenger or two appeared to be attached to the bus only by an arm, feet scrabbling to find purchase, body swinging in the wind. Then, as the bus pulled away from the curb, a clutch of daring young men invariably dashed out from among the remaining crowd of would-be passengers and flung themselves in the direction of the human mass on the bottommost steps, front and rear, trusting the arms outstretched to pull them onboard. There was no lining up. Invariably, in its wake, as the monster puffed off in a smelly black cloud, left on the street were large batches of the disappointed, who had either failed in their efforts to get on the bus or whose nerve had abandoned them before they'd made the attempt. Meanwhile, those few lucky ones who had made it inside the bus were confronted by rows of already crammed seats and forced to squeeze into the center aisle.

Despite the phenomenal overcrowding and the fact that buses were the only affordable means of transportation for manual and office workers alike, not once during the year I rode Egyptian buses did any other passenger show the slightest resentment of this light-skinned foreigner, obviously a Westerner, by definition able to pay for more expensive transportation. Quite the opposite: every time I rode a bus, people were unfailingly friendly and polite, even protective, despite the fact that I was taking the place of someone who had no other choice of transportation. All this, while I, always the only foreigner onboard, dared to feel proud, considering myself the only Westerner valiant enough to choose the less comfortable means of transportation in order to "mingle with 'The People.'" Only later did it occur to me that my fellow Westerners must have been either smarter than I or more thoughtful of their Egyptian counterparts.

Stepping into any street in Egypt felt like lowering myself into a rushing river. If I allowed myself to float amiably where the stream led, I would be safe, entertained, and supported. There was not a day that year in Cairo that I was not warmed and lightened by the expressions in people's eyes—the middle-aged woman, dressed all in black, who sat on the sidewalk and from whom I bought the English-language newspaper each morning, the tea seller who greeted me with his gentle smile when I passed his shop each day. Countless and precious, such moments kept occurring, day after day.

That first morning in Cairo when I took a bus on my own, yet another of Egypt's seemingly endless supply of helpful young men accompanied me until I found myself aground amid the traffic spinning in an impressive Parisian-type roundabout. There I was offered differing (and sometimes contradictory) sets of directions by numerous people— men, women, and children—to whom I showed the scrap of paper on which Halim had written his family's address in both English and Arabic. Each person peered at the writing and, either unsure of the address or unable to read, carried the little paper over to someone else to study. Each person who could read the paper and who presumably had some knowledge of the neighborhood would then lead me hither and thither with such goodwill that the experience was a happy one, although I ended up several times on wrong streets, and on the correct street at last, still had difficulty finding Building #2.

I was eventually led into the right building. I remember it as a tall, concrete apartment building, with perhaps five floors, three or four apartments on each floor, in a row of other buildings like it. When we stepped inside, the interior was dark. There was no lift in sight, and so my guide led me up several flights in a dark stairwell. On the correct floor, I waited while my guide knocked first on one door, then another, until the last was finally opened, and, yes, it was the right one! I had arrived at Halim's family home in Cairo, less than three months after I had first met Halim.

I thanked my guide and was invited in by a woman of about my age and height, but with the more substantial build and lovely dark hair of an Egyptian woman.

"I'm Chivvis Moore," I began. "Are you Nahid?"

"Yes, I am," came the reply, friendly, but puzzled.

"I am a friend of Halim's, and he sent me to you," I said in English, and then stopped, unsure whether I should have come, since it seemed my name was not familiar. Hadn't they been told I was coming? But before I could experience more than a second's doubt, Nahid reached for my hand and drew me into the large front room.

"Welcome, welcome!" she said warmly, also in English. From the hallway appeared three children, two girls, the elder probably about fourteen, the second quite a bit younger, and the littlest, a two- or three-year-old boy, toddling behind. All wore Western clothes, which I had by then seen were common in the streets of Cairo. The three children came forward and were introduced: the older girl was Heba; the younger, Rania; and the toddler, Ibrahim. I shook hands with all of them, and Nahid led me to a seat on a couch just inside the door, in what seemed a casual and comfortable living room. Nahid sat with me, while Heba vanished for a few moments and came back with glasses of an orange drink. The littler ones stared, looking down shyly when I looked back at them.

"How is Halim? Is he happy?" Nahid asked, and from the way she said it, I knew she loved her brother very much. "When is he coming?"

"Didn't Halim tell you I was coming?" I asked, and the answer was no, he hadn't. In this pre-Internet age, and in a country where telephones, where they existed, were likely to be out of order, the family had received no letter telling them about me.

Regardless, I was welcomed like a queen.

Throughout my first visit with Halim's family, it was clear I was being welcomed as *une amie de Halim* (a friend of Halim's), who had come to Egypt in hopes of meeting Hassan Fathy, the famous architect and city planner whose address Halim had also given me. Yet I was unable to answer Nahid's question as to whether he was *content*, and I knew nothing about his family. I took care to say I had just met Halim and that I did not know him well.

Soon after I had arrived, Nahid's husband, Muhammad, came into the room. We were introduced, and I learned that he worked as a distributor of cigarettes for a US company—Winston. Nahid told me that the two girls attended school, forty students to a class. Even the younger daughter, five-year-old Rania, was going to school part time to learn English. The little boy, Ibrahim, was always with Nahid.

Heba soon discovered that the three of us spoke French—in my case, a fortunate memory from high school, for them, a holdover from the days of the brief French occupation of Egypt. From then on, French was the language she and Nahid and I used to speak to one another.

We talked, of course, about the role of women. Heba brought up the issue of veiling, which in recent decades has galvanized many Westerners, including governments and non-Muslim feminist writers, many of whom assume the custom is not only a patriarchal imposition but also indicative of a regrettable lack of self-esteem in women who elect to cover their heads.

Heba, herself not wearing a headscarf, volunteered that although she and her family were Muslim, none of the women in her family wore Islamic dress. She said she wore jeans with her parents' approval. Women in the cities, she said, had a choice—in dress, in career, in husbands—but women in the villages had less freedom to choose. Some village women came to work in Cairo, she said, as laundresses and maids.

Nahid had many questions:

"What do university professors in the USA earn, and engineers, compared to manual workers—tradespeople—carpenters, mechanics, and the rest?

"What does a government engineer earn as opposed to one who works in private industry?

"What percentage of US citizens can be classified as poor?

"What does it cost a person to attend a state university, and what percentage of people have scholarships, with either loans or total freedom from paying?

"Does a woman professor who works at a university earn as much as a male professor?

"What percentage do women earn in all professions as compared to men?"

I answered her questions as well as I could, very much aware that these last two were questions that Second Wave feminists in 1970s USA had only recently begun addressing.

In striking contrast to the Western image of the helpless, unthinking, beaten-down Arab woman, Nahid was a natural homegrown feminist, the first of the many women I met during my years in the Arab world whom I respected and admired for the strength, inner fortitude, and self-esteem that I came to see as characteristic of Arab women.

In Egypt in 1978, as today, most women had harder lives than women in the USA. They were poorer, had less opportunity for education, and did more physical work, without the aid of washing machines and dryers, gas stoves, and dishwashers. In Egypt, fewer families had cars than families in the US; shopping was more difficult, traffic and stores more congested, buildings had no lifts. . . . Egyptian women confronted the whole array of challenges that all women, except the wealthy, have to face—having to work outside the home and yet do all the work inside the home as well.

"The life of a woman in Egypt is *dûr* [hard]," Nahid said.

But from Nahid and the other Egyptian women I met, I got the distinct impression they valued and respected themselves more than I or many women in my own society did. With freedoms more limited than those of women in the USA, Egyptian women, it seemed to me, nevertheless carried their heads more proudly, seemed surer of themselves, and appeared more comfortable in their own bodies. I wondered if we in the USA had to a greater extent internalized our oppression than women who had far less freedom of choice than we.

When I met her, Nahid was taking time off, due to a bad back, from her job at a bank. Even so, she worked at home every day, cleaning the apartment, cooking, hanging loads of laundry, and shopping for her own family and two of her unmarried brothers, who shared the apartment with Nahid, her husband, and their children. The apartment in Giza, I learned, belonged to Nahid's and her brothers' parents. Their mother had died the year before, and their father six years earlier.

When Nahid admitted that her back hurt and that she had been resting when I arrived, I offered to stay with Ibrahim one day, but she wouldn't hear of it: "Oh no! You have come to see the old things."

She served me dates and later Coca-Cola with ice cream in it. Little Ibrahim kept offering more, while Rania read her English book. Nahid showed me Heba's room and invited me to stay there with her if I found nowhere else after my stay at the hostel was over.

Nahid and I spoke of the USA, which she referred to as "America," as do most people in the Middle East and in many other developing countries.

"To call the USA 'America' feels unfair to all the other countries of the two American continents, like Mexico, El Salvador, Venezuela, and all the others," I tried to explain. "People in those countries resent being lumped with us, as if their nations were just territories or colonies, or some other appendage of the USA. Even to call the United States of America 'the US' is to ignore Brazil, formally the United States of Brazil." Yet I find myself doing the same.

At one point I commented that many of the goods imported from the USA by other countries seemed to be *toujours les choses bizarres* (always strange things), like war toys and odd T-shirts like the one little Ibrahim was wearing, which read, "What's up, Doc?"

"That T-shirt was made in Egypt," Nahid told me; and Heba added, "There are shirts made in Egypt with Elvis Presley on them."

This took me aback—*Egyptians make T-shirts!*

"These are not the kind of shirts I expected to see in Egypt," I said, "especially decorated with US cartoon figures and rock stars." It was my first inkling of the popularity abroad of aspects of US culture that I would not have thought would appeal to people whose cultures seemed so much richer than mine.

Before I left that first day, Nahid said that she and her husband would pick me up at the hostel the next morning to drive me to meet Hassan Fathy. I protested—but only weakly—for I knew that if she and her husband did not escort me, other strangers would.

"It's *un plaisir*," she insisted, "because it's for *une amie de* Halim."

3: THE CITADEL

The very next day, in Muhammad's white car carrying the big red WINSTON sign on the side, I rode with Nahid, Muhammad, Heba, and Ibrahim through parts of Cairo I'd not yet seen. It was odd to be on the demon end of the street battle that seemed to rage day and night, guerrilla-style, between motor vehicles and pedestrians.

At one point, Muhammad backed the car into a tiny alley, and the bumper upset a chair. The accident could hardly have been prevented, given the contrast between the size of the car, modest as it was, and the narrow unpaved lanes we traveled. Everywhere we saw outdoor markets, street vendors, people sitting outside their tiny shops, tables and chairs overflowing small eating places. I saw women veiled—not in the gauzy black see-through veils I'd seen in Latakia, Syria, when our boat stopped there, but—more shocking to me—even more covered, only their eyes visible from between two pieces of thick white cloth.

"Nuns?" I asked. "Are they nuns?"

"No, no," Nahid said. "Most women who veil themselves in this way are from the more religiously conservative states on the Arabian Peninsula—Saudi Arabia, Kuwait, and the others."

Never having spent any time in the Gulf countries, I found the unaccustomed sight somewhat chilling— women without heads. Ghosts? Robbers? Are these the connotations the clothing brings to mind? I think the foreign reaction comes from our own inability to understand how a woman could consider it a positive act to hide herself away.

What surprised me those first days in Cairo was finding women living in the same city dressing so differently from one another. Some women, like Nahid and Heba, wore no head covering at all and clothes no different from anything worn by most Euro-ethnic women in the United States. Other women wore Western clothing, but with the addition of headscarves. Still other women wore headscarves and hid the shapes of their bodies with an ankle-length coat, still looking more Western than what I thought of as Eastern. And then there were the most conservative women, who covered their faces except for their eyes and hid their forms completely in flowing robes. I could not with any accuracy generalize about Muslim women's dress, much less understand what the variations meant to different Muslim women.

∽

At last, after much asking of directions and many zigzags in our route, we reached what Heba called the "mountains" that rose steeply at the end of the plain. Growing from them was a mighty cream-colored mosque, with a great dome and tall towers, atop the great rock mountain, and walled all around.

"*Al Qal'a*," said Heba, then translated for me, "The Citadel."

This was the Citadel of Salah ad-Din (known in the West as Saladin), the Kurdish ruler and founder of the Ayyubid dynasty who had fortified the structure in the twelfth century to protect it from the Crusaders. I mostly heard it referred to as the Muhammad Ali Citadel, so named for the distinctive domed mosque built by Muhammad Ali, the Ottoman ruler of Egypt in the early nineteenth century. Unlike the pyramids and the sphinx, this architectural marvel had not been imprinted on my mind from pictures, and was therefore all the more amazing.

The closer we came, the more intriguing the sights, accentuated by the contrasts that were everywhere in Cairo—some of the old buildings crumbling in decay, and next to them, others standing strong and beautiful. We drove through streets of sand at the foot of the rock, barely missing pedestrians, asking directions at every turn, told first to go one way, then another. Finally Muhammad parked the car at the foot of a stairway, and we climbed worn stairs, passed through a doorway, and stepped into corridors rounded with white plaster. A man in robes, who lay on a mat, apparently sleeping, outside a doorway, rose when he saw us and directed us up even more flights of steep stairs. A wondrous experience, climbing and climbing, turning sharply through these corridors.

"*Une aventure!*" I exclaimed, and saw that Nahid appeared to be enjoying it as much as I. "Did the man say Fathy is home?"

"Yes!"

The door at the top of the stairs was opened by a woman with her arm in a cast. Her arm had been broken, we learned, *dans l'autobus* (as she was trying to get on a bus). We were led into a spacious room comfortably furnished with pillow-covered wooden benches, a few chairs, and a table, at which sat a young woman and Dr. Fathy, whom I could not mistake, his mottled skin and short stature just as Jean, my architect friend, had described. Born in 1900, he was seventy-eight years old when we met.

He looked openhearted and calm despite our five new presences interrupting what was obviously an interview. We were offered seats and hot coffee—what I thought of as "Turkish" but which was in fact Arabic coffee—with at least two extra cups appearing, in case, I supposed, more of us appeared. Nahid motioned for me to sit beside the man himself, while the others scattered round.

Hassan Fathy shook hands with us all, obviously enjoying the children, and interrupting himself several times during the discussion to joke or laugh with one or the other of them. No sooner had we drunk the coffee than tea was brought, and cakes. I realized that Halim had not been using a figure of speech: Hassan Fathy was in fact offering us *both* coffee and tea. Impressed by his graciousness, his ability to absorb all the newcomers without a sign of tension or dis-ease, I waited as he continued his conversation with the Frenchwoman.

He was describing, as I would find he often did, to visitors from across the world, the Institute, which at that time was still a dream. It would be a gathering of everyone who had a part in building—architects, engineers, carpenters, masons, all working together. He said that the houses the Institute would build would not be of mud alone. Windows and doors would be of wood. A Russian study had confirmed his view that wood is the best material, while steel and concrete are the worst. Trees, he said, are natural conductors of light and nutrition. As for mud, the study had not specified, but he guessed it fell somewhere in between.

"The main door of each house must open not into the street but be set off by passageways, because the Arab house turns inward, away from the harshness of the environment," he said. "And in addition to beauty and utility, the house must have humanity."

When at last Nahid said we must leave soon because her husband had to go to work, I asked Dr. Fathy if I might meet him another time, or stay and speak to him after he had finished with his French guest. But immediately, he turned his attention to me and so I explained my mission, showing him the photo album with photographs of some of the work the other women carpenters and I had done in the United States.

"I've come here to ask you if there's any way I might be of use to your project," I said.

Gently, Hassan Fathy told me that all his current projects were still in the planning stages. At present, he said, he was seeking funding. The village he had built at Gourna, near the city of Luxor, south of Cairo, was standing, and I would see it, but he had no actual construction work at present.

"But—" I began.

"Yes," Dr. Fathy assured me, "there will be a place for you in the Institute. How long can you stay in Egypt?"

"As long as it takes to learn. Probably about a year," I said. "I have some money, and when that is gone, I can teach English to support myself."

"Well, then," he said, "we must get you work immediately."

Get me work immediately? I was stunned. Hassan Fathy would find me work until the Institute could be built? I could hardly believe what I'd heard. When foreigners come to the US, no one offers to find them jobs! He thought a moment, and his next words astonished me yet more. There was a young man, a carpenter, he said, who was working at the time in Alexandria, but who would be returning soon to work in his father's woodworking shop in Cairo.

"You might work with him," he said.

By then I had seen the incredible doors on the mosques and other buildings, spectacularly beautiful and unlike any I had ever seen, made of small pieces of wood set in Islamic designs and fitted together without glue or nails. The wood used was of small pieces, Hassan Fathy explained, because Egypt had few trees. Dovetailing each piece to the others ensured that the wood could expand in summer heat and contract in winter cold in a way a large wooden panel could not, thus keeping the doors from warping. On some of the doors I'd seen, the wooden pieces were individually carved and inlaid with ivory.

So the gorgeous doors I had been admiring, or some variation on them, were the very kind Dr. Fathy would include in the houses he designed, and the kind I would learn to build. The intricate woodworking involved in making the doors was an entirely different craft from the one I had come to Egypt to learn, but it was work, I knew, that I was more suited to do than working with mud brick. I knew I would love it.

How different this was from the way things worked in the United States, where I had been refused at seventy-six job sites before I got my first job as a union carpenter!

"Come back Thursday afternoon at one," Hassan Fathy said. "By then the young man should be back in town." He waved away my thanks as if he had done the most natural thing possible.

Astounded, grateful, I took my leave and floated down the stairs.

4: LIKE A CHILD LEARNING TO WALK

I wandered through Cairo amazed.

Like a child learning to walk, I was happy when I could pronounce a word, ask a bus driver if the direction was correct, or find my way at all. Everything felt like learning a new game. I learned that instead of dashing for each bus and asking either the driver, who was always blocked from sight anyway, or the would-be passengers struggling through the crush of people to get on, I could, before the bus arrived at the stop, ask someone standing there if the bus coming into view was the right one.

Sometimes I still didn't understand what was happening at all.

I was intrigued one morning when a man, with whom I had boarded after asking him whether the bus was the right one, kept hissing at me to come several seats back and sit with him—but in the same single seat. One evening, a man changed seats to sit behind me—was he a pickpocket, someone trying to help, just curious, or none of the above? As it turned out, he helped me with directions, but before he did, I had no idea which he would prove to be. I was in the position of never knowing for sure other people's intentions.

Another time a man got on at a stop after mine, holding an open newspaper. He jostled me, and a woman nearby spoke to him—chidingly, it seemed—and tried to draw me near her, though she was already smashed up against the driver's seat. Still the man with the newspaper pressed against me. The woman spoke to him again, and then she reached out and put her arm around me. Sure enough, a hand snaked out from under cover of his newspaper and moved toward one of the zippered pockets in the satchel I was carrying. It was the pocket into which I had replaced my wallet after paying the conductor.

"No, no!" I said—not loudly, but rather as one would reprove a child, looking up at the two grown men who were standing nearest to me, not one hundred percent sure which man's hand had attempted the deed. One of the two said something in Arabic, speaking so forcefully that I decided he must be protesting, "It wasn't me!" The other man looked nervous. I moved my satchel away from the man who had not spoken. I felt like a selfish child holding a cookie just out of reach, refusing to share. At that point the thief apparently gave me up as a bad job, for he slunk off at the next stop. So many warnings I'd had, and luckily, or I'd not have been left feeling so smug. Still, pickpocketing seemed such a peaceful crime, lit with a certain Dickensian glamour, that despite the woman's attempts to protect me, I was pleased, rather than put off, to have at last witnessed an attempt.

One of the greatest pleasures was discovering that Egyptians are known for their laughter and good humor. That year in Egypt, I also came to laugh more easily and often. Waiting one afternoon for Julia, the Frenchwoman I'd met at Hassan Fathy's house, outside the French school where she taught, I bought a Coke where several men were sitting at a little outdoor café. Standing there, I got a close look at the men's water pipe, a pretty affair: water bubbles in a bowl beneath a little fire burning in a metal saucer, and the smoker draws in the smoke through a metal mouthpiece at the end of a flexible hose.

"*Hashish*," one of the men said, as if in explanation, looking my way. I was as easily taken in as he might have hoped.

"It *is*?"

I had heard of *hashish*; were these guys smoking *opium?*

Well, in the first place, *hashish* is made from cannabis, while opium comes from the poppy plant. In the second place, it was clear from the men's smiles and a whiff from the package one held out to me that they were smoking ordinary, if rose-scented, tobacco. Years later, I was to fall for a similar trick in a completely different context before I learned that the word *hashish* can also refer to common grass.

✑

At noon on the appointed day, I went back to Hassan
Fathy's house to meet the carpenter he'd mentioned.

There I found Mustafa, a slight man in his late
twenties or early thirties and, like many Egyptians, short
by US standards. He had a small mustache and brown,
darting eyes. His motions were quick and nervous, his
smile tentative, his welcome polite.

After introducing us, Hassan Fathy went back to sorting
abstractedly through his slides. For a while we watched
him, Mustafa on one side of the table, I on the other, both
silent, while Hassan Fathy muttered names of slides and
left us to each other. At last Mustafa spoke to me in Arabic.
Hassan Fathy translated:

"Did you bring some of your work to show him?"

I brought out the album of photographs. I had no idea
what Mustafa thought of me, this American woman foisted
on him by Hassan Fathy. Whether he was being gracious,
hospitable to a foreigner, or whether he wanted a bit of time
together to evaluate this possible associate, he arranged to
take me the next day to see, not his father's shop, as I had
expected, but, as he put it, "how things are made."

My Arabic, of course, was at that time nonexistent, his
English sparse, and he didn't speak French at all. Unlike
the generation before that included Halim's sister, Mustafa
had attended school when French was no longer required
of students in public schools. But we did fine, that day and
all the days to follow.

He took me to see a great complex of artisan workshops, all of them producing artworks made by hand, without the use of machines. He showed me first the extraordinary woodworking he called *claustra*, using the French word for mud latticework in a house of mud brick, but by which he meant the wooden bar-like artwork that allows light and air to come in through windows but keeps direct sun from the rooms inside.

We came to a man who was seated on the floor with one leg outstretched and a string attached to his big toe, which he was pumping quickly back and forth. The other end of the string was attached to a long wooden cylinder, held in place at one end by the man's other foot, which was not moving, and at the other end with a metal clamp. The movement of the man's toe was causing the stick of wood to revolve rapidly, and, as it turned, he was carving the wood into shapes with a hand kept steady by the foot that was stationary.

Mustafa said, "Six years I have worked to learn the art, carving the wood with a chisel as it turns on a machine-driven lathe in my father's shop, but only this year have I begun to actually make the pieces for the *claustra*."

But this man was spinning the wood with his toe, connected to the wood with string! It was an amazing process to watch—a human-powered lathe. With such skill the sharp chisel cut fine wooden feathers, ridges, and curves. No machine, only a keen eye and a skillful hand. I could not have dreamed such a thing was possible.

And the wonders did not end there. On the wall hung

examples of different possible *claustra* designs. Mustafa took care to show me that some were made in patterns of six, others four, and to point out variations within the basic designs.

Downstairs, he showed me a shop where furniture and doors were made. He explained that there were three ways of making doors.

In the first, pieces of wood are cut, each in the shape of one tiny part of a geometric design. Then, every edge of each piece of wood is chiseled by hand to create either a tongue or a groove, and the pieces are joined rather like pieces of a jigsaw puzzle, without glue or nails. Thus the whole door is made of separate interlocking pieces that can slide together and apart, until they are all enclosed in a wooden frame.

I studied the work as he talked.

"This first kind of door is the most difficult and time-consuming to make. In my father's shop," he said, "my father and I make furniture this way."

A second way of making doors is more affordable, and therefore most common. In this second method, the wood is cut into geometric shapes, but without the rabbeting— without the tongues and grooves to join the pieces together—and these shapes are then glued and/or nailed to a solid backing. These are the doors called *sabras*, most usual in modern times. In the third method, just a single block of wood is used, and the design is carved upon it.

Mustafa joked with me: "You will learn this, and we will not be able to speak to you! You will be above us!"

But, awed by all I had seen, I said, "Then I shouldn't be speaking to you, for you already do this work."

Carving did turn out to be what I loved doing most in Mustafa's father's shop, although my skill never came close to the level he predicted.

〜

Upstairs, Mustafa showed me how plaster is used to make lanterns and a certain kind of window. Designs are drawn in pencil on a plaster sheet about an inch and a half thick, which has been set in a rabbeted wooden frame. With a sharp pointed tool, twirled like a drill, the first hole is bored. Next a tiny saw, like a small keyhole saw, is inserted into the hole and carves away the gypsum-like material, with the edges often ending at an angle to the surface, and coming very clean. Pieces of colored glass are then cut and attached to the back of the sheet with more of the same kind of plaster, so that colored light comes through the openings.

Mustafa also showed me drawings he had made of Islamic architecture in all its various periods. Some of the drawings he had made from studying art in museums and in private homes; others he had copied from designs in books. The drawings, done with exquisite care, were to be patterns for his own artwork. Proudly, he pointed out the detail in one of the drawings he had made.

"Look!" he said, pointing to birds, rabbits, and strange animals nestling among intricately drawn flowers and leaves. "These are all worked in wood." Later he told me

that the representation of birds, animals, or human figures
in painting or carving was not traditional in most Islamic art.
In creating these, he considered himself a kind of pioneer. I
was surprised to learn that in Islam it was possible, even for
a devout Muslim, to bend artistic rules. I was impressed by
Mustafa's unconventionality and by the fact that his father,
who I expected was even more traditional, presumably did
not object.

5: Morning of Goodness, Morning of Light

After two days of exploring artisan workshops and markets, I began thinking about finding a permanent place to live, as well as a school where I could study Arabic.

After visiting various Arabic-teaching schools, I settled for the best one I could afford. This was not the renowned intensive CASA program offered by the American University in Cairo, which was too expensive. Nor was it Berlitz, which taught the language through transliteration only. If you learned through Berlitz, whenever you heard a new word, you wouldn't be sure you were pronouncing it properly, since you wouldn't know which Arabic letters were used to spell it. Nor would you become familiar with what I later found was the lovely structural mapping of the language. Arabic vocabulary grows like leaves on a many-limbed grammatical tree, each branch representing three letters. From each, sprout whole clusters of words in different grammatical forms. And I was shocked that anyone would think of teaching Arabic without imparting the gorgeous lettering that is an art form in itself.

In the end, I chose the inexpensive evening classes offered by the Egyptian Ministry of Culture at the Egyptian Cultural Center on the island of Zamalek, in the Nile. Government sponsored, the school turned out to have excellent, dedicated teachers who were a joy to learn from and to know.

On my first journey to the Center, I was offered help so many times that I realized I must always stop, shake hands, and make it clear I was okay before anyone would leave my side.

I had already learned the importance of another ritual. I had been having trouble one day persuading an obviously reluctant taxi driver to take me a far distance, when a stranger stepped up unasked and spoke with the driver. A moment later, the driver and I were on our way. The driver warmed as we went, accepted a Winston cigarette that Nahid's brother Muhammad had given me, and seemed pleased by that and my gratitude. When we reached our destination, I gave him a few extra coins, but he only tried to give them back. I smiled, insisted, and he finally accepted. I realized one must insist to give the gift, or one always ends the taker.

When I arrived at the Center, there was no one there to answer my questions, but help of another sort was offered when the doorman undertook to rehearse with me the pronunciation of Arabic numbers.

Doorkeepers, I found, were outside doors when you

needed them but mysteriously absent when you didn't. The man had been at Hassan Fathy's door when Nahid and her family and I needed to ask directions, and this man was outside the Egyptian Center when I needed to get in. But neither man was to be seen when the visits were done and I wished to thank him.

The word for doorman in Arabic is *bawwab*, from the Arabic word *bab*, or door. The ones I met were always men, always old, and appeared to live on the premises they were protecting. When not in action, they disappeared into some hidden crevice or shaded spot from which they could keep watch. They had the power to give or to withhold much more than simple entries and exits. Since they knew the movements of everyone on the street, doormen were valuable sources of information about the neighborhood, even though they appeared to be napping when a visitor arrived. They were capable of performing many other functions, too. For instance, the doorman at a Coptic church I visited took me down a long, dark stairway made of worn, irregular stone to show me, when we reached the bottom, thousands of bats hanging upside down from the ceiling of a dark cave. Sleeping during the day, as vampires are said to do.

Doormen reminded me of Khidr, the spiritual guide who appears in stories from the Arab world and Central Asia, materializing suddenly with a flash of green—the color of the cloak he wears—only to disappear just as quickly. The image chosen by storytellers from this part of the world was apt, for Khidr seemed to be everywhere in

Egypt—and not only in the guise of doorkeeper, but also as stranger, traveler, teacher, guide.

∽

Meanwhile, the hostel where I was staying was supposed to accept travelers for just three nights, and I had been there more than a week. To the rescue came two other foreigners in Egypt—two women from Sudan, named Maha and Samia, who were staying in the same hostel. They introduced themselves and offered me "any help," as Arabic speakers tend to phrase the offer in English. They promised that as they looked for a room for themselves, they would also look for me.

"It's better if you don't come with me," Maha said. "If you are there, the price will be much higher." She didn't have to tell me why. I already knew my pale skin and light hair color would communicate that I had a lot of money, whether I did or not.

Maha's own situation in Cairo was the reverse of mine:

"People look down on me in Cairo, because I'm blacker than most Egyptian women."

Even in Sudan, she said, in a country and on a continent where people knew about the color prejudice they would face outside Africa, many northerners looked down on their blacker sisters and brothers in the south. Racism existed even in Arab and Muslim countries. Both she and Samia were studying mass communications, Samia hoping to work in public relations, Maha for a newspaper or radio station.

"Yes," she confirmed when I asked, "there are some female news reporters in Sudan, but such a job is unusual for a woman."

In the meantime, until I found a place, Samia said I could stay with her brother, a student of political and social science at Cairo University who shared a flat with another friend.

"This cannot be proper!" I exclaimed. "A woman staying in the same apartment as men to whom she is not related?"

Both women assured me that, while such an arrangement would not be permissible for themselves, or any other Sudanese woman, for me it would be perfectly okay. They were expected to obey not only Samia's brother, but also any Sudanese man, for all Sudanese men claimed responsibility for Maha and Samia as if these men were their brothers too.

"Sudanese men ask us, 'Where did you go? And with whom?'" For that reason, the women told me, they said nothing of their doings to any man. Because the hostel curfew was so early, they simply signed out overnight to an uncle—but stayed with their boyfriends.

This was my second encounter with the bizarre status granted in Egypt and in other Arab countries to an adult unmarried female who was neither Arab nor Muslim. I found I was treated by many people as neither fully male nor female. The extent to which I was treated as either sex depended on the circumstance. For instance, I could walk in the streets at night without provoking comment, which most Egyptian women could not. When I was eventually invited into Mustafa's family home, I was treated at first as a male guest would be. I ate with the men of the family, while invisible women cooked. On my first visit, I saw just the woman who brought food to the table from the kitchen. But later I was allowed to associate with the women of the house in ways a man who was not related could never have done.

The next day, Samia brought her brother, 'Adil Sharfi, and three more of his Sudanese friends—Nader Muhammad Al Kheir, Anwar 'Abbas Ahmed, and Muhammad Kheir Al Taher—to the hostel to meet me. Scarcely had we been introduced when Nader, incidentally a young man of exceptional beauty, gave me my first keys to the Arabic language. On the spot, in the common room in the hostel, he initiated a lesson, drawing the Arabic letters and explaining the sounds for which they stand. He showed how letters change appearance depending on whether they appear at the beginning, middle, or end of a word. He explained the endings given to words to show possession, and he told me that a person's name almost always has meaning.

He said that his own, Al Kheir, meant "rare blessed goodness," and that Al Taher meant "clean before God." He taught me the literal meaning of the Arabic morning greeting, which, instead of "good morning," is "morning of goodness." The greeting is met with its own response, which means "morning of light." He taught me "good-bye." As the young men left, I said, "I'm glad to have met you," and received the answer, "Glad! I'm more than glad. I'm happy!"

This was another experience with an Arab custom I loved from the first—the exchange of greetings or compliments, each one more extravagant than the last.

Although it was during that first year in Egypt that I heard the most elaborate exchanges, years later in Egypt and in other Arab countries, I could still draw a laugh by continuing up the scale:

First speaker: "Morning of goodness!"

Second speaker: "Morning of light!"

First speaker: "Morning of honey!"

Second speaker: "Morning of jasmine!"

First speaker: "Morning of roses!" and so on, until one or the other finally surpassed them all with the highest possible greeting: "Morning of 'ishta [cream]!"

This was always the last, though it took me some time to grasp that, since in my own personal hierarchy, honey always ranked highest of all.

I never caught on to the subtleties of the proper pairing or ranking of all the possible items. For quite a while, whenever I thought I was saying "Morning of jasmine!" I was in fact saying "Morning of fava beans!" since in Arabic, the word for "jasmine" sounds something like the English word "full," while "fava beans" sounds more like "fool." Even in Palestine, where things were always hard, I could get an appreciative grin on all but the grimmest days by tossing in "Morning of onion!" as in the Arabic expression "Days of honey, days of onion"—wry acknowledgment of the bad fortune that comes along with, and in Palestine often far outweighs, the good.

The next morning, Samia and Maha waited with me for 'Adil Sharfi to come and take me in a taxi to his apartment. Only when I got there did I learn that he lived in the apartment with not just one friend, but with at least five other male students in their early twenties, three of whom I'd met the day before. Even so, I was warmly welcomed and quickly learned that all of them assumed I would stay with them until I could find my own place to live.

The apartment had almost no furniture. All the young men were studying full-time at Cairo University, without jobs or money coming from home, and making do with almost nothing. In the kitchen there was only a single table (no chairs), around which we all gathered at dinnertime. Standing, we bent to dip pieces of the round brown bread into a large plate of macaroni someone had cooked up on the little stove. This was my first experience, most common in poor or rural communities, of eating food from a common plate, using little pieces of bread as forks. I liked the custom, and came to dislike the cold metal of the fork used mostly in Western countries. The young men were sharing with me everything they had, and I was overwhelmed by their kindness and generosity.

But it was only when night came that I realized the full extent of their hospitality. It turned out that there was only one bed in the flat—a huge bed, where I guessed at least four of the young men had been sleeping each night side by side. It went without saying, apparently, that from then on, as long as I stayed with them, those who had been sleeping in the bed would vacate it and leave the entire expanse of bed for me. Everyone else would sleep on the floor.

I was horrified. It had never been mentioned, of course, that there was only one bed in the apartment, much less that I would be the only one to sleep in it that night and for three more nights after that. All my protests were promptly, firmly, and unanimously laid aside.

∽

Inevitably, my conversations with the Sudanese, as with everyone else, turned to politics. The bind in which Third World countries found themselves as the result of the rivalry between the USA and the USSR was becoming increasingly clear to me. The so-called "developing countries," the former colonies, always had to choose one side or the other. When I was there in the late seventies, Sudan and Egypt were turning to the US, not for ideological reasons, but because the US had more money to give and because Saudi Arabia would not give money to governments working with the USSR. Hence Egypt's switch from a position close to the USSR, which had lasted all through the Nasser years, to the new orientation to the USA.

The US and USSR, it seemed, were using Third World countries like pawns on a chessboard. Not only that, but citizens of Middle Eastern countries (as well as of other countries in the Global South, I was to learn) were quite aware of the fact. The Sudanese students I was staying with were too polite to say so, but Egyptians and other Arabs I got to know better made it clear they knew that US actions in the Middle East did not stem from charitable impulses. To the extent that US citizens believed that they did, we were fooling only ourselves.

But English had become the language most widely spoken throughout the world; and success in any field, in any country, was becoming ever more dependent on learning it. Less predictable, in my view, was the fact that all the Sudanese I met that year in Egypt wanted to go to America to study. But I understood why when they spoke of university professors in Arab countries demanding rote regurgitation of textbook material on exams. In addition, like Maha and Samia, they said they were being discriminated against in Egypt.

"There is prejudice in the US, too," I warned them.

"We know that," one said, "but we're already being discriminated against in Egypt, not only because our skin is darker, but because we're not Egyptian. The situation in the US probably won't be worse." One told of an Egyptian landlady who kept his rent deposit even after he informed her that he had decided not to move into her building. Another said the Sudanese were made to pay more than Egyptians in taxi fares and university fees. They agreed that the resentment they felt coming from Egyptians paralleled resentments Egyptians felt among themselves due to class differences. University professors and doctors, they told me, made only 28-30 Egyptian pounds ($56-60) per month, while owners of buildings might appear poor and in fact be very rich. The prospect of Sudanese students gaining some benefit from the

United States was appealing, but I knew as well as they did that the likelihood of their being admitted to study there, much less funded, was small.

$$\backsim$$

One evening, as I was writing my mother a letter, Nader asked my mother's name and then wrote something in Arabic on the same page. He translated it for me:

Jane Moore, we send our greetings and yearning. We hope that you are okay. Chivvis is spending a beautiful time with us.

Thus I encountered the custom of sending greetings to a friend's mother—even though you had never met her and probably never would. Years later, the custom continued to surprise me each time it occurred.

Like Nahid, Nader told me that Egyptians would not want to live in houses of mud brick. "Will Americans?" he asked. "Will Americans want to live in houses made of mud?" Hearing it put this way, I found it hard to imagine that poor Americans would consider living in mud houses an improvement in their lot. An uncomfortable doubt entered into the picture I had fashioned.

6: COME EVERY DAY!

Over the weeks, Nahid continued to invite me to visit. Halim's introduction to his family, and his family's acceptance of me, were gifts of inestimable value. Halim's sister and his brothers and their families, all of whom spoke either some French or English in addition to Arabic, made me feel welcome each time I appeared, sharing with me their lives and their views of Egypt and the world, offering me a deeper understanding of Egypt than I could otherwise have had. It was a welcome I still cannot imagine offering—a house that's always open. Throughout my later years in Arab countries I was met with the invitation, the standard Arabic phrase, "Come visit us! Come every day!"

What I didn't realize that first year in Egypt was that the welcome lingered from a social code that had existed in the ancient Arab world. Among desert tribes, who traveled great distances, with food and water nonexistent between oases, the custom was a vital one: to be turned away from pasture, from well water and date palms, was to die. Arabs who settled in cities continued the tradition. Like many Arab offers and expressions, the urging to "Come every day!" was meant to be accepted in spirit, but not necessarily in fact—or, at least, not without checking to make sure the offer was indeed meant literally. If accepted, then in time the kindness would be answered with another.

To someone unfamiliar with Arab culture, and particularly, perhaps, to someone raised mostly in Euro-ethnic, upper-middle-class suburbs in the United States, where you neither visit nor expect guests without having beforehand agreed on a specific date and time, such invitations were disconcerting. To what degree were they sincere? They were repeated with such emphasis—if I did not visit for a week or two or less, I was scolded for desertion—that it was easy to believe that my presence was really that desirable.

And yet—how could that be? Any idiot could see that if the person you were visiting was in the middle of washing the floor, she probably would have chosen another time to entertain you. This would be even truer in a culture in which the arrival of a visitor meant that the hostess not only stopped what she was doing but also prepared pots of tea, served plates heaping with fruit or bowls of nuts or seeds, and sat with you as long as you chose to stay. No casual "Come on in and make yourself at home while I finish this" or, "Well, it's been great seeing you; now I should be getting back to work." In Arab culture, such remarks would be unbelievably rude.

I must have spent a whole year in Egypt—and possibly

several more in other Arab countries—without knowing how to interpret invitations to "Visit every day!" "Sit down and eat with us!" and other similarly extravagant offers. People would pass me food from their own plates; and if I complimented a woman on a scarf or a pair of earrings, she would whip off the item I admired, hand it over, and urge me to keep it for life.

Eventually I decided that the welcoming words, generous offerings, and invitations extended to a neighbor (or a stranger) passing by, although always graciously followed through whenever some foreign ignoramus like myself took them at face value, were in themselves gifts. They were expressions of friendliness and goodwill, all aiming to create a climate of warmth and welcome. And that is exactly what they did. Even though each Egyptian individual or family may have, in the end, given and received no more or less than one would in the United States, the custom of offering generously made people happy. It made *me* happy! Instead of carefully dividing up a bill in a restaurant, or each person smoking cigarettes from his or her own pack, we enjoyed offering and being offered.

Of course, a stranger might altogether misunderstand a ritual exchange if she had never seen it in action. When one of the first buses I rode in Cairo stopped for a few moments to let passengers off, I was startled to see two men arguing. It looked to me as if they were both angry—but my guide-of-the-moment explained that each was urging the other to come to *his own* family's house for the afternoon meal that day.

Something else I failed to grasp was the fact that both sides in the mock battle had to participate equally in the struggle to give to the other, or the system would quickly fall apart. Returning to the US after that first year in Egypt, I began to give away more money and possessions than I had before and to work without pay, only to find after a short while that this lifestyle—big surprise!—was unsustainable in a culture in which two sides didn't play. Much later, hearing from a traveler that Egyptians were no longer so unstinting, I was not surprised. They'd likely worn themselves out, being always in the giving role, with foreigners taking all they were offered but giving little in return.

On one of these many visits, I ate the afternoon meal—the main meal of the day—with Nahid and her family. The bread eaten at the afternoon meal, I saw, might be different from the brown, crusty-topped rounds I'd gotten used to. Instead, the afternoon breads Nahid served were long and white and soft, and shaped like miniature loaves of French bread, but without the crusty outside. We ate them with local honey, dripping heavy and sweet, or *halaawa* (some say halva) to my surprise. *Halaawa* on bread—why not? It was utterly delicious!

Nahid described for me some differences between ancient, more educated cultures such as Egypt, Syria, and Lebanon, on the one hand, and on the other, some of the Arabs states made rich by the relatively recent discovery of oil.

"Maids earn twice as much in Saudi Arabia as they do here in Egypt, and they are given clothes and food in addition to wages," she told me. Libya had discovered oil on its land just nine years earlier. But Libya's educational system, compared to Egypt's, was poor. "So Egypt, Syria, and Lebanon, although heir to ancient cultures and possessors of better educational systems, are less well-off materially than the oil-rich Arab countries." I was so grateful for everything Nahid and everyone else was taking the time to tell me. In each conversation I learned things I had never known.

Yet each time I visited, I could also see that Nahid was tired. She was taking radioactive treatment, having massages, and doing special exercises for calcium deposits in her back.

"I'd rather work outside my home," she said, "since at home, not only on Friday [her day off], but *chaque jour* [every day], I have to cook a big meal like the one we've just eaten."

Nahid's husband, Muhammad, was applying for a job as distributor with British American Tobacco, based in London. In former years, he had played squash and tennis. He had even served as referee in national tennis games, but no more.

"No time now," he said.

∽

In the meantime, like many other people, both Egyptian and foreign, I continued to visit Hassan Fathy. There was no telephoning or other advance arrangement, at least in part because telephone service was so iffy; and in those days, there was no Internet. It seemed to be expected that if you wanted to visit someone, you just dropped by. Hassan Fathy's home, in particular, seemed to be something of an ongoing open house, a kind of salon. It was not unusual on arriving to find a large group of people already present.

Arriving one night at Hassan Fathy's house, I found ten or twelve people gathered around building plans. There were a number of foreigners, all casually dressed, and the rest Egyptians, the men attired in the short-sleeved lightweight and light-colored suits that I'd seen many Egyptian office workers wear. Much of the talking was in English, with some French and Arabic. Hassan Fathy showed a model of a complex of domes, apparently guest sleeping quarters for a hotel, since the houses did not have kitchens. Each building was to be different. The listeners murmured: How could this be? But Hassan Fathy insisted.

Someone brought *baklaawa*, made of layers of pastry filled with chopped nuts and honey, and insisted I eat.

"It's like a Rembrandt, no? With your signature," one woman said of the plans, and I got my second taste of Fathy adoration, the first coming from a young architect who had said earlier, "We are all his students." A Fathy cult? I wondered. That night one of the Egyptian architects offered me his house to live in. Although grateful for the offer, I thanked him and declined.

When the visitors left, Dr. Fathy said, "You will stay and

eat with me. If I were alone, I'd go to bed, but I think it is good to eat with someone."

We ate rice soup and breadsticks, then chicken and macaroni, tomatoes, and a sweet fleshy roll, and last, *guafa* cold in a sweet syrup. We scarcely spoke, and I restrained myself from asking questions, for it was clear Dr. Fathy was tired. He asked if I thought one of the men who had been there earlier was Italian; I didn't know. I did ask him about Sadat Village, which he was planning at the time.

"The government is insisting on the wrong site," he said. "I want to build on two other sites instead. I arranged to meet someone from the government, but he never showed up. I have to write him a note. I'm not going to work unless I have complete control."

Hassan Fathy asked me why I was a carpenter. I said I had been a newspaper reporter, but had had to find a way of earning my living when I eventually rejected the political constraints under which reporters must work. I said I'd decided to do work that showed tangible results each day. In addition, when I had first become a carpenter, I knew no other women in the trades; entering the field appealed in its pioneering aspect.

"Have you read the book *Her-Bak*, by Isha Schwaller de Lubicz, about apprenticeship in ancient Egypt?" Hassan Fathy asked then.

"No," I answered, but guessing that he might be trying to tell me something about my own role in the carpentry shop, I determined to find a copy.

Another afternoon, as visitors were leaving and I was

preparing to leave also, Hassan Fathy said again, "You will stay and eat with me"; and eat we did, mostly in silence as before, and the same meal.

But this time we were interrupted by a call from Tokyo. After the call, unable to restrain my curiosity, I asked, "Are people in Japan interested in building houses of mud brick?"

"Yes. A group of Japanese architects want to build a school of mud brick, and I've told them they can publish something I've written."

Dr. Fathy worked awhile at his drawing table while I studied Arabic. Then he asked if I would stay while he went out with a prince from Kuwait so that I could receive visitors who were to come at five. He changed into a suit, and shortly afterward, a tall and handsome black man with a short Afro arrived, and the two men left together.

"My friends," Dr. Fathy called everyone. The prince from Kuwait was his "friend," and so were the others who came—two Swiss architects who were hoping to work with him in Nubia, and three others working on an exhibition of Islamic architecture.

Often Mustafa joined the group, and one Friday, he invited me to visit what he called the "beautiful houses." These were the exquisite old houses turned museums that, along with caravansaries, *madrasas* (religious schools), mausoleums, palaces, citadels, and mosques, grace the older parts of Cairo. Despite the poverty and the crowdedness of too many people sharing spaces too small for them, including the flat roofs of apartment buildings, where entire families lived in makeshift shelters, and despite the fact that the city was always swept by the dust carried from the desert on the wind, Cairo was incredibly beautiful.

From Mustafa's patient tours about the city, I got my first bits of information about this art he loved and of which, as an Egyptian, a Muslim, and a lover of art and architecture, he was understandably proud. Through his eyes I glimpsed the treasure trove that is Islamic civilization—the woodworking, architecture, and other Islamic arts that make Cairo the glorious city it is. From him I learned that each of the distinctive kinds of Islamic architecture is characteristic of a different era, many named for the various dynasties that held political and religious leadership in the Muslim world—Tulunid, Fatimud, Ayyubid, Mamluke, Ottoman. . . .

In an article published that year, 1978, by John Russell, I read a description of Egypt that expressed what I was finding: "The centuries in Egypt do not line up like pearls on a string. They come tumbling in, just anyhow, the way the treasures of Tutankhamen were tumbled in his tomb. . . . It is for us to do the work of disentanglement; and we can do it well, or badly, or not at all. . . ."

I also learned about different forms of Arabic scripts— *Kufic, Fatimid, Naskh, Thuluth, Ta'lqz,* and others, some originating in Baghdad, some in Persia, others in Turkey, the elaborate lettering sometimes forming shapes—a bird, a boat, a pear. Verses from the Qur'an were painted in the various scripts on paper, glass, and ceramic. They were carved in plaster, gypsum, stone, or wood, on elaborate doors or above arched doorways, on coffered ceilings. Even advertisements were written in gorgeous Arabic script. The charm of these, however, lasted longer if I didn't understand the ad. Years later, studying Arabic in Syria, looking up at a great billboard and slowly mouthing out the first word I was able to understand outside my schoolbook, I was chagrined to find that the word, which looked so lovely, was nothing more than the name of a US product, and an unhealthy one at that: *Muh-arrrl-boo-roo—Marlboro!*

So many other things in the look, the sounds, the smells of Cairo—indeed, in all of Egypt—from the Nile Delta in the north, up the great river and out to the desert, to the beginnings of Africa in the south—intrigued and delighted as well. Unlike US malls and supermarkets, with their walled-in stores selling tight-wrapped dried fruit, coffee, grains, herbs, and soups in packages, bottles, cans, and jars, Cairo's streets teased and tempted with scents of coffee, cardamom, curry, peppermint, dried apricot, and fig, all in sacks or bins open to passersby. Raw smells of animal dung, fish, meat, or rotting vegetables added dimensions beyond the sanitized, homogenized environments in which I had grown up. I was charmed by the small, gracefully curved glasses and ceramic cups in which tea and coffee were served. Women's scarves, hung out on stalls for sale, sparkled with threads of silver or gold. The pale blue *gallabiyyas* worn by men from Upper (southern) Egypt hung full and slanted outward as they neared the ground.

And the sound! Cairo was a city of voices—of hawkers

calling, people walking and talking, cars honking seemingly without reason, and music—always music, in the streets, pouring from cars and apartment windows, a little radio accompanying each roving street vendor. At first I did not appreciate Arabic music, but one day, I heard a woman singing on the radio, and I was amazed: Who was this? I loved hearing her. That was the first time Arabic music moved me. I recalled the sound of that woman's voice often, and yearned to know who she was and to hear and see her in person.

In time I would discover that this was Om Kalthoum, the most beloved of Egyptian singers and possibly the most beloved in the entire Arab world. Years later, in Palestine, the drivers of the *services*, or shared taxis, would tell me, as they played music on their car radios or tape decks, driving me to and from work: "Fairouz [the famous Lebanese singer] in the morning, and Om Kalthoum at night." And that's how I listened as well. The song I heard that first day was *"Enta 'Omri"* ("You Are My Life"), which I learned was a trademark piece of Om Kalthoum's later years. When she died at the age of seventy-seven in 1975, just three years before I arrived in Egypt, Egyptians had poured into the streets in the millions to mourn her loss.

My favorite of all sounds were the calls to prayer. Cairo, I learned, is known as "the city of a thousand minarets," and no wonder! In every neighborhood where I rode or walked were mosques. Five times each day, unearthly calls sounded through loudspeakers from all one thousand minarets at once—well, not quite at once, but in overlapping waves of poetry—beyond music, beyond speech—rolling through neighborhoods across the city.

In all these ways, Cairo was magic.

∽

My two Sudanese friends Samia and Maha found me a place to stay. In the end, the family who owned the room behind the mechanic's garage had decided not to rent to me. But the women had found me a place just down the street from the garage. It was a room in an apartment in Dokki, then a rural neighborhood, with two Egyptian women, sisters in their fifties or sixties; it was hard to tell. The apartment building was near Cairo University, which was a fine place to be. The sisters owned the entire building but rented me a room in their own apartment. They fed me and showed me how to wash my clothes properly by hand, grumbled at me with a wink if I forgot to wear my flip-flops, and said they were my mothers—all in Arabic, but the meaning was clear. One night, mulling over a word a grandchild had written for an English lesson, they were delighted when I could translate the word as *shakoosh*—hammer. Lucky for me—at the time, it was one of only about ten words I knew.

7: *Ahlan! Ahlan!*

At last the day came when Mustafa walked me down the hill from Hassan Fathy's home to his father's shop in the warren of streets below. There I met Mustafa's father, Hassan Ali Ibrahim. He was a short man, even by Egyptian standards, with a round brown face, and eyes that evaluated me shrewdly as he shook my hand and greeted me, *"Ahlan! Ahlan!"* ("Welcome! Welcome!") in gracious Egyptian style.

"Thank you, *M'alim* Hassan! Thank you!" I replied. Egyptians so often said something more than once that I found myself doing it too.

By then I knew that in Arab society the title goes with the first name, not the last, and so I addressed my teacher as *M'alim*, or Master, Hassan, rather than as Master Ibrahim. Eventually I addressed Hassan Fathy as "Hassan *Bey*," using, as his other guests did, a title of respect dating from Ottoman times. I never heard anyone call him

"Dr. Fathy," as I had done at first. Another polite title for Mustafa's father was *hagg* (for a woman, it would be *hagga*), respectful acknowledgment that the person had made the *hagg* (in some other Arabic dialects, *hajj*), the pilgrimage to Mecca, which each Muslim who can afford it is to make at least once in his or her lifetime.

At the time I met him, Master Hassan was sixty-five years old but looked forty or forty-five. Mustafa had told me that three years earlier, his father had founded Sinary House, the large artisans' workshop Mustafa and I had visited together. *M'alim* Hassan introduced me to his younger son, Mahmud, tall and thin, with gentle eyes and a wide smile. Mahmud hardly spoke that day, except to make me welcome; I learned that he was a quiet soul, particularly when contrasted with his more voluble father and brother. It was Mahmud who used a chisel to carve long wooden rods into the shapes that would decorate the window openings. The day I met him, he stood the whole time, working at the lathe; and that, I learned, was where I'd always find him. One of my first tasks would be to cut apart with a small handsaw the pieces Mahmud had fashioned.

Mustafa showed me around the shop, its floor sprinkled with blond wood shavings, while Mahmud, as befitting the younger son, at a word from his father, made us tea. Mustafa brought out a chest he was making, which was to be decorated with panels of *mashrabiyya*, with brass hinges holding the lid and handles on two sides.

"Can you do this?" he asked.

"No, of course not."

"I promise you that you'll learn to produce a chest like this in three months' time!"

He showed me carved figures he had made as a table base, other wooden pieces he would fit into a door that needed repair, and pictures of work he had done for an exhibition held at the French Institute in Cairo. He gave me a remnant of old *mashrabiyya*, a network of rounded wooden jewels. Each polished brown bead was joined to others by tiny wooden fingers, every finger fitting beautifully into a hole carved in the adjoining piece. I have it still.

As I was shown around, it became clear that I was being offered the opportunity of a lifetime—a chance to work in the shop of one of Cairo's finest carpenters. I was being invited to spend my days with this man and his sons, learning what I could of a craft that had been integral to Islamic art and architecture for centuries. I would work with wood, a medium to which I was more drawn than I was to stone, plaster, or mud brick. I would learn to use hand tools instead of the electric tools we used in the United States. And I would be making doors that were the most beautiful I had ever seen. Never had I been offered a gift of such value.

By now I had made a habit of asking the meaning of people's names; and so, to the names I'd learned—which meant "rare," "goodness," "one who is always serious," "stronger light," "noble," "one who can struggle against anything," "clean before God," "chosen," "beautiful," and "highly placed"—I added the word for "blessed." The name, it seemed, should be mine.

"This is beyond my wildest dreams!" I exclaimed the next time I visited Hassan Fathy. "But why am I, rather than an Egyptian, being taken into the shop to learn?"

"I have supported them for many years," Hassan *Bey* answered, "commissioning them to do the woodworking on many of my projects. That's why they wish to be good and kind to you."

∽

And so my daily life began, helping with the work when I could, which was little enough, and learning what I was able to learn.

Each morning I would leave my room and ride two buses across the city. I got off the second bus under the long, sturdy branches of the tamarack tree at the bottom of the steep hill on which stood the magnificent Muhammad Ali Mosque. This was the neighborhood I came to think of as the true heart of the city. The area, called Islamic Cairo, is richest in the schools and mosques built centuries ago in Islamic style, in contrast to so much of the rest of Cairo, where the newer architecture resembles that in more modern Western cities. Through a sky veiled with smog and dust—in what proportions I was never sure—I caught sight each morning of the Rifa'i Mosque's tall minarets rising high over the narrow street in the Midan Salah ad-Din. The square is named, like the Citadel, for the Kurdish military leader widely respected for his humane treatment of both Christians and Jews when in 1187 he recaptured Jerusalem from the Crusaders. The Christian soldiers had taken the city in a bloodbath and occupied it for nearly ninety years.

I walked a short way down an unpaved road that looked then probably much the same as it had thousands of years ago, to a small dirt space shaded by a couple of trees. Seated on wooden chairs in the open were the readers, writers, and translators—men skilled enough to handwrite or type a document or to translate a letter for someone who had never been taught to read or write. In those days, most children attended public school, but boys from poor families often worked at jobs throughout the city. Not so long before, reading and writing had been a skill limited to the few, some of whom grew the fingernail on their littlest finger long to show they were educated people who did not work with their hands. Despite the fact that he often did work with his hands, Mustafa kept one fingernail long, I guessed to show he had book learning in addition to knowledge of the craft.

Along with the translators, there were throngs of schoolchildren milling about on their way to school. They gathered round the little gaily painted wooden carts so common then in Cairo. Some of the carts carried little burners under pots of frying oil, into which the vendor popped the round green balls of *falafel*, or *ta'miyya*, in the Egyptian dialect, and cooked them on the spot. Plucked from the deep oil and drained, the *ta'miyya* was mashed slightly, along with chopped tomato and lettuce, into a small round pouch of white bread, and offered to the customer. Other vendors sold *ful* (the fava beans I had earlier mistaken for jasmine), serving them in tin bowls, with lime and sometimes tomato and cucumber, and a round of brown bread, fresh that morning.

If I had time, I'd perch on a chair or, if a chair was not at hand, on a rock. Whichever it was, it would have been carefully dusted by the proprietor of the makeshift outdoor "restaurant." From there I'd gaze at the high walls built by Saladin to enclose this part of the city, at the great buildings of limestone, and especially at the Muhammad Ali Mosque, high up on the rock, with its great dome and two tall slender minarets. Sometimes as I sat there, I'd read a little, or study Arabic. If I did the latter, then I never lacked for teachers: whoever was sitting nearby, or someone passing, mostly a gaggle of schoolchildren, took pleasure in helping me pronounce or spell the words I learned so laboriously. From the first, I loved the language even though I found it tremendously difficult. I valued each small gain. Schoolchildren laughed at my scrawl—the Arabic equivalent of "Dick ran"—and admired my book with pictures showing the meanings of the words.

After I'd eaten, I'd walk the short way to a little stand down the road, where, after being warmly welcomed by the owner, Muhammad, I'd sit on a wooden bench and watch the old man reach up and carefully lift down one of his beloved, delicate porcelain cups and matching saucer. In the bottom of the cup he would heap small spoonfuls (three, by request—"Ah, like the *fellahin* [the farmers]," they'd say) of coarse-grain sugar. I'd watch as he lifted the large dented aluminum kettle off the fire and pour from it the strong dark tea that had been simmering there, then fill the rest of the cup to the brim from a pot of water on the stove, also piping hot. Only then would I be served.

The sweet black tea became a much-desired treat for me, and in any company I'd hope to be offered tea, instead of coffee or a Coke. From that time on, everywhere I lived in the Arab world, I always made sure I knew the nearest tea maker, easily found by tracking the man or boy who raced along the streets, tray of glasses held high in one hand, serving shopkeepers and the visitors in their shops. Eventually I caught on to a method of making "instant" tea—dumping an individual serving of tea leaves and sugar into a cup, then pouring in boiling water and stirring rapidly. The tea would be ready to drink right away. I quickly learned, however, that if the water was not hot enough, the tea leaves would float on top in a miniature whirlpool of undesirable whitish foam, and the tea would not taste good.

After a couple of glasses of tea, I'd walk down the road, passing each day the same tradesmen in their little shops, at work from early morning until late at night—mending shoes, shaping aluminum stoves, ironing clothes, serving tea. Each morning and evening, I would see these workers standing or sitting at their jobs. The ironer would take a sip of water from a plastic bottle, bend over his ironing board, and shoot from his mouth an admirably uniform watery mist—*sasssssssssssst!*—to moisten the material before ironing it. A human spray bottle!

A few minutes before 9:30, I'd make my way down the

street into the labyrinth of narrow roads that comprised this and other older sections of the city, take a sharp left onto a tiny sandy lane, greet the chairmaker across the way, and knock on a great wooden door set in a high brick wall. This was the entrance to the tiny woodworking shop situated between two of Cairo's most famous Islamic monuments, the Mosque and *madrasa* of Sultan Hassan, and the Mosque of Ibn Tulun.

The door would be opened by Master Hassan or one of his sons, and we'd exchange the greetings—"Morning of goodness!" "Morning of light!" I'd step into the pretty little courtyard, with its banana tree and cactus, other small trees I didn't know, and the lavender flowers that in Brazil we used to call "Mary without Shame" in Portuguese. In English the flowers are called impatiens, and I thought them fitting for me to have at hand, since I was such a beginner in everything.

The courtyard had a floor of hard-packed dirt, and when we were working on a big project, some of the work was laid out on sawhorses on this surface outside. Otherwise we worked inside the shop, but even then, the light was with us, as the shop's fourth side had neither wall nor door but opened directly onto the yard.

A small, whitewashed building stood across the courtyard from the shop. One room of the structure stored the beautiful windows and doors before they were installed. The second room's single window, latticed with the wood Mahmud had worked on his lathe, looked out onto the courtyard. This was a comfortable room. Two walls were lined with cushioned benches, and in front of the window, a high wooden stool stood before a drafting table.

This was where Mustafa showed me how to draw the geometric designs that in the shop were translated into wood. At the drafting table, he taught me to draw the patterns used to make furniture and doors. He showed me how to work with a T square, protractor, and sharp pencil, and set me to memorizing the processes involved in drawing each pattern. There were more than three hundred of these patterns to learn, and in the first days I learned only two.

Here, also, Mustafa and I ate lunch until the four of us, Master Hassan and Mahmud, Mustafa and I, began eating lunch together. It was in the privacy of this room that I exchanged each morning the long loose cotton pants and long-sleeved shirt I wore on the street for a gray cotton *gallabiyya*, the men's gown I chose to wear in the shop to attract less attention to my female self. That must have looked a little weird, since although the men wore *gallabiyyas* at home, they wore Western shirts and pants when they worked in the shop. Only the foreigner wore traditional Egyptian clothes.

Wearing my *gallabiyya*, I'd step into the shop, breathe in with pleasure the smells of fresh-cut wood, and make my way to a workspace, standing on the blond wooden curls that had fallen on the concrete floor. Thick golden glue would already be simmering on the single-burner, three-legged, old-time brass kerosene stove. Hardened glue would be spilled over the edges of the messy glue pot, its distinctive, delicious smell sweetening the air.

When tea was needed, for us or for visitors, the glue pot would be removed and set on the rough wood table alongside the little stove, and a pot of sugared water placed on the flame instead, until sugar and water came to a boil. Then tea was added, just until the liquid welled up again into a second boil, after which the hot, sweet brew, the sugar almost caramelized, was poured into tiny fluted glasses. Each time that happened was, for me, a favorite time of day.

The work in the shop was organized so that while Mahmud carved the *mashrabiyya*, Master Hassan and Mustafa designed and built furniture and doors, repaired and renovated old pieces of furniture, and prepared the wooden frames into which they joined and set the wood Mahmud had carved. Mustafa and his father also negotiated the price and nature of the work, went on-site to install the doors and windows in the houses whose owners had commissioned them, and dealt with customers, both in and outside the shop. Most of the work was for new houses, much of it commissioned through Hassan Fathy for buildings he'd designed.

Except for the mechanical lathe and a small table saw, all the tools in the shop were hand tools. Virtually all the work that would have been done by power tools in the USA was done by hand. That meant that each board was rendered flat and smooth with a handheld plane, each wooden tongue, each groove hand-chiseled, and the finished work sanded by hand. No power sanders, saws, drills, or routers. Working in the shop, I came to value, more than I ever had, works made by hand. How much more beautiful were the wooden cabinets, tables, and doors produced here than the mass-produced furniture churned out in the United States by the thousands, each piece just like all the others. Unlike the plastics, polyester, and cement used in US industries, many of the materials Egyptian craftspeople were using had once been alive—wood made from trees, rugs and cloth woven from plant fibers and natural dyes. Even materials not usually considered living, such as mud, clay, and glass, were transformed, shaped, and decorated with an artist's skill. Slight variations in cloth, rugs, pottery, glass, and woodwork all signaled that each piece had been loved into existence completely by the eye, imagination, and the human touch.

So I would learn not only the use of a shop and hand tools, the finer work I'd wanted to learn ever since I began carpentry, but also ancient styles of woodworking, historically one of the finest forms of Islamic art. In the shop I was *M'alim* Hassan's "daughter," and a "sister" to his sons. Thus I was welcomed into yet another Egyptian family and offered yet another priceless gift, the chance to learn a craft from a master. I had come to Egypt not only to learn, but also to be of use in some way to Hassan Fathy's project. Instead, day after day I was being heaped with gifts and was finding no way to give back to those who were giving to me. And everything I was being given was something I needed, something I lacked. I wondered about this American who wanted so much to be of service, yet found herself continually on the receiving end. What would I find to give?

8: Two Kinds of Wealth

From a world of lesbian feminist tradeswomen in the San Francisco Bay Area, I was plunged into a world of men as well as women. I found much to appreciate and admire. I was surprised to feel this way in the Middle East, where most women have less freedom than women in the West. I was privileged to be treated as that anomaly, an "American woman," not subject to the rules Egyptian women were, and I was astonished by the ease with which this treatment was given. At work there was none of the condescension, barbed putdowns, or even open hostility I had experienced in the company of many male carpenters in America. No one tried to humiliate me or scare me off the job the way one union carpenter had by chasing me with a forklift, and another by jumping on the scaffolding that supported us, trying to make me fall. No one asked me why I wasn't home with my husband and children or claimed that men would fall and injure themselves because of the distraction of my female presence on the job. My life felt better balanced than it had before.

And yet—I was a lesbian. I had to decide what to do with that aspect of myself during the year I was in Egypt and later, when I lived in countries even more homophobic than my own.

Among lesbian feminists in the San Francisco Bay Area, it had by then become a matter of both pride and honor to refuse to hide your sexual orientation. Lesbians and gay men were standing up to denigration and abuse. To some of my friends in California, not to do so was not only unhelpful but also cowardly. No doubt some of them would have felt the same way in countries other than their own.

But I did not. My identity as a lesbian is only one part of who I am, and I felt strongly that I was in Egypt to learn, not to try to change another culture. Equally important, though hardly commendable, I was afraid that the Egyptians who cared about me would be appalled and reject me if they knew I was a lesbian. When attractions arose, as they did from time to time in later years in other Arab countries, I let them go. Halim knew; and in later years I told friends in Palestine who had lived for a time in the US and who I guessed would be more accepting. Mostly, though, my silence limited my friendships. It did not feel good not to be completely honest about who I was.

᭄

Egyptians asked me, "How do you like Cairo?" And when I answered that I loved it, they persisted, "Even though it is so poor, so crowded?" They asked me if I did not miss all I'd left behind in America.

I answered that I missed nothing. "I've learned that America is rich in material things, but poor in spirit." I was thinking of consumerism and of a certain negative edge to individualism in the country at large.

Of the two kinds of wealth, I told them, I'd pick that of Egypt. The openness and kindness I experienced in casual daily encounters, the warmth and generosity from women, men, and children to whom I was a stranger, continued to astonish me. In Egypt, both Islam and Christianity held a deeper place in people's lives than I had known religion to inhabit.

I saw much love of children in the faces and actions of their fathers, mothers, sisters, and brothers. A small child would reach out to offer me whatever she or he held—a cookie, a toy. So young, children were learning generosity. I liked the physical demonstrations of affection between adults of the same sex, appreciated seeing men or women walk through the streets holding hands, kissing one another's cheeks—once, twice, three times, right cheek, left cheek, right again—or walking arm in arm. I watched *M'alim* Hassan taking food from our lunch each day to give to poorer people on the street. And although expressions of love among family members are certainly prevalent in the West, I especially loved the directness with which people spoke in Egypt. One day I heard Halim encouraging his younger brother Muhammad, saying, "Find the beauty in yourself, and then you will be able to see it in others.

You will find yourself in a community of beautiful people,"
Halim said to me: "We used to call him *ya gameel* [O,
beautiful one] when he was young. He is very beautiful."

ᔐ

The intensely personal nature of my time in Egypt, while
infinitely precious and rare for the depth of experience it
gave me, did not provide me with much of the "big picture."
I had no means of knowing what reprehensible things the
Egyptian government might have been doing at the time.
I was not aware, for example, that the Egyptian President
Anwar Sadat, the darling of Western governments, was
imprisoning political opponents, among them Nawal El
Saadawi, the woman doctor whose feminist writings were
becoming known in the West.

Still, some of what I saw did begin to trouble me.
Everywhere I saw generosity, so why was there the same
contrast between rich and poor that existed in other
countries, including my own? Why were so many children
working? Women, for all the strength and positive self-
image that had so impressed me, did not have the same
freedoms as men. The women in *M'alim* Hassan's family,
though treated with respect, were far more protected than
men—their whereabouts were always known and excursions
outside the home monitored. They were the ones cooking
meals on kitchen floors. Like women everywhere, Egyptian
women were expected to cook and clean, do laundry, and
run the household. Many also worked outside their homes.

Nahid worked at a bank and did all the housework

too, for her sizeable extended family. *M'alim* Hassan's daughters could not have become carpenters. Women who were poor, unlike Nahid or *M'alim* Hassan's daughters, may have looked as if they had more freedom, for they could be seen working outside in the fields or in the streets selling cigarettes, matches, candy, or newspapers to passersby. But most of these women probably would not have chosen these exhausting and repetitive jobs, and they still did double duty at home.

Perhaps it was to be expected that I'd eventually develop a more realistic view of the vast and complex reality that was Egypt after that first month of ecstatic response to everything I heard and saw and everyone I met. After a month or so of euphoria, my spirits sagged.

I was becoming aware of how much more generous many people seemed to be with a foreigner—that is, myself—than with other Egyptians. I was offered a job; and although at first I refused pay, I was offered a wage, while little boys, in need of basic necessities, ran about the streets delivering tea or performing errands. A number of times, first on the train from Alexandria, I witnessed boys or young men being struck and run off buses, off trains, out of parking lots, with the men giving the beating saying that their targets were thieves. There was also much pushing and shoving getting on and off buses, which was how the woman who worked for Hassan Fathy had got her arm broken.

Might the physical demonstrations of affection I had observed and admired on the streets—men to men, women to women—not mean, after all, that Egyptians were warmer and more openhearted than Anglo residents of the US? Might these signs of affection simply be, instead, consistent with the Egyptian manner of showing more openly whatever they felt?

Evidence of poverty and the lack of health care were staggering. On the bus one night on my way home from work, a boy of eight or ten, terribly disabled, dragged himself, in evident pain, to the seat a young man vacated for him. The child could barely make it down the stairs of the bus when the time came for us both to get off. In the street, he slumped down onto the curb and walked just a few paces with his arm around my waist, until another traveler asked him, "*Rayah feyn?*" ("Where are you going?") and interpreted for me his answer: he would be taking another bus. The pain in the boy's eyes and in his movements stayed with me.

Another day I watched aghast as a man with no legs crossed a street. He lay just at the edge of the road, his body parallel to it. When he saw that no cars were coming, in a flash he rolled himself right across to the other side and arrived wrapped in dust.

If I had taken in at a deeper level the words of the Sudanese students, or noticed the difference with which I was treated and Egyptians sometimes treated each other, I might not have bumped down so hard from my little cloud. I might have understood better many of the problems in the city if I had been able to grasp, too, the fact that the population of Cairo, between nine and eleven million, possibly more, had tripled in the last decade, in the era before population control.

Two other sentences from Russell's 1978 article especially struck me: "Egypt is an experience that shakes us up and dares us to put ourselves together again," he wrote. "The Egyptian experience cannot be simplified. It is a manifold and disunited experience." Not only in centuries and material treasures but in so many other dimensions as well, his observations were proving true.

∽

Some of what was upsetting had as much to do with the US as with Egypt.

One evening after Arabic class, I went home with Mary, another American student, to eat with her, her husband, Luke, and their friend David, to stay the night. They lived in a huge apartment in a building in Zamalek, a part of the city where many rich people, including wealthy foreigners, lived. From their ceilings hung gilt candelabra, and their floor-to-ceiling windows were covered by draped curtains of thick velvet tied with cords wound with threads of gold. This was a world of difference compared to Nahid's home, not to mention mine.

"Oh no," Mary and Luke insisted, after I raised the question, "We could never live like this in the US."

Luke and David both worked for US companies engaged in construction and provision of other services to oil companies. When I met them, they were stationed on a barge near Suez, laying pipe for the canal Saudi Arabia was building from the Persian Gulf to the Red Sea. They and the other employees from the US were being paid a US wage, while the Egyptian workers, required by Egyptian law to be 65 percent of the workforce, held lower jobs, were paid far less, and were not given the chance to learn the technology that the Americans understood and that Egyptians required if they were to unearth, refine, and transport their own petroleum. The American and European workers were unwilling to give up their status as "know-it-alls," Luke said.

But Luke believed there was another reason that Egyptians were not being trained to take the higher positions. He said Egyptian workers were lazy and not so bright, and thus essentially un-trainable—"unable to work" was how he put it. This statement recalled to me similar racist views I'd heard adults express twenty-five years earlier in Brazil, and I was appalled that the same ignorant rubbish was still in circulation. Not much had changed, it seemed, since I was a child. I was so taken aback by the comment that, I am ashamed to say, I did not question or contradict him. But the next time I heard such a remark I was ready, and challenging bigotry in this new context, relating to Arabs and Islam, quickly became second nature.

The American couple, conceiving of Egyptians only as servants, employees, and lesser beings, had come to Egypt, one of the world's poorest countries, their move paid for by Luke's company, and they were living like kings, rent-free, in Cairo's equivalent of Beverly Hills. The contrast in the standard of living between these Americans and the

Egyptians I saw was nothing less than stupefying. This pattern was to be the same in every Arab country I lived in after that.

∽

"Think of the interchange between people who have less and people who have more as an investment," another American, Wayne, suggested one evening at Seigi and Mieko's dinner table.

A group of us from Italy, France, Yugoslavia, Spain, Brazil, Pakistan, India, and Japan, as well as Egyptians and an American—myself—would gather from time to time in the Japanese couple's apartment, some of us from Mieko's Arabic class, others people Seigi met through work. We would eat Mieko's superb dinners, fresh Nile fish cooked with specialties from Japan, and discuss the world. That night the subjects included socialism, capitalism, Egypt, and the United States. Wayne was an agriculturalist working for the US Food and Agriculture Organization. His theory was that everyone needed to be "invested in" and was a potential "investor" in others. Phrasing human need in business terms seemed odd to me, but at least he wasn't advocating blundering liberalism or misdirected Christian charity.

Of course Wayne's view of Egypt grew out of his contact and struggles with the Egyptian bureaucracy, with what he described as its greedy *kabirs* (literally, "big ones," as in "fat cats") and underpaid, under-worked, and enormous staff whose efforts did not translate to success.

His perspective was so very different from mine, which came from my current life among the tiny workshops in "old Cairo," where carpenter and ironer, old man and child worked hard from dawn until after dark. The chairmaker across the way from the shop was standing at his bench each morning when I arrived at the shop and was still working late in the evenings when I left. The owner of a car repair shop worked all day as an accountant in the School of Fine Arts at the University of Cairo, came home, slept awhile, then went out to the garage and worked there with his brothers. And on, and on, and on. People worked because they had to.

Wayne saw the farmers, too, and respected them, but he said his contact with the "higher-ups" was giving him a far less optimistic view of human nature than he had had before he'd come to Egypt. He disliked socialism for what he saw as fostering dependence on government. He disliked the Egyptian government's policy of subsidizing food prices at the expense of the farmer, who was forced to grow cotton instead of the food he needed to nourish his family and the rest of the population. The government bought the cotton cheaply from the farmers and sold it abroad at a profit, then used the money to subsidize much of the food that cost so little. And *that's* why a great round of wholesome brown bread cost just one *piaster* (less than 2 cents).

∾

An American woman I met living in Cairo saw the new situation in Egypt as "the worst of capitalism." She said that the US Agency for International Development (USAID) was using one-third of the economic aid the US gave Egypt that year for industrialization, ignoring small businesses. She criticized a system that involved middlemen who skimmed the profit, and which required a surplus labor force—women in Egypt and in the rest of the "developing" world or "Third World," now more commonly called the Global South—to keep wages low.

9: HALIM

Halim, the Egyptian architecture student whom I had met in Berkeley, who had told me about Hassan Fathy and given me his family's address in Cairo, returned to Egypt about a month after I arrived. He would give himself two months, he said, to decide if he wished to remain in Egypt, or return to the United States.

After nine years in the United States, he, too, was to some extent a stranger to Egypt. At that moment in time, we were both newcomers there. We began taking walks through various sections of Cairo, talking the world over. On the night of my thirty-fourth birthday, we walked in beauty along the Nile, golden with the lights reflected off the El Gama'a Bridge, sat a long while on one of the restaurant boats, and talked. At dawn, we were still strolling and humming down the wide avenues, lovely in their empty expanse. We walked under trees, past soldiers in their greatcoats with their guns and berets, warming their hands at the little fires they'd built on broken curbs. We admired the fragile baskets piled high on horse-drawn carts, and the loads of green hay and leafy plants. We talked of Egypt, and Halim described "the terror" he sensed in the attitudes of people around him. It was a fear, he said, that sprang from people's unease with who they had become. The city had "lost its center" due to the invasion of foreigners. These foreigners, he predicted, "in ten years will milk the country dry."

"Would Egypt be better off continuing to accept aid from Russia and maintaining closer ties with the USSR than with the US?" I asked.

"It's a matter of personal opinion," he said. "But in my view, the answer would be yes, because Russian aid does not bring with it the army of businessmen and investors, along with the propagation of the American image that comes with US aid. Egypt must take aid from both East and West, without allowing the evil aspects of either."

Halim described a job he'd had in Nigeria, where he became friends with his driver. One day he was reprimanded by the Egyptian who employed them both.

"Keep the distance between high and low," he was told, "or the system will never work."

"Luke and David are being paid to help create the distance between master and slave," Halim said. "This is a conscious act on the part of the companies who pay them." Hence the big houses, lavishly furnished, the parties, the chauffeur-driven cars—to perpetuate the gap between rulers and the ruled that capitalism requires.

Halim said he found creativity in the bustle of New

York, but not in Cairo. For me, it was the reverse: I found
creativity everywhere. In every street, in all the tiny shops,
people were hard at work, creating things—furniture,
doors, horseshoes, pots of brass, plates of copper with
filaments of other materials, the red hats called fezzes,
carpets, and cloth. Or they were baking bread or milling
spices or processing any of the other foods we ate. Much
of the work done in Cairo, unlike that in America, was un-
fragmented. The worker performed the whole task, as we in
the West had done some two hundred years ago. To work in
this way, I thought, must surely give a spiritual satisfaction
many of us lack.

Hassan Fathy had written in his book of the spiritual
growth that comes from learning to build one's own house.
All around me, people were performing entire tasks and
seeing for themselves their meaning and relevance to the
life of a community.

"Isn't this creative," I asked, "in a way the West no
longer knows?"

"People no longer take care of one another," Halim
said. "Perhaps they do in the neighborhood of the Citadel,
but here no longer." I was to hear this sentiment echoed
many times over the years I lived in Arab countries: "We
don't care for each other as we once did. In the old days,
we'd stop on the street and exchange elaborate greetings—
now we barely say hi! When someone was in the hospital,
we always went to visit. Now we do not."

Each time I heard these comments, pronounced with
such regret, in societies where it seemed people *were*

showing so much concern for one another, I could only wonder: What must life here have been like before?

"Sexual repression," Halim said, "is everywhere in Egypt, channeled into what is called spirituality." But again I could not see it. Religion in Egypt seemed to me a creative force, not a stagnant repertoire. The speech and behavior of Muslims I listened to or whose actions I observed—Mustafa, the Sudanese, *M'alim* Hassan, strangers on the street—suggested to me that Islam was important to them in a way most Americans, certainly myself, did not experience religion.

Halim mourned the changes in his own community, Giza. He pointed up to the apartment building we were passing.

"That's the product of the idea of the individual—each family for itself."

"But what do you expect? Against what standard do you measure Egypt? Certainly not the US!"

"I measure Cairo against the Cairo of yesterday, or against other countries now. Raise your standards."

Stop excusing people! I said to myself. *Is this a form of racism in myself? Expect the best from Egypt just as you expect the best from the United States!*

"I realized I need pass no tests," Halim said, "and coming to Egypt for two months like this is a regression from that realization."

"But you came to test the place," I objected.

"Never," he answered. "One thinks one tests others, and only and always is testing oneself."

∾

"I want to ask you something very important," Hassan Fathy said once when I was visiting. "Are you learning the joinery? It is very important that you do. Save the *mashrabiyya*, to the fifteenth millimeter, for afterward. The fancy stuff can come later." He said also, "See if you can learn a few words of Arabic."

I told him, "I will do as you say."

∾

One day at work, I learned about what seemed to me a very handy business. Mustafa's briefcase was stolen, and in it were documents valuable to him, though without monetary worth. Instead of darting frantically around looking for his briefcase or for the documents, as someone in the US might, hoping the thief might have discarded them in his rush, Mustafa just grimaced with annoyance. He looked resigned, rather than anxious. He told me he was going out to seek the "master *kleftees*."

"*Kleftees*?"

Mustafa pantomimed snatching something from the air, turning to run. Thieves. But *master* thieves?

"There are five master thieves," he said. "I have to find one of them to get my briefcase back."

Hours later, Mustafa returned to the shop, suitcase in hand, important documents inside. Sure enough, he had located one of the master thieves, been told the price he needed to pay to get his briefcase back, had crossed the city to his bank to take out the required funds, and then traveled all the way back across town again to pay the *kleftee's* ransom fee.

What a clever enterprise! The thief who had stolen the briefcase was protected. A wage, presumably satisfactory, was generated for both thief and "master thief." And the stolen goods were returned to their rightful owner, who surely ended up relieved and grateful, quite possibly happier than he had been before (although Mustafa, hot and grumpy after his trips across the city, might not have agreed).

∾

One cool overcast day, the air had an uncanny feel, a sense of before-holiday but of something more than that, something momentous, for which we were all collectively waiting. In the streets hung expectation, strung tight on a thin, taut cord that bound us all together, as if the city's millions were all holding our breath.

The following day would bring the *'eid*, or festival, of *as-sadaqa*—almsgiving, "a grant from the rich to the poor"; *Beiram*, Hassan Fathy called it. It was to be a holiday, but it held none of the personal, material anxiety of Western Christmases I had known.

Large gatherings of sheep, and here and there a great cow, were crowded unnaturally in the roads. The animals' cries held for me the sound of death, and no wonder: in many of the small shops near the Citadel, great carcasses of sheep, blood-red, stripped of their skins, hung upside down on butchers' hooks.

The holiday celebrates God's mercy in allowing Abraham to sacrifice a lamb instead of his son Isaac, and so in Egypt sheep are killed to mark God's grace, and alms are given to the poor. Mustafa explained to me why he would drop me off at Tahrir Square instead of driving me home.

"Because my father must go to the bank—'Take this . . . Take this.'" He mimed his father handing money to the poor.

That evening, as Halim washed dishes and cooked an omelet for us in Nahid's tiny kitchen, he told me the fullest version of the story I'd yet heard, which, to my surprise, was like the one I was taught as a child from the Bible. The Qur'an, I learned, contains a number of stories similar to those in the Jewish Torah and the Christian Bible.

As Halim told it, God told Abraham that he was to kill his son Isaac when he had reached the end of all his resources. But when the time came, the bitterest hour of Abraham's journey to Mecca, an angel of the Lord appeared to him and told him he need not kill his son after all but that he might sacrifice a sheep instead.

Halim said as a child he'd watched as the butchers, dressed in pure white, slit the throats of the animals. Children dipped their hands in the blood as it ran in the street and patterned handprints in bright red on the butchers' snowy robes. Mary said later that she and Luke, driving north to Dumyat, had seen houses with red marks on the outer walls.

The night before the holiday, after hearing music with Nahid, I went with Halim to a friend's house and sat long hours with the men there. At last I slept, under a thin blanket, a chilled sleep on an empty bed in the next room. At four or five a.m., Halim woke me up:

"Do you want to sleep, or do you want to come with us?" The air was filled with an unearthly drumming, the pounding of feet in the streets all around, the thunder of what must have been a million voices chanting. I had never—and have never since—heard anything approaching that sound. Joining Halim and his friends, who were still awake and talking, I looked out the upper-story window and saw that the entire city, as far as I could see, was packed with slowly moving masses of people, all headed in the same direction, to the center of Cairo. Men, women, and children—the country's entire population, it seemed— were flooding into the capital on every thoroughfare, traveling by every conceivable means—on foot, in cars, on motorcycles, atop wooden wagons. They had walked or driven or ridden all night long, Halim told me, to reach the city, some stopping along the way to pray.

The radio boomed, magnifying the crowd's chorus, while outside in the streets streamed men wearing *gallabiyyas* and turbans and scarves; women, too, were in long gowns. Others stood at corners chanting, or prostrating themselves in the streets in prayer. Halim and the other men in the apartment recited, over and over, words of praise for God.

"Wash your feet," Halim told me. "It's a ritual. You must do it, if you'll be praying with the women."

Six of us crammed into someone's tiny Volkswagen and headed in the same direction as the others, the car a speck in the moving mass of humanity. Now people were moving almost silently through the broad streets. Men on motorcycles, women in flowing black clothing riding on the rear, squeezed past us.

We parked, and Halim arranged a scarf about my head. I followed other women to the brightly colored, busily patterned tent-like structure open to the sky, its sides hung with material effectively concealing us all from the sight of the male crowd we could hear rumbling around outside. We were few, we women, who bent to remove our shoes at the tent entrance, ducked our heads under the material, and took places in rows on carpets cold from the chilly dawn air. Then we waited a long time, during which women near me smiled and welcomed me; several young women, veiled and gloved, faces covered all but the eyes, introduced themselves.

Then: *Allaho akbar!* (God is great!) five times, with the women helping me to perform with them the movements of the prayer—bending, prostrating until our foreheads touched the ground, standing once more. Then, recitations I didn't understand because my guides' explanations were cut short by the prayer. Only the first I understood: "God is great!"—and after that I heard it always from the mosques. As the prayer ended—could I wait? the women asked. Could I come home with them now? Could I go to the mosque with them? No, for Halim and Muhammad were waiting for me. In a flurry of thanks and an exchange of addresses, I left and joined the brothers waiting.

Later, exhausted, I went home to bed, chilled and

feverish. The teeming, overcast afternoon of the *'eid* became for me a memory of a people's passionate evocation of their God, amid movement and dust, with the clarity and timelessness that come when one has not slept.

10: THE END IS UNKNOWN

For days after that, I stayed in bed, through the remainder of the holiday and beyond, as sick as I'd ever been. When I did not return to work after the *'eid*, Mustafa appeared at my bedside. Solicitous, sympathetic, he drove me to their family doctor, who gave me medicine for a "gastrointestinal infection" brought on, he thought, by the chill. I should have recognized the signs of cold weather when well-to-do Egyptian women began appearing in the streets wearing high boots and woolen coats. Instead I had been thinking, *What in the world . . . ?* Having assumed that Egypt was always hot, I hadn't brought warm clothes from the United States.

Wrong! Egypt is not always hot. From late November to sometime in April each year, poor people suffer as much as or more than they do in the heat of summer. The sisters sold me some used clothes, of which it turned out they had a tremendous stash. Later, I found a vast and wonderful market heaped only with used items. There I found a tall pair of leather boots and a baggy, full-length wool coat.

The two weeks following the *'eid* were the roughest I'd had since I'd left America three months before. Certain that solitude would help, as it had in the past, I appealed once more to a family down the street who had turned me down earlier in my bid to rent the room behind their garage. To my relief, I was accepted. Still weak from the sickness, I moved out of the room I was renting with the *deux dames* and into a space by myself.

My room, a cold cell detached from the main building, could be reached only through the auto service garage managed by the old couple's four grown sons. Between the garage and my room ran a narrow concrete alleyway. Off that was an even smaller room containing a showerhead, a sink, and a toilet—it struck me that this was what was meant by a "water closet," the original WC—which I shared during the workday (and into the work-night) with the brothers and another tenant whom I never saw. His room, which seemed to be mostly underground, opened off the alley outside my door.

The alley was just wide enough so that in warm weather I could set out my chair and read, though there were many flies. The brothers were kind and friendly to me, and one of them, Munir, eventually became a friend. The whole situation—a single foreign woman living alone among all these men—must have been a bit bizarre for Egypt, but by the time I asked again if I could move in, the family had probably decided I was someone who was polite and well-behaved, a reliable tenant. The rent was low—the owners hadn't taken advantage of my foreignness to charge me more than they had the two Sudanese women—and the people were kind.

Still, I found it difficult to get used to my new home. The square building had one small wire-covered window high above the narrow cot on which I slept, along with a desk, chair, small metal wardrobe for my clothes, and a sink in the corner. There was no hot water in the sink or the shower, no heat in winter cold or cooling in summer heat. The door couldn't be left open without exposing me to the view of the brothers working in the garage and of passersby on the street. The concrete walls and ceiling had once been painted a pale blue, but now the paint was peeling off, and the walls were stained.

$$\backsim$$

There was another element to the sinking spirits I began to feel a month or two into my stay. It was not only an increased awareness of "real life" intruding into my blissful bubble. The real intruder was the inner world I had brought with me—the figurative luggage I'd grown accustomed to hauling about with me, and which a simple change of location could not eliminate. I was negative and easily depressed. When I encountered difficulties of any sort, the result was not a happy one.

As I continued to visit Hassan Fathy, I came to see that all my protestations had quite a negative effect on the ones who wanted to arrange things for me, include me, make me happy, feed me, and care for me. It seemed I must be very poor in spirit if I was so concerned that in taking I would incur obligations I would not be able to repay.

For all my newfound love of things Egyptian, my thoughts were still for the most part centered on myself. No sooner had I begun to grasp the dire living conditions of so many Egyptians than I lost sight of the real poverty all around me: living on so little, I began to feel anxious about my own diminishing funds. It was often hard to get facts straight, for my Arabic was stuck and wasn't moving ahead. My slowness in learning the language was demoralizing. Many times, when trying to understand something, I not only got it wrong but heard the exact opposite of what the person was trying to tell me. Instead of the voice of wonder, it was the voice of discouragement I was now quick to hear: *You can't learn Arabic. You've never been able to draw—you don't have the talent. You've clearly not got the mind for geometry—I could have told you that before you began.*

Sometimes my world crumbled when I could not draw a geometric figure or cut the tiny strips of wood to fit together. The boards I planed by hand did not come out smooth and flat but looked like waves in the Mediterranean. Mustafa and Master Hassan encouraged me as any good teachers would, assuring me that I would learn *shiwayya, shiwayya*—"little by little," or "step by step." But to me it seemed I was utterly unsuited to learning the geometric forms so fundamental to Islamic art.

Answering my discouragement, Mustafa told me he'd been for four years studying in an Islamic art institute, and five years before that learning about Islamic art. "It's hard," he said. "You cannot expect to do it *'alatool* [straightaway, or all at once]."

Mustafa and I joked that we were "bracken," which is to say "broken," from our efforts—his to teach me and mine to learn. But for all his and his father's kindness and encouragement, I began to question the path I was on. Why was I trying to learn something for which I had no talent?

∽

One of the most important things that happened to me during this difficult time—in fact, during that entire year in Egypt—occurred one morning when I came to work with a badly twisted ankle. My ankle throbbed and swelled, but I knew that if I didn't walk on it, I would have to stay home, and the last thing I needed was a day at home alone.

I was, quite simply, in a bad mood. As soon as I stepped through the door and into the courtyard of the shop, my grumpiness and negativity were apparent to *M'alim* Hassan. Still, as he always did, he warmly greeted me and asked how I was.

In reply I grumbled, "Not so good," and complained that I had hurt my ankle.

To my surprise, instead of answering sympathetically, *M'alim* Hassan stopped me as I was about to step up onto the concrete floor of the shop. Gravely, he looked at me and spoke to me severely. In that moment, something rather amazing happened. Although I still spoke only a few words of Arabic, I had no trouble at all understanding the words he spoke to me.

He pointed to the sky. A great stream of words poured from him and washed over me as the Arabic language does, sweeping up listeners and carrying them away on a beauteous, hypnotic tide. I could not have translated directly a single word he used. Yet I had no doubt that he was scolding me, almost as if I had blasphemed, for feeling sorry for myself. I understood that I had, unwittingly, committed a colossal blunder. I was, instead of complaining, to be grateful for everything I had.

He lifted his hand toward the sun slanting into a perfect circle on the clean-swept courtyard floor. I must always thank God, he was saying, for all I had been given. No matter what my problems, I must give thanks to God. In Arabic, the expression "Thanks be to God" sounds like "*Alhamdulillah*."

After that day, in every Arab country I lived in or visited, I was to hear and recognize these words spoken by Muslims dozens of times a day. They were said almost always as a reflexive initial answer to the question, "How are you?" To that query, there was no lukewarm "Okay," not even a "Fine." Instead, the first response was to thank a greater, more generous force than we humans could ever hope to be. I found it a good grounding, a way to put into perspective my tendency to gravitate toward the negative.

The words lifted up instead of casting down. It was not that people avoided speaking honestly to their friends about things that went wrong. But before anything else came the reminder to be grateful for all that was right. As my understanding of the language grew, I noticed with interest that the same words of thanks might be spoken in sympathy or condolence, even for a tragic loss. These words offered a way through sorrow. After that first time, although I was not a follower of any religion, whenever I heard or spoke the words, I felt and acknowledged gratitude. From then on, I too included in my response to the question "How are you?" acknowledgment of something greater and better than myself.

∽

Each night after I returned from work, I began to read anything I thought might help me with my various dilemmas. The problems were not new ones; I'd always suffered from self-centeredness, impatience, a diffuse anxiety, lack of perspective, negativity. Self-doubt. But in Egypt, where I was living without the clutter of an "ordinary" daily life, a life that was fast-paced, crammed with errands and habits and complicated schedules, and without millions of words, all of which I understood, streaming into my ears, the qualities that bothered me were crystallized. And they were easier to see in Egypt also because they contrasted so dramatically with the attitudes of so many of the people around me. Here was a different culture on which I might draw. So I read—books on Islam, fiction and nonfiction about Egypt. I read in translation any Arabic literature I could find, including stories and novels by the famous Egyptian author Naguib Mahfouz. So that I would not forget, I wrote or copied out small reflections from the books I was reading. Two in particular still strike me. One read:

> The student . . . should be able to say . . . "Do I always have to be dependent on 'seeing a man with no feet' . . . before I realize that 'I have feet'?"
>   —Shah 1979. "The Sanctuary of John the Baptist," *Wisdom of the Idiots,* 157

And this, from an Indian Muslim:

> The subject should always disappear in the object. In our ordinary affections for one another, in our daily work with hand or brain, most of us discover soon enough that any lasting satisfaction, any contentment that we can achieve, is the result of forgetting self, of merging subject with object in a harmony that is of body, mind and spirit.
>   —Muhammad Aga Khan, 1877-1957, Imam of the Khoja Ismailis, India, "Looking Forward," from his autobiography *World Enough and Time,* quoted in Kritzeck 1970, 274

But the state of being for which I strived was easier to read about than to practice. One day in the shop, I took a piece of wood without asking, determined to carry out a project on my own. Until then, I had hesitated to undertake anything independently, mostly out of fear of wasting expensive wood. But that day, silently, I worked alone, and when *M'alim* Hassan asked, I refused to show him my work, partly because I knew the work itself was not good, and partly because I dreaded his telling me so.

"I am the teacher!" he said, angry with me at last. "Didn't I show you how to make the *sabras*, the *mafrooka*, the stool that holds the Qur'an? I help you do one thing, but you turn away and do another! You are hardheaded, Chivvis!" Immediately, of course, I felt terrible, and I apologized. I was forgiven, it appeared, for *M'alim* Hassan then stopped his own work and redrew the lines for me, so that I could start again. The second time, I did the project well.

To be told by Mustafa that I was hardheaded was one thing; to be told the same thing by *M'alim* Hassan quite another. Chastened, I again examined my attitude and actions. I wasn't entirely sure I understood why he had been so angry. I wasn't sure if it was because of ego, his dislike of anything done incorrectly, or his deep belief in the system of training in which the student worked under the direction of a master. I decided it was the last: I had violated the teaching method to which we, in our carpentry sisterhood in Berkeley, California, were such strangers.

In the US, each or several of us would plunge into a project, knowing little or nothing—and emerge, with or without someone else's help, after a shorter or longer time, triumphant. In relating to *M'alim* Hassan as "master," I was committing myself to learning his way, entering, at least for the time being, a different kind of relationship than I had ever had.

When I first arrived in Cairo, I had been flattered that Maha's brother and the other Sudanese students, as well as Mustafa and Mahmud, all said they were my "brothers." But now I knew they called themselves my brothers because there was no other category into which I could fit in the cultural scheme. I was beginning to understand more clearly what relationships entailed in the Arab world. I was *M'alim* Hassan's daughter—he had even suggested I call him Baba, or Father, Hassan—and I was sister to his sons. It seemed there was no category outside "family" to which a woman, whether married or unmarried, could belong and associate with men.

In *M'alim* Hassan's case, though, the father-daughter relationship was to some extent confused with the master-helper, employer-employee relationship of the everyday business world.

What precisely did it mean to him that I was still eating my breakfast in the square? That I could be seen in his neighborhood speaking to someone on the street? That I might not go directly home each evening after my work in the shop was finished? I knew these things were anathema to him. And the longer I worked with him, and the closer the relationship between us grew, the more he tried to act toward me like a father.

In that role his instinct was to pull me *away* from the shop, put me in the home, and protect me from outside influence, certainly from manual labor. At the same time, I was a guest, and he would not violate the responsibility he felt to act graciously to a guest. My role was further complicated by the fact that I had been foisted upon him by his patron, Hassan Fathy. It would be no wonder, I reflected, if *M'alim* Hassan had a headache every day, even if he had nothing to worry about but me.

But there was more to come. Grand dreams, fattened on Mustafa's predictions about the speed and quantity of what I would learn, and on Hassan Fathy's recommendation that I read *Her-Bak* "about apprenticeship in ancient Egypt," whooshed to a more realistic size just a few days later.

This occurred in a talk with *M'alim* Hassan, with Halim acting as translator and intermediary. I have forgotten what the precise trigger was this time; it was probably my impatience with the little I was doing in the shop, for I was often impatient, sitting through days when there was no work I was qualified to do. There were times when Mahmud was working on the lathe but had not completed enough work to supply the rest of us with the material we needed for the next steps. Sometimes, business was slow. Mostly, I had simply not achieved a level of competence that allowed me to be useful. Uncomfortable doing nothing, not understanding the way *M'alim* Hassan viewed my role in the shop, frustrated at my own lack of skill, I grumbled like a spoiled child in a way that shames me when I recall it now.

Whatever the initiating incident, there was Halim, to my embarrassment, mediating for me at my work, where a meeting had been called to explain to me my position in the shop. In the course of the discussion, I came to view teaching and learning in ways I never had before. Learning in the shop of a master carpenter in the traditional way in Egypt was not like working at an ordinary job in the US, I was told. For one thing, the kind of teaching I wanted from *M'alim* Hassan would have required from me a lifetime commitment. Stripped of all *M'alim* Hassan's politeness and razed to the truth, Halim's translation was blunt:

"*M'alim* Hassan cannot take you as an apprentice. An apprentice makes a long-term commitment. He is placed, usually by his own father, in the hands of the master. He is there, after that, for the master to direct as he chooses."

Certainly I had made no such commitment, to the teacher, to the place, or in time. And even if I did want to make this my life choice, even if I chose to stay and work, "This would be impossible," Halim said, "unless you made a cultural commitment.

"You may feel it is not enough for you," Halim said, then added, more gently, "It's not only you who have to make such choices. I do, too. I'm having to make such choices now.

"On the positive side, *M'alim* Hassan—because of his code of ethics—feels bound to teach you the craft, because the ethics of the craft require that the master be open with the knowledge to those who ask and seriously want to learn. He will teach you, not because of anything about you, but because it is in his nature to do so. The individual here is not what the individual is in the West."

I had gotten a glimmer of this fact in the shop just a few days before, when I'd noticed a lack of attachment to projects on the part of both Mustafa and his father. This surprised me, since carpenters I knew in the US took pride in completing a project on their own. I, too, would have viewed another person's work on a task I'd begun to be inappropriate interference.

Mustafa, in contrast, would begin a wood carving, turn it over to me to work on, and take it back to add a touch or two. This happened in the case of the blocks I carved for a box he was making to show in an exhibition at the French Cultural Institute. Or we'd both begin work on a *sabras* door, and then I'd leave to teach. Returning the next day, I'd find myself instinctively seeking the place he had not been working when I left, looking for "my side," only to find that the evening before he had switched sides and begun working on the part of the project I had been thinking of as "mine." He showed no concern if I took up the work right where he left off. He began a cabinet for a friend's shop; his father came in and put in all the shelves.

Sometimes, when the tasks were very different, there was a logical division of labor. But it was not at all uncommon to see Mustafa come in and pick up a plane or chisel or saw and begin working on the very board his father had left some minutes before, without any communication between them.

I was barely conscious of my reaction to this until I put all the incidents together, and realized how different this was from our way of working in the West. I wondered if there was more of a communal feeling about work in Egypt. Was there less sense of the importance of one's own self or of one's own work? Was each project seen not as an individual product, but as the artistic creation of all? Yes, it seemed.

During the conversation with Halim, *M'alim* Hassan offered to pay me at the role of "helper"—LE 6 per week, or LE 1 per day (at the time, about $12 per week, or $2 per day). In importance, "helper" was one rung below apprentice.

"An apprentice is one who can be left alone three days in the shop, and you cannot," Halim said. "Mustafa is at the level of apprentice. You are not even as much help as 'Adil [a young boy *M'alim* Hassan had recently hired], who is at his beck and call, whom he can send anywhere and have do all kinds of other things perhaps not even connected with carpentry."

M'alim Hassan spoke then, and Halim, with a smile, told me, "*M'alim* Hassan says there are four levels in the craft: master, apprentice, helper, and—"

"—American guest," I interrupted, and was instantly sorry that I had.

"Yes," Halim said, but I asked him to explain the fourth. "It's called 'boy,'" he replied. "This is the one who is ordered to fetch and carry. You are here in the shop because you are lucky. You are fortunate to be in this place at this time. You are not being taught because of qualities you have, but because you happen to be here now. Someone in Switzerland wanting to learn *mashrabiyya* would be out of luck.

"But," he added, "you can learn only what you are capable of learning." As if in direct response to my

impatience and my frustration—at my slowness and
mistakes, at the periods in which there was no one actively
"teaching" me, at my lack of productivity—*M'alim* Hassan
and Halim were both giving me the message: "One learns
in accordance with one's capacity to learn."

You will learn what you are able to learn: of all the words,
these spoke most forcefully to me.

It occurred to me, also, that a particular attitude toward
life I'd noticed among Egyptians might be connected with
this idea of recognizing one's own limits. In Egypt, I didn't
find the straining against life's constraints that I did in
America. People seemed to live with an acceptance I had
never felt, as if they believed that once they had done their
best, done all they could do, they could trust that some force
greater than their own would ensure their well-being. This
attitude underlay the words of the Prophet Muhammad,
which I was to hear quoted more than once: "First tie
your camel, then trust in God." Generalized anxiety was
replaced by a sense of ease.

"There's no use trying to push it," Halim said. "It's a
different concept than the one prevalent in America,"
he suggested, "where we think we can learn anything,
everything. *M'alim* Hassan is saying that you will learn, as
you are able, within the limits set—if you want to learn at
all. It's crucial, and complex; and it's something you must
accept. Or you may decide it's not worth it, that you are not
getting enough.

"He cannot take you as an apprentice, because the end
is unknown."

Before he left, Halim relayed to me *M'alim* Hassan's insistence that I not speak, beyond politeness, to people on the street—that I not "engage in conversation," was the way he put it.

"At this point, you are past the stage of 'guest,'" Halim said. "You are his daughter. Everyone on the street now associates you with him. This places limits on you that you might not like. It's the same with me. In the street I am known as 'friend of Hassan Fathy.' I don't know if I like that—it limits me. But," he added, "now *M'alim* Hassan is telling you nicely. But if you fail to obey—"

"—Out!" I interrupted again; but Halim continued, "You will see another side, and it will be very different from the one you've seen."

When later, I finally was able to read *Her-Bak*, I found the lessons I was in the process of learning so painfully were described, just as I was living them, in this tale of ancient Egypt. The novel tells the story of Chick-Pea, an Egyptian boy who sought to become a disciple in the mysteries of the Egyptian temple. But instead of teaching him in the way he had expected, Chick-Pea's spiritual teacher apprenticed the boy to a craft. First he set Chick-Pea to learn pottery. But each vessel Chick-Pea made in the pottery shop lost its shape and crumpled. Chick-Pea went back to his teacher. He complained that the work was boring and objected to the rules of the trade.

Next the teacher set Chick-Pea to carve stone vessels. But the stone didn't yield to his hand as clay had done. Chick-Pea complained and kept asking questions of the stone carver instead of concentrating on the work. Again the boy appealed to his teacher: "Why am I being apprenticed to this trade?"

His teacher answered sternly. "What you are doing does not matter so much as what you are learning from doing it. You will stay at this trade until you have mastered cowardice."

A few days later Chick-Pea went back to his teacher and told him that he had cut his vase the wrong way. Another day he reported that his drill had gone through the stone by accident and wrecked it. Day after day he returned downcast to his teacher: he had cut a block badly, had gauged poorly the way of the thread. So it went, "until the time came when Chick-Pea appeared evening after evening with a serene look on his face." Only then was he released from his apprenticeship to the stone carver and shown the unprecedented favor of selecting his next trade.

✍

Gradually, talking and listening to Halim and interacting with other members of his family, hearing of their situations and problems, affirming what each of us gets from the others—all this helped me to feel better. The fear I felt at returning to my room each night faded. As I sat down to write, I'd ask myself:

"Okay, what's happening now? . . . and now? . . . and now? At any moment, is there cause for terror?" And of course, at each moment, the answer was "No, everything's okay; life's going on." I needed to recapture the ease I'd felt as I traveled across Europe on my way to Egypt. Then, positive feeling had come from the fact that I was constantly moving, always looking forward expectantly to what might be over the next hill. Learning to find the same calm in the stillness of remaining in one place was the challenge.

On one of our walks, Halim told of the doves that mated outside his window on Benvenue Avenue in Berkeley. His love of that memory of the doves reminded me that of course there are always doves outside one's window. So I described the tree and the patch of sky outside my little room, and the chickens, and the kindness of the brothers working in their garage.

"Maybe Egypt will get you writing again," he said.

Gradually, instead of viewing my cold stone room as a prison cell, a place of confinement and depression, I came to see its very barrenness as making space for me. Living with the two women, I had felt stifled by the constant darkness, the sense of being underground—for they, like many living in the dusty desert world, always closed the shutters to keep out the dust and sun. In my new room with its tiny window, through which I could see a tree and patterned sunlight, I felt free to read and write, and my mind felt free to move as it wanted.

One evening I wrote:

I begin to care for this room, with the very solitude I dreaded so. It's not so lonely here, really. I hear the voices of the men in the garage down the alley, present but never troublesome—the brothers talking,

music from the radio. . . . One of the men recited
verses from the Qur'an tonight. They're close enough
to my room for a kind of company, but not oppressive
in the way I found the lights, talking, television,
the eating of the women in the underground house,
which was so green and dark, and the alienation that
comes with meaningless proximity.

I'm helped too by the morning breakfasts in Al
Qal'a, by my friend who gives me always the white
china dish painted with red roses and the crate to sit
upon while I eat his ful and falafel, and who never
lets me pay until after I have eaten.

∽

About this time, Munir, one of the brothers who worked
in the garage just in front of my room, befriended me as I
passed by their shop. I liked Munir, and I got the impression that he wanted someone to talk to just as I did. In time,
living in other countries, I found not only that many people
shared my interest in hearing someone with perspectives
different from theirs, but also that people sometimes felt
they could confide in me something for which they would
be criticized by people within their own culture. Munir's
and my common language was French.

He and his mother visited me one evening when I was
sick, his mother making him bring me tea and the "little
breads" she had made, and laughing at our communication
gap. Munir stayed after she left and told me, among other
things, that he and other male friends shared an apartment

in a building where they drank whiskey, smoked hashish, and were "with women," where they did "all things *mauvaise*." He said he went to the apartment once a month to relieve the suffering that was part of his life. To atone, he read the Qur'an, prayed, and gave money to the poor. His home, he said, was like a mosque; he would never behave so at home. That was why he would not rent to Halim or other Egyptians:

"Because I am that way, I assume others are the same."

Somehow we got onto the subject of smoking. Munir never smoked in front of his mother. Even as a guest, I wasn't supposed to smoke in front of her either, although I hadn't known that when I met her. Munir said that he had made allowances for my foreignness and didn't hold it against me. He had decided, in spite of my smoking, that I was "good." Somewhat contradictorily, he praised me for being open when I smoked, for doing in public the thing others sometimes did, but only behind closed doors. There were women in Egypt who smoked, he said, but they were "*mauvaise*."

"But why are they not to be praised, like myself, for doing in public what they do in private?" I asked.

But he answered, "They're just . . . *mauvaise*."

∽

"So," Hassan *Bey* asked me one evening, "you are continuing to learn some things? You are learning something new?" When I assured him I was, he asked, "Will you be able to use in America what you are learning here?"

"Yes, positively."

"Yes, because a door such as this"—he gestured to one of his massive works of art—"can help the most barren room." I was reminded of his houses at Gourna, built for such low cost, and for the poorest people, but nevertheless adorned with the beautiful *sabras* art.

That night Hassan Fathy spoke of not adding "one *piaster*" to the cost of any dwelling to be built in the desert for the poor, for to do so would deprive "one million" people. Yet I knew he intended that the simplest of houses should each have some work of wooden art in them.

He spoke of the reversal he saw the Institute as bringing about: Americans and others would come to Egypt to learn, and Egyptians would no longer be seeking knowledge always from the West.

∽

After Halim suggested I write, and I'd begun, I found myself looking forward each day to returning to my little home. As the days went on, I worked with my hands, practiced giving, and lived in the present moment, strangely unburdened by my own personal history. Each day I did the carpentry, I grew more in love with it. It was growing into a love such as I had never experienced, accompanied by more patience and less fear than I had known before in any learning process. I began once more to enjoy the bright swept courtyard. I felt the calm that comes from acceptance and gratitude.

∽

One aspect of life that gave me increasing pleasure was the sound of spoken Arabic. One afternoon, listening to the boy 'Adil as he stood before *M'alim* Hassan, talking, I was spellbound. I decided that there was something in the Arabic language, and in the speaker's use of it, that fascinates. Much conversation took place with this mesmeric intensity. Person after person talked uninterrupted for long spells; everything that was said seemed to matter to speaker and listeners alike.

'Adil was giving a performance, I realized as I listened, using words and tone of voice, with a pause, a lilt, a run, repetition, sometimes rhyme. He was magnificent. I looked away but always found my gaze coming directly back, and I felt like applauding when he finished.

"Blah, blah, blah," *M'alim* Hassan mimicked, but not unkindly, when 'Adil finally stopped talking and turned away.

11: KINDS OF FULFILLMENT

Nahid and I often talked about work, hers and mine. Several times she said to me, "Here we do not leave a job." She seemed to be saying, "How rich you must be, if you could leave your job!" But one day, she said she understood my situation for the first time—that I worked with other women in a company, and that I would return to work, perhaps while others traveled.

I asked her what job she would have if she could have any in the world.

"*La traduction* [Translation]," she answered, and I remembered the words scrawled in a child's handwriting in the front of the dictionary Heba used: "*Le premier cadeau de mon père—Nahid* [The first gift from my father—Nahid]." She wanted to work for the UN, perhaps, or another organization.

The dream didn't seem unrealistic. Her French was good. Banks and other groups needed translators, and her first job at the bank had been translation. She told me she had recently called a supervisor who told her if she would call him back in a few days, he would see if her position in the bank could be changed to one she would like better.

We agreed that if a person does not do what she needs to do, *elle commence á mourir* (she begins to die). In French, Nahid said, there is an expression to describe what happens to someone who fails to do what her nature prescribes—something about being consumed by fire: she grows smaller and smaller. I began to think that Nahid and I understood each other very well. Like the spirits of her brother Halim and their younger brother Muhammad, hers was one I was beginning to love.

$$\backsim$$

At last one day, *M'alim* Hassan and I finished one of the doors I'd worked so hard to plane—and it looked fine! Earlier, Mustafa's friend Gamal had informed me that a box for which I'd carved nine blocks of deer and flowers was a project Mustafa had started three years earlier. That day, I also finished a small wood carving of a geometric design that had distressed me when I had first tried to learn it.

Suddenly, outside in the street, we heard the unmistakable braying of a donkey, and a cry—"*Khass kabir! Khass kabir!*"—and *M'alim* Hassan rushed out to buy great heads of romaine lettuce delivered by donkey cart. He called me to come, and handed me a fresh, stiff head of my own. We washed them at the stone basin in the courtyard, and then, sitting side by side, we devoured them entirely. I copied him in this, as I did in carpentry, first stripping the long stems of their green leaves, tossing these away, and eating instead the watery, crisp stalk. When all the "branches" were gone, *M'alim* Hassan took a chisel from the shop and cleaned the main stalk, and I found that this, like the heart of an artichoke, had the best taste of all. Like rabbits we munched, fast, and when we were done, the parched earth all around was littered with limp pages of pale green.

That afternoon after I left work, I was making my way up the hill toward El Midan Salah ad-Din and the bus stop, when two officers—whether police or soldiers, I could never tell—one of whom was handcuffed to a prisoner, stepped up to the little stand under the tree in the square and bought cigarettes. The prisoner was a woman, her reddish hair falling thick to her shoulders. She was wearing a red sweater and black corduroy pants, all fitting nicely to show her figure, a style unusual in Egypt, especially in the conservative Al Qal'a neighborhood. She leaned toward one of the men, laughing, and reached up a hand as if to pat the other on the cheek, her face close to his.

I recalled a remark Halim had made about the growing number of prostitutes in Cairo. She must have been one, and once I had seen her, she reappeared often in my mind, flaunting, so attractive, moving handcuffed to the stand to buy her cigarettes, while men passing by stared at her and laughed, and not behind their hands. Yes, a prostitute, in red and black, on the sandy floor beneath the tree, among the stands of *ful* and cigarettes and newspapers, in Midan Salah ad-Din, on her way to the police station. She repeats her dance inside my head.

～

The sight of the prostitute recalled to me an explanation Halim had given me a day or so before about why I should not speak to everyone in the street.

"The dictum applies not only to women; *M'alim* Hassan would tell his sons the same thing," Halim said. "It has to do with a concept of privacy. One does not spread oneself around. One walks down the street, remaining somehow intact."

I was intrigued by the concept. I had never in my life considered a prohibition on talking to someone in the street. And it occurred to me that the prostitute, an anomaly in any society I knew, must be very alone indeed, and brave— or desperate?—to act the way she did in a culture such as this one.

It seemed that the concept of privacy extended to actions other than speech. Each time I was about to carry something of mine from the shop out to the street, *M'alim* Hassan would reach gently for whatever I was holding, and I would hand it to him. It might be a pair of sandals to be fixed. It might be the English books I needed for my tutoring later that afternoon. Or it might be my *gallabiyya*, which I was taking home to wash. Whatever it was, *M'alim* Hassan always wrapped it carefully in part of the newspaper he had been looking through that morning, packing it all up tight. Then he'd hand it back to me.

I knew he didn't do this to please me, but because it was something that should be done. And although I supposed I wouldn't carry dirty underwear unwrapped, even in a street in the US, I'd never considered that it might be unseemly in some cultures to carry anything at all unwrapped on the street, or in front of strangers. I guessed it was one more way to avoid "spreading oneself around," another way of remaining private. Later, in Palestine, I learned that among stricter Muslims, both male and female, the rule applied to eye contact as well. It was better not to walk down the street looking strangers in the eye. That one was for me the most difficult of all. I did get used to wrapping things I carried, but when it came to glances and speaking, I admit I never succeeded. The exchanges with people in the street were too nourishing to me, too precious to give up.

ࢯ

One workday, Mustafa and Mahmud both away, *M'alim* Hassan took me firmly in hand as we skirted muddy places in the streets and led me the short walk round the corner to *Shari'a as-Sufeyia* (Sufi Street), then up dark flights of stairs to a narrow door at the top, and into his home. At the door, we were greeted by a young woman, who I later learned was one of *M'alim* Hassan's daughters, with a baby in her arms. We saw no one for the remainder of the hour or so we were there, except for a grandchild, who behaved outrageously, climbing onto tables and chairs and laughing, while his grandfather tried to catch him.

When we first entered, I was seated in a large living room, or parlor, while *M'alim* Hassan vanished to another portion of the house, separated from the part I was in by

the open-air courtyard through which we had entered
the house. All the apartments in the building were built
around this courtyard. The section of the house where I
was seated consisted of a dining room, and off the dining
room, a small sitting room. Off the living room I could see
a large bedroom, with an enormous double bed and a tall
wardrobe.

The parlor was furnished with large chairs and
couches—enough to seat nine or so—with puffed and
decorated leather pillows that looked Moroccan. Each
tall window was hung with material. Worn Persian rugs
covered the floors, and two massive sideboards lined the
walls. There were also two big tables and a chest. All the
furniture was crafted of interlocking wooden pieces and
was either carved or decorated with *mashrabiyya* or lovely
strips of inlaid wood. Some of the pieces had been made by
Mustafa, and some by *M'alim* Hassan.

All of these opened my eyes to other possible uses
for the skills I was learning: they could be used in various
combinations to craft tables, chests, mirror frames,
cabinets, and many other pieces in a home. I loved the
design Mustafa had carved for a wooden tabletop, covered
with a piece of glass.

Even after *M'alim* Hassan had returned to the parlor,
I took my time looking around, since this was the first
time he and I had been together in a social situation, and
we were (at least I was) shy. And alone it was, for unseen
hands served us (food was placed on the dining-room table
while I waited in the parlor) and removed the plates only

after I had left the room. Only once did someone appear, bringing us tea, and that was the same young woman who had answered the door.

I sensed a lively, self-contained women's world existing somewhere in another part of the house: Why was I not allowed to see it? Did the men always eat alone? We were served fish, one a medium-sized fish of what I thought of as a "normal" fish shape, and then others that looked like eels, slender for their length, twisted in the crisp batter in which they had been fried. We ate "French-fried" potatoes and chunks of even tastier meat, along with the round brown bread, and greens.

Afterward, sitting in the living room talking, *M'alim* Hassan and I found that in this, our first extended conversation, we could understand each other well enough, although I still spoke only a few words of Arabic and *M'alim* Hassan spoke no English or French at all.

Before I left for Egypt, I had wondered in what ways my life would be restricted due to Islam. Would I have to cover my head? Not go out alone? Wear only skirts, no pants? In Egypt it was never suggested that I do any of these. Nothing was said if I forgot to keep both feet on the floor when I was sitting down or if I smoked in the presence of my elders. Here I was, infidel, agnostic, unmarried, female, a twentieth-century American, a feminist, in the house of a man to whom the Qur'an came first, who lived his life in accordance with the teachings of Islam. Never could I have envisioned the riches that could accrue from living within the few limits that were set.

Again the next day, *M'alim* Hassan and I went to his home for lunch, this time Mustafa with us. On this second visit, I felt as if I had passed a test, even though again we ate alone, because I was introduced to Mustafa's mother, *M'alim* Hassan's wife, a lovely, imposing woman. Her gray hair was pinned to the top of her head, and she wore no head covering, since no unrelated male was present. She was tall and carried herself with grace and authority; and from the gentle deference with which her son and husband treated her, I gathered she was both respected and much loved. She spoke little to me on that visit, or any other time I saw her, but her manner was not unfriendly; rather, she seemed self-contained, "intact," the way *M'alim* Hassan wanted me to be. The only other woman I saw that day was a young woman I glimpsed in another room, who was taking keen and vocal interest in the Zamalek soccer game showing on TV.

Had I proved myself worthy of being seen by the women of the house? Apparently so, for one afternoon soon afterward, I was invited to leave the dining room at *M'alim* Hassan's home, and enter the kitchen at the end of the hall.

There, sure enough, were the women and girls of the house, washing up after our lunch and preparing more food—and they were doing much of it on the floor, on a portion slightly raised from the rest. Food was cooked on a two-burner stove set on a table. Dishes were washed by one woman squatting on the floor of a little shower stall. Another rinsed, rising and bending with each dish, and a third stood outside the shower stall and placed the wet dishes on the rack. The two rooms off the raised portion of the floor were tiny, like miniature closets, or bathrooms. Why no shelving or counters? I wondered.

A low table was brought out at which Madame and at least four other women ate, sitting on the floor. I learned that the name of the young woman who had let us in the door the first time I came was Tahani. When everyone had finished eating, she washed the floor clean and dried it all, even the water sitting along the low part, near the wall.

∽

In one place or another, pretty, many-colored lights decorated trees or houses from time to time throughout Cairo.

"Are there always lights like these?" I asked Nahid.

"Only when there is something special," she answered, "like a wedding. Thursdays and Sundays are the days for weddings."

Red, green, blue, and yellow, the lights were strung like pieces of Christmas amid dusty lower tree branches or around a balcony in a building topped with rubble and missing brick and plaster up and down its sides. I loved to wonder what special event was lighting up a particular corner of Cairo.

One night Mustafa and I drove by a candlelit procession in the dark, and heard music in Midan Salah ad-Din, moving round the earthen triangle and up the way the buses went.

"Do you understand . . . like this?" Mustafa asked me, rubbing together the forefingers of his two hands.

"A wedding?"

"Yes. A man and a woman."

Later that night, I wrote:

Twice, now, I have heard the jangle of the tambourine,
singing, and the clapping of hands, seen the candles
shine along the dingy walls of the apartment building
at Giza, watched guests being borne up, stiff figures
in a balloon, through the elevator's wide-grilled walls.
People marrying.

One of the brothers who ran the garage in front of the room where I lived told Halim that he wanted to marry, but that it would cost him $10,000. In Arab countries, not only is a wedding expensive, but the apartment where the couple will live is bought and fully furnished before the groom and bride move in. I wondered if he had anyone in mind, thinking, if so, what a tragedy. Meaning in our Western, romantic sense, here were two beloved ones, separated by lack of means. I guessed that he had no one special in mind; he was of an age and it was mating time. The idea of wanting to marry with no specific loved one in mind no longer shocked me as it used to.

"A repressed people," Halim said, and I wondered.

I found out later that the young man did have someone in mind—the daughter of the pharmacist across the street. But since he did not have the money to marry, he could not ask her. She worked with his brother Munir, who passed indirect messages back and forth between them.

"And you, will you marry?" I asked Mustafa. He answered, "When my father tells me to, I will."

These words surprised me. The Western world was awash with the stereotypical image of an Arab woman, especially an Arab Muslim woman, being married off against her will. But a man?

Egyptian women, and later, women in Syria and Palestine, too, explained to me that parental pressure—or the lack of it—on both son and daughter to marry covered the entire spectrum. In some families, the pressure might be intense; in others, no greater than it would be in a family in the West where parents hoped for the best for their children. Reasons for the differences were just as varied. A daughter might be pressed to marry if her parents felt marriage might protect her, as in Palestine, where the population is living under military occupation. The family's financial situation might affect the pressure. Cultural traditions played an important part in such decisions; Muslims struggle to achieve the same kinds of legal rights and protections that Western women either have won or are fighting for still. The major difference from the West seemed to lie in the degree of separation of the sexes, which in Egypt made it less likely that unmarried men and women would know each other well.

In more traditional, often rural areas, marriage might be viewed, as it was earlier in the West and still is in some other cultures, more as an alliance for the good of two families than a contract between two individuals; and parents might be thought to have a better sense of their children's natures and needs than emotional and sexual attraction, possibly fleeting, might predict. It did occur to me, odd as this might sound to a Westerner, that the divorce rate in the US (generally thought to be as high as fifty percent) could conceivably suggest that traditional methods had at least as good a chance at bringing felicity and longevity to a marriage as Western reliance on "romantic love."

"A Muslim man and woman do not marry for love," I read in the English-language newspaper one morning. "Love brings a merger, a destruction of the individual. In marriage, two people come together for practical reasons, each to do a share of the job, and in the arrangement there is no room for dissolution of identity." I had no way to know how widespread that belief was, but it seemed that in urban areas, where married adults were likely to have to live apart from their families and were subject to more varied influences, old customs were giving way to new.

ᔕ

The evening of December 24, we stood the three doors each of us had finished that day, *M'alim* Hassan, Mustafa, and I, in the courtyard, and turned out the light in the shop behind, the better to admire them. Two of the doors were ones I had worked on, and one I had completed mostly alone.

They were the three loveliest doors I had ever seen. Other doors might be more intricate in design or varied in technique and materials, combining carving, ivory inlay, and *mashrabiyya*, as well as interlocking wooden pieces.

But these were stunning, made of new wood of red and blond. I had worked on the door with the diamond-shaped pattern for four or five days solidly, with Mustafa and *M'alim* Hassan helping off and on.

That last night, as I was inserting the last pieces, the door was descended upon—*M'alim* Hassan helping place more pieces, 'Adil setting nails, *M'alim* Hassan filing and planing, then all of us setting nails and sanding, picking the corn-colored *humus* nuts from the grooves where I'd spilled them and popping them in our mouths.

"*Anti quoisse kiteer* [you're very good]," *M'alim* Hassan told me. The words made me feel honored and happy; the first real praise I'd had from him. Mostly, though, I felt the satisfaction of a job well done, by all three of us, a team, and felt wonder at our having created something so beautiful.

"*Ahsan bab* [the best kind of door]," I said, my Arabic still too limited for a more eloquent description. Then *M'alim* Hassan and I sat on chairs in the courtyard. In celebration, I accepted the first cigarette I'd had since I'd most recently quit; and we sat smoking side by side like two old cronies, admiring our work and complimenting each other. We spoke about America, and whether it would be possible to earn a living making these "best doors" there. We said we would take pictures of our doors and invite Hassan Fathy to look at them. At last *M'alim* Hassan went back to work, laying out new wood for Mahmud to work on the lathe, while I swept the courtyard clear of the wooden diamonds, drank tea, then took the buses home.

12: FELLOW TRAVELER

In December, the nights grew even colder, continuing to surprise me, given my foreigner's notions of Egypt. In Cairo, thin young soldiers, posted outside Sadat's house, embassies, and consulates, still hunched over their tiny fires, rubbing their hands before the red and yellow flame. By day the child in my neighborhood still led the horse by the bridle, the boy's mother, I supposed, riding the wagon among the heaps of turnips, while a brother walked alongside. The child called and called for people to come and buy.

"Is there any public presence of Christmas?" Jean asked in a letter to me that month. It was Jean who had first introduced me to Halim. The answer was no, there was not. Christmas was not real enough in Egypt even to be boycotted or played down. Publicly, at least, it just "wasn't." Its presence, if there was one at all, must have been wholly private. The buses seemed no emptier on Christmas, and the visit I made that day to the Coptic churches in Old

Cairo, where a sign said that 10,000 Christians had once lived, showed none of what Americans typically think of as Christmas decorations.

But to me, Cairo always looked a little like Christmas; and so, to answer Jean's question, I counted up the signs: the colored bulbs lighting so many of the little shops, sitting on the rectangular tops of the outdoor food wagons—red and yellow, red and green, all sparkling above the big brass or silver-colored *ful* pots, or shining on mounds of apples, pomegranates, dates, and bananas. In December, oranges heaped on flat wagons glowed yellow, the way pumpkins do in late October in the foggy fields of San Francisco's Half Moon Bay, sunny pyramids lit by Aladdin lamps against dark buildings and the darker ground. Bells jingled on the horses and donkeys that pulled the carts all day, and chandeliers glittered in lighting shops.

At night, small fires glowed in the streets by little stands selling cigarettes, pens, biscuits, and candy. Fires burned in every building under construction where homeless families took shelter, or shone through chinks in the makeshift brick or slat wood walls of tiny living quarters erected in streets and vacant lots. Balconies and trees sparkled with strings of lights; and taxis often looked like Christmas, with red, white, green, yellow, and blue lights along their dashboards and around their front windows.

Bells, color, and light—but no rushing about to buy, buy, buy; no loudspeakers piping Christmas music, no hauling about of fresh-cut trees, no alcohol or empty reaching for gaiety, no anxiety, no sense of loss. I visited the Coptic churches, several of which were said to have sheltered the Holy Family in little crypts behind dwarf-size doors as they made their way through Egypt. Instead of a desperate expending of resources, tangible and intangible, the mood felt like the sober remembrance of one people's claim to a part of their own history.

∽

One morning in January of the New Year, Mustafa and I had what may have been our first real conversation. We were both more open, I think, than either of us had ever been with the other, unmarred by frustration at the other's view or styles, both of us really trying to communicate and to understand. It was like one of our old-time lazy days, both tired, but in good moods, and I, probably for the first time, willing to sit and talk, not impatient for work to begin. The subject: the role of women.

"Why are you a carpenter?" Mustafa asked. "Your hand"—he pointed to mine—"is soft. Your muscle"—he touched his bicep—"is little. Did you go to school to be a carpenter? Were you always a carpenter?"

I told him that I had been a newspaper reporter before I became a carpenter, and that mostly I'd learned carpentry from other women, not in a school, although I'd attended school for a year as an apprentice in the carpenters' union. "I am a carpenter," I said, "because I don't want to be a desk worker, looking up to a boss or a husband at home, cooking three meals a day and washing clothes and dishes. I want to see other parts of the world. I want to experience many things—to read and write, to learn. I love the wood and its beauty; I love working with it."

"How long will you stay in Egypt?" he wanted to know. "You could stay one or two years, but not forever, for you are not suited for the work. You are not a man."

Mustafa, I knew, had gone to school to study both Pharaonic and Coptic art, as well as Islamic architecture, carpentry, and design. He made the gesture now, so frequent in my lessons with him and his father, his two hands serving as side blinders to the eyes, then falling straight and firm ahead—'ala tool—direct, the straight and narrow. The way I was told to walk in the street, speaking to no one, going directly from work to school, and back home again.

"In the Qur'an," Mustafa said, "man is business, woman is house. No business. Or business, mumkin [maybe], but"—he flourished his thumb and forefinger as if he were scribbling on the page—"secretary, office work, teacher. No carpenter"—he made motions of hammering, lifting. "Woman is soft. And, says Qur'an, women and men shall not be left in the same room alone, or there may be . . ."—he made gestures of hugging and kissing, followed by appropriate signals of horror and disapproval. The very attitudes that had kept my mother from working in an office when she graduated from school.

"Because you are American, I can be with you," he said. "But even for me, the limits are strict."

To Mustafa I said, "Americans are in a state of change. We're only two hundred years old. We have no traditions like yours. We have no Qur'an. Family members live far apart in different parts of the country, so individuals rule themselves. My mother and father don't tell me what to do; they say, 'Be happy, be honest, and we are here to help you if we can.'"

∽

Munir's mother was hit by an *autobus* and had broken her arm. That evening I visited her with Munir as she lay in bed. She said that now that she and Munir's father had a house and money, and their sons were grown and working, all that remained was for them to make the pilgrimage to Mecca. After that, their lives could end. Munir translated for me. After that, "*C'est fini* [it's over]," he said.

Munir came sometimes to my room and read to me in Arabic from the Qur'an. He showed me how the verses rhyme at the end of each sentence. He said an American had counted electronically all the letters in the Qur'an and found there were almost equal numbers of each letter. For instance, throughout the entire book there were as many of the letter *jeem* as the letter *meem*.

But several letters were lacking, to make the count exactly even; and so, Munir said, "We sometimes find *ameen*," which sounds a little like the English word "amen." He told me, as others have since, that each verse in the Qur'an contains seven different levels of meaning. *No wonder*, I thought, *I can't find a satisfactory translation of the Qur'an!*

One night when Munir and his brothers were working in the shop, I wrote this:

*Tonight the biggest sheep, its reddish-brown wool
wet from the rain, bleats in the garage while the four
brothers laugh and talk around it. They will soon kill
it as a gift to the poor, an offering to God in thanks
for the opening of their auto repair shop and for its
doing well. The shop is the culmination of one of the
brothers' years of work and study in Italy.*

Sarwat, the youngest of the four brothers who worked in
the garage, kissed the sheep on the top of its head, in a
private, at least partly playful, spirit. Munir bound her feet,
and, holding her head over one of two large metal pans,
proceeded to cut with great slashes into her throat. The
animal did not make a cry, only tried heavily to get breath
for a few moments; then she was dead, head dangling into
the pan, one great green eye catching the light, staring glas-
sily. I found a kind of comfort in Madame's appearance just
before the sheep died, as if her presence and her direction (she seemed to know better how to perform the ritual
sacrifice than her sons) sanctioned the slaughter, removing
from it the aura of an evil deed "the boys" were perpet-
uating there in the garage at midnight. Afterward, Munir
assured me that his brother had said "in secret" the first
words of the Qur'an, giving thanks, avowing the purpose of
the sacrifice.

Then Munir poked a hole with a screwdriver (after an
unsuccessful try with a knife) in a foreleg while another
brother applied the air hose to the hole Munir had made

and pumped the sheep full of air until it was bloated to nearly twice its size. Next he beat it with the sawed-off handle of a broom—hard whacks. Afterward they let the air out by turning off the hose, and Munir slit the skin down the center, his brothers parting the wool before his hands. With a knife another brother periodically sharpened on a grinder, Munir proceeded neatly to pull off the skin; it came easily, leaving a white film and all the sheep's muscles and organs covered and intact. I did not stay, since it was late, but I would have liked to see how they went about draining the blood, for it is unlawful for Muslims to eat meat with blood in it. Munir had once told me that that was why so much of the meat we ate was dry; the blood is taken before the animal is sold. The sheep was to be divided among poor families they knew, "in this house" and around the neighborhood.

Having witnessed this, it occurred to me that Mary's and Luke's repugnance at seeing children patterning bloody handprints on outer house walls after the religious sacrifice on the holiday was probably due more to the fact that many Westerners' only encounters with dead animals are with bloodless chicken, beef, or lamb wrapped in cellophane in supermarket coolers than to the correctness of their conclusion that Arabs are unnatural, bloodthirsty beings, different from them.

∽

It was the *mawlidu n-nabiyyi as-shareef*, birthday of the Prophet Muhammad, after whose name Muslims pronounce the words *salla Allahu 'alayhi wa salaam* (May God bless him and grant him peace). Coming home in the afternoon after a light rain, disappointed to have found the library at the American University closed, and feeling a little dreary, I met two young women walking on a road near my house. All three of us were dressed in our "Muslim uniforms"—knitted caps covering our heads, the caps partially covered with close-fitting hoods, open to show our faces, with extra material reaching down to our shoulders. They also wore long, graceful garments reaching to their shoes. I had on, over a pair of loose pants, an old wool coat reaching only to mid-calf, bulky, brownish, and not the slightest bit attractive, which I had found in the used-clothes market. (When I got to know the women better, I was surprised to learn that both wore jeans under their long, proper coats. And the woman who had introduced herself as Gigi (*Gigi!*) had a package of Marlboros rolled up in the short sleeve of her T-shirt just the way a working man proud of his muscles, or a butch-leaning lesbian proud of *her* muscles, might carry cigarettes in the US.)

So there I was walking along, looking, without knowing it, pretty much like a Muslim woman somewhat on the conservative side. They looked at me, I looked at them, and we all smiled. Just after I had passed them, though, to my surprise they hissed, just like an Arab man might if he were up to no good. But apparently there was no disrespect in one woman's hissing to another; and after a few paces of this, I turned and saw them beckoning to me. Like so many other young Muslim women I have met, their faces shone with an inner beauty I do not find in most women's faces in the United States.

Then, all in Arabic—I was proud!—we talked. As I understood it (my understandings subject, as ever, to revision with the advent of new information), both women were students at Al-Azhar, Cairo's famous Islamic university. They promised to come for me the following Friday morning to take me to the mosque.

This was the third time young Muslim women had approached me and said they would come for me one day. The first time had been at the Beiram prayers, the next on the bus on the way to work. But the other women had not come. Would these, I wondered? I liked them, wanted to know something of their lives, and was pleased at the invitation to accompany them to Al-Azhar, which I'd been waiting to visit until I had a Muslim guide.

∽

In fact, both women did come to get me on the day they said they would. In time, they also took me to the Islamic university. Sometimes I met them at the "House of Guests" near my house, where Gigi's grandmother lived and where they were headed the day I had met them.

I was surprised to learn there was an institution where old people could be cared for outside their homes; the phenomenon, increasingly common in the USA, was practically nonexistent in Egypt. In fact, Egyptians sometimes asked me about these care centers they'd heard of in the West, their expressions suggesting that they viewed as somewhat shocking the prospect of sending one's parents to an institution when they'd grown too old to care for themselves. In the "old folks' home" for people over sixty, we visited Gigi's grandmother, introduced to me as *Madame* Ikram. It was she who first explained to me a larger meaning behind the Arabic greeting code I had been learning to use.

I knew that each greeting should be more elaborate than the one before. If, for instance, one said *salaam 'aleikom* (peace be with you), the person responding will say *'aleikom salaam, wa rahmat Allah wa barakato* (peace be with you, and the compassion of God and His blessing). I knew that when I returned the greeting, I must give more than I had received.

But Madame told me that the pattern of exchange operated on other levels as well. Not only verbal exchanges, but actions, should be ever more generous. If I am happy, I must give some of that happiness to others. If I am in good health and another is not, I must help. If I have money, I *must* give money to those who have less.

All this she explained to me, and if I had remembered her words, I would not have been surprised later when, teaching in the West Bank, I saw them in practice. Whenever the wife of a colleague had a new baby, or a student passed a special exam or received a fellowship, or one of us returned from a trip, the person who was happy and grateful would bring cake or candy or some other treat to the people with whom he or she lived or worked.

To understand the Qur'an, I would have to be able

to read the elaborate Arabic in which it was written; but Madame Ikram said, "We can speak of the spirit of Islam, and of the life it requires—we can speak of marriage, of giving." And so we did, over the time I visited her.

Things always got sticky when I tried to explain my relationship to religion. I told Madame Ikram I had no trouble believing that an energy had created the universe; agreeing, she offered proof: every mammal has seven vertebrae; one plant will respond to another plant's being cut. How, she asked, could the structures of living things be so patterned, and sentient beings so connected, if there were no God? My difficulty, I said, was making the jump from belief in a diffuse kind of spirit to belief in a "God" with supernatural powers, whom one must love and obey. And why the emphasis on *one* God?

"All the prophets," she said, "Muhammad—may God bless him and grant him peace—Jesus, Moses, and those that came before, were sent as messengers for this very 'energy' you speak of, to tell mankind how to act. Belief in one God is important to ensure that humankind recognizes the voice of the one energy and doesn't fall prey to conflicting voices giving contradictory information on how to act. Then, in order to help people believe that each of these prophets was indeed God's messenger, each was able to perform acts miraculous for their time. Jesus came with the gift of healing, the Prophet Muhammad came with the poetry of the Qur'an for the poetry-loving Arab soul."

"How do we know the Qur'an came from God?"

"How could it have come from anyone *but* God,"

Madame said, "since it contains information about the splitting of atoms and the gestation of a child in its mother's womb, things that were unknown to science until centuries later?"

I had heard these things before, for I was often asked if I were Muslim. I never argued. How could I? I had no idea what was true. Often people simply wanted to tell me more about Islam, and I was glad to have the chance to ask questions and to learn how Muslims viewed this religion of which I knew so little. When asked what I believed, I'd say that I did believe something, but that my belief was "without clothes," that it did not include mosques or churches, rituals or special apparel.

I dreaded answering questions about my beliefs the first times the issue arose, knowing the central place religion played in Egyptians' lives and fearing I would be judged harshly because I didn't follow some established religion. But every time I was asked—and this continued to be true all the years I lived among Muslims—I found people tolerant of my position. Sometimes there was even a familiar nod.

"Ah," said one old man as he served me tea early one morning in a shady grove by the Nile, "People like you are mentioned in the Qur'an. You are called 'fellow travelers.'" The term was positive: I was recognized and respected even though I didn't really fit the mold.

I reflected on the existence of extraordinarily gifted human beings who dream, heal, create art of great beauty, or predict the future, without being called prophets or messengers. Where did these abilities come from, if not from tapping into a great central pool? And might that "central pool" be called God? I searched for signs. The possibility hung suspended in my mind as I walked the streets of Cairo, half-hoping to catch a glimpse of the green the wise man Khidr is said to wear beneath his cloak in the ancient stories.

ᔐ

One evening Madame Ikram told me that Gigi was married and had a child. But she said that Gigi had left her husband and had for a time lived with her mother, because her mother threatened to commit suicide if she were parted from her daughter. She said that Gigi's father was alive, but divorced from her mother.

"What was wrong with her mother?" I asked. "Did she have a physical problem?"

"She was not normal," I was told. "Gigi's brother was killed in the 1967 war, and she has a sister, who is also not normal. Now Gigi lives in her mother's house alone. She had money but has spent it, and now she needs work. She should go to her husband in Switzerland."

She cited a story from the Qur'an in which the Prophet told a woman to obey her husband, even though he had forbidden her to visit her father as he lay dying.

"But Gigi talks of going to study in London," I said. "She doesn't talk of going to Switzerland."

"The marriage is finished," Madame Ikram said.

And so, in the midst of this strange land, with its strong

religious and family ties, I found that I had stepped into a reality that was not so different from the one I knew.

∽

One day I had a painful conversation with *M'alim* Hassan. Someone had told him that people in Western countries welcomed a stranger only if he had money, and shooed him away or arrested him as a *kleftee*, a thief, if he had none. The person who told him had returned from visiting both the USA and Europe, and said the two continents were alike in this.

"You can starve in America," the man had told him. "If you enter a house and people are eating, if you are lucky, they might ask you once if you are hungry—and that's it! Not again. Much less three times." That was how I learned that in Arab society it is polite to decline an offer twice, and to accept only when the invitation has been extended a third time.

"I'll stay here," *M'alim* Hassan said.

"You wouldn't visit even for a *fantasía*?" I asked, using his word for visits to beautiful places. He had spoken many times about wanting to visit the United States.

"No," he replied. "Here, I have *fantasía*—I have Luxor, Aswan, Abu Simbel. . . . Here, people say *sabah al kheir, sabah an-nour* [the elaborate Arabic equivalent of "good morning" and its response], *ahlan wa sahlan* [welcome] and *marhaban* [hello], whether you have money or not."

I asked *M'alim* Hassan how many carpenters there were in Cairo of his caliber—*quoisse, quoisse owie* (good, very good). Three or four, he said, but they did not know how to do the work on the mosques that he had done. He had been working as a carpenter for more than forty years, since he was twelve. He was one of the few left, then, of the masters.

"And here I am, an American, coming to learn from you," I said. "Where are the Egyptians?"

"I need them; I have looked for them," he said. "But they want to make money, and I cannot afford to pay them what they want."

"*Ba'den, ba'den?*" I asked, meaning, "And then what will happen to the trade?"

"*Khalas,*" he said. (It will be) finished.

13: "Use It for Whatever Purpose You Choose"

Of the words I learned in Arabic that year, among those I heard most often from *M'alim* Hassan were *shiwayya, shiwayya*, translated as "little by little," or "step by step." In short, take it easy.

In the shop, beginning with plane and chisel and dovetail saw, I was a bungler. In design, too, and in all the early fittings of the wood, I was terrible, and felt my old despair: *I can't do it!*

The response of *M'alim* Hassan and Mustafa was always to take the bungled work from me and to finish it themselves as I watched, which frustrated me even more. How could I learn, unless I practiced? Yet, slowly, slowly, trying and being stopped, only to try again and be stopped again, I found myself improving—though sometimes long periods went by between opportunities to practice; and these opportunities were often very brief.

Sometimes Mustafa would challenge me by saying,

"You can't do it"—whatever "it" happened to be. But when I grew defiant and angry, agreeing with him, but hating to hear him echo my worst judgment of myself, he explained that he spoke this way only to provoke in me the opposite reaction: "Yes, I can *too* do it!"

Only once, *M'alim* Hassan said, to my protests, "No, you *don't* want to learn!" This caused me to examine myself: Did I?

Muhannad, a new boy in the shop, had been kicked out of school, I was told, for being "slow in the head." *M'alim* Hassan demonstrated by gesturing a wheel rolling, then skipping, missing a cog, and dropping into dysfunction. Yet here he was in the shop, with *M'alim* Hassan drilling him in the alphabet, and his little city-wise comrade 'Adil teaching him how to plane a board. He was an apprentice in one of Egypt's finest woodworking shops. One day, he might be a fine carpenter, a master, even. The question mark about myself was the residue of my own upbringing—doubt. What is "talent"? What is "innate ability"? Muhannad entered the shop at ten years old and would leave it when he died. He might progress more slowly than some, but where in this scheme was room for the concept that he might "fail"?

One evening I approached Hassan Fathy with my doubts. Two young architects, Omar, who was Egyptian, and Thomas, who was German, were working quietly by themselves at a table in another part of the room. I said I had doubts that the carpentry I was learning could be for the benefit of the poor.

"It's the rich who buy the fancy doors and windows and furniture, both here in Egypt and elsewhere," I said. "But I want to be of use now, or at least know that I am learning something that I'll be able to use in the future to benefit people who have less money."

"There are two things," Hassan Fathy said. "One is the craft, the other the use to which it is put."

I didn't understand how his words related to my question.

"Even the wood costs money," I said. "Here it is imported and so is expensive; and in America, too, only the rich can afford the houses we build of wood."

One of the young architects working nearby reminded me that every carpenter has a scrap pile, and it is wood from this scrap pile from which are made *mashrabiyya* and the small pieces that are worked into designs for the doors.

"Even the long sticks of wood into which the smaller turned pieces are inserted can be made of small bits of wood, held together by a metal rod," Hassan Fathy said, and he drew me a picture. "It is the craftsmen who are charging higher prices than they need. It didn't use to be that way."

I appealed to him again. "Hassan *Bey*," I appealed, "I need to learn how to learn, faster and better. I'm slow. I'm not good at the work. Because I'm not skilled enough, I watch and watch, and feel I must work at it, but cannot, so I watch and watch some more. Is there something you have seen from my words or my manner that would enable you to say what I could do, so that I could learn more quickly?"

What this great man thought of this American woman, an adult in her thirties, coming to him and questioning the gift she had been given, I never knew.

"There are," Hassan Fathy said again, "two things. One is learning with the mind. The other is learning with the fingers. Do not be impatient with the time it takes."

And then he said the words that have been so important to me.

"Once you have mastered the craft," he told me, "you can use it for whatever purpose you choose."

The conversation wandered after that to some of the dilemmas architects face. Omar described how Hassan *Bey*, in discussing the Saudis who wanted to design embassies in the Islamic tradition in eight countries in different parts of the world, had said:

"Ask yourselves, what would occur if Islam *did* move to Latin America, or to Sweden. What architecture *would* grow out of the joining of Islam with the existing traditions and culture?"

And Thomas's chuckle: "Ah, I love it: We'd be asking, 'What do the buildings want?'"

Hassan Fathy told us of the glass university in Algeria: the students broke the windows when the air conditioning went off. The windows were fixed, and broken again. Wouldn't you think that the university would have installed windows that would open? Now, he said, another university has been planned, also of glass. And a mosque "for the sardines, for the fish"—a mosque floating in water! A man from the Institute of Management described how in Saudi

Arabia, young Saudis, educated in America, hire Americans "for tens of thousands of dollars, for 'pre-feasibility' studies, *ad infinitum.*"

"We get what we deserve," Thomas said of the glass university, the floating mosque.

"No," said Hassan Fathy, "these people are victims of the architects, and of the schools."

"Not so in the old days, was it?" Omar asked.

"No, it wasn't." Hassan *Bey* described the old system of education in which a Sufi master taught both the craft and the "revealed knowledge."

"What ended it?" asked Thomas.

"The end began with Lord Cromer," Hassan *Bey* replied. Lord Cromer was the British consul general, the imperialist governor in Egypt from 1883 to 1907, who reshaped the country's educational system into one aimed at increasing Egyptian agricultural output. Then Hassan *Bey* was called away to answer the door. When he came back, I asked, "How could such a fine system be destroyed by Lord Cromer?"

"The old masters," explained Hassan *Bey*, "knew too many apprentices would create competition, which would lower the standards of the craft. When the British introduced competition, the apprentices welcomed it, thinking it would be to their advantage." Cromer warned that "any education, technical or general, which tended to leave the fields untilled, or to lessen the fitness or disposition of the people for agricultural employment, would be a national evil." Village schools had to compete for grants, leaving the masses with only a few years of elementary education. Egyptians were educated to fill posts in the local civil service and, later, to become a "thrifty peasantry and an artisan class skilled in European manufactures." The days of long apprenticeships, in which the selected few studied over a lifetime to learn a particular craft, were over.

As I left, I thanked Hassan *Bey* for answering my questions. "There is not just one thing," he said again. "You are learning several things at the same time with the carpentry," he said, "all of them important."

᠅

Omar and Thomas and I worked at Hassan Fathy's house once while he was away on business, cleaning and painting the kitchen, feeding the cats. In the end we left a single pink rose in the kitchen window and white bright paint all around. While a first coat of paint was drying (our excuse for temporarily abandoning the job), we left the air empty of our talking and rushed out of the house to visit the Mosque of Sultan Hassan down the street. There the men took interminable measurements of floor and wall designs, of wood, mosaic, and stone, to find what they called "the module," "the unit of measurement," while I hung about in the spare, pure beauty of the great space, the outline of ornamented walls against a blue sky. I watched a golden afternoon sun wash with light the expanse below the blue.

"There are two kinds of buildings," Omar said. "One overwhelms you, and the other overwhelms you in such a way that you rise to meet it." Westminster Abbey versus Sultan Hassan. In Sultan Hassan, I rose to meet the greatness. I was glad I had waited so long to enter there.

One evening after he returned, instead of doing business with anyone, Dr. Fathy told a long story. He had been speaking with his French visitors, but when I entered the room with a tray of cups and a pot of tea, he stopped. When he was to resume, he said he felt like a Biblical figure with his head chopped off. I think he meant he couldn't remember what he had wanted to say.

Instead, he told a story about a couple who sought to find utopia by reading a single page in a book each day. Each page gave the couple their itinerary for the day. First they visited the Country of Red. Next they visited the Country of Blue, and after that, the Country of White. Finally, they visited the Country of Green, which, however, was no longer green because, with a big machine, people had greedily taken from the earth all the substance that made the earth fertile. The couple had been seeking a land where material was transparent and one could see the truth.

At one point the man and woman got into an argument because the man used a long abstract scientific term instead of asking for "bread" right out. The woman thought that pompous and unnecessary, and the man thought her bourgeois for thinking so. They fought without words. In a cave one night they saw a flickering fire, which appeared to be a demon. Then a "*chevalier*" appeared and suggested that the woman return to the metropolis. She was angry, but inside herself knew she wanted to go. She was with child, though neither she nor the man knew it.

She went back, and the man went on alone. But the next day, when he opened the book to consult the itinerary, he found that the pages of the book were blank. The demon said, "You don't want to go. It's too hard," whereupon the man and the demon had a long discussion. The man saw the demon voice as evil: it was the same voice he had heard as a child from the man who sought to sell slingshots so children could kill birds. It was also the voice of a schoolmate who had urged him to do wrong. The man at last fell asleep and died. And the demon said to him, "You are even now choosing to die, just as every time before, you chose to wake up." In the morning the man was a block of ice.

When he had finished telling the story, Hassan Fathy said he was very tired and could write no report that night. He said he had told the story to take the conversation from grittier matters. It was an allegory of today, he said, with the Country of Red being Russia, the Country of White, the United States (composed of people of all colors, and therefore none) and Egypt, the Country of Green. (I never did learn the equivalent of the Country of Blue.) Someone asked if he had written it, and Hassan Fathy said that he had, and that it had been published but he had just one copy.

I don't know what the others made of it, but I found the story odd. Now, many years later, it seems a sad prediction of the plight that would come to pass in Egypt through the time ahead when the US would have its way. Egypt's soil—her entire political and economic life—would become depleted, until thousands of people demonstrated in the streets and in Tahrir Square, demanding democratic change. They succeeded in overthrowing Hosni Mubarak, the dictator supported by the US and the Egyptian military. Mubarak ruled from Sadat's assassination in 1981, two years after I left Egypt, until he was deposed during the uprisings known as the "Arab Spring" in 2011. Five years have passed, and Egypt is no closer to democracy.

∽

By mid-June in the summer of 1979, I would awaken each night in the usual sweat, heat sitting like a clamp on a board in my little room while outside the door, the breeze blew cool. On one such night I woke and, sitting at my table, wrote:

> *The muezzin calls and sings (yes—sings!) of God. A woman groans in a bed nearby. Through the window comes the stink of sewage, and I picture the green slime that oozes back into the open sewer out in the street. I am appalled at the extremes Egyptians— and most of the rest of the world—suffer in physical things—first bitter cold, now this terrible heat. I marvel at the climate of the pearl, San Francisco: at work, as I cut the sabras pieces, flashes of her hilly streets and cool sunshine flicker across my inner eye. It is a little peninsula that even all our human*

devastations cannot make unlivable.

I am not sad, or lonely. The gentle, steady state persists; I continue to work, and look, and learn, to probe this many-sided being that is Egypt. Increasingly, now, I take the two of them in my hand, Egypt and America, and weigh them, turning each about. I feel balanced, in the center of the world. Everything is here to comprehend—if only I could! As soon as I begin to generalize, the creature shifts slightly: I catch a glint in the eye, a wind-tossed forelock, a patterned thigh I had not seen before, and any label I might have had is ducked out from under. I know this is a good deal of the attraction. Egypt, the East (anywhere?), bends you, imperceptibly, to its nature, if you want to know it.

"Don't judge another language by your own," Dr. Makki said last week when I balked at some peculiarity of Arabic grammar.

$\backsim$

My Arabic teacher, Dr. Makki, had been interested in Dun Nun the Egyptian since Dr. Makki was in his teens. He grew up in Giza, where Dun Nun's tomb is. That was news to me, but then what wasn't? Dr. Makki was originally drawn to Dun Nun, he said, because they came from the same province.

"What province?" I asked.

"Divine love. The province of divine love and unity with

God. Dun Nun was the first of the mystics to speak of the stages one must pass through in order to reach the highest stage, union with God, in the process influencing Christianity."

Among intellectuals, he said, there was a growing movement toward Sufism in Europe and America, and also in the Middle East.

"I am not one of them, but I respect Sufis," he said. "I think highly of them."

He had left Kuwait and returned to Egypt, because "the Arab states, Saudi Arabia and Kuwait, are happy spending their wealth, but don't look to the future. They do nothing to create a civilization. We are poorer, but better. Morocco is most akin to Egypt. Libya is the worst."

It was the first time I understood that many members of states that Westerners would call Arab, such as Egypt, Palestine, Lebanon, and Syria—famous sites of early civilization that are especially known for their culture and traditions—don't refer to themselves for the most part as "Arab," but rather as "Egyptian," "Palestinian," "Lebanese," or "Syrian." In their view, "Arabs" are those who live in the Gulf states, the "new oil" states—Saudi Arabia, Kuwait, Bahrain, and the United Arab Emirates.

ᔕ

In July, two friends of mine came to visit from the United States. They stayed with me, on two extra cots, in my little room. For both, it was their first trip to Egypt, and since I had seen nothing yet of Upper Egypt, *M'alim* Hassan urged me to take some time off for a short trip to the south. My tutees were happy to have a holiday as well.

On this trip I was at last able to see Hassan Fathy's vision incarnate: the village he had made of mud brick. It was in a place called New Gourna, across the river from Luxor. The houses and courtyards, the vaulted market, the pigeon tower—all the buildings in New Gourna—were designed to replicate the structures that had existed in the original village of Old Gourna.

Houses of mud brick, set on broad streets, with courtyards, arches, domes, vaulted arcades, lacework done in mud brick and plaster, and *sabras* doors—there they all were, just as Hassan Fathy described in the book I had read. There were laundries, latrines, and the village's own water supply, facilities for baking, for bathing, stables for the animals. Not only was the whole village gorgeous, it also stood as proof that this radical new concept in rural housing was both affordable and practical.

But the houses and streets stood empty, as I'd known they would. The village's only occupants were a few men who showed us around. From the start, Hassan Fathy had objected to the building site. Instead of housing people who were already living in Old Gourna in their old, tumbledown houses without any modern features, the village had been built on a site where no one lived.

The Egyptian government had wanted to force the 7,000 people currently living in Old Gourna, on the site of the Tombs of the Nobles, to relocate to the new village. The land around Old Gourna could not support the population and was mostly owned by rich landowners. Residents of the town had been working as laborers on archaeological excavations, as guides for tourists visiting the ancient tombs, even as tomb robbers.

Gradually, however, that source of income was drying up, due to exhaustion of the tombs and increased government vigilance against thieves. The land on which Hassan Fathy was allowed to build could not have supported the population the government wanted moved there, and so the idea was that the villagers, in building the village together in voluntary cooperation as was the custom, would in the process receive on-the-job training in various crafts, by means of which they could support themselves. But, as Hassan Fathy explained in his book, *Architecture for the Poor*, none of this could occur when the proposed new occupants of the village balked at undergoing the increased hardship such a move would involve. Because it was not preceded by careful study of socioeconomic factors and realistic long-term regional governmental planning, the village was, at least for the present, fated to remain empty.

14: RAMADAN

As my friends left, we entered Ramadan, as the month is called in the Muslim lunar calendar. In 1979, the holy month began on July 26, in the hottest part of the summer. Ramadan is the month of fasting, when observant Muslims do not eat or drink from dawn to dusk. They fast to purify their souls and to experience the suffering of those less fortunate than they.

> Fasting is a religious institution almost as universal as prayer. . . . But Islam has introduced quite a new meaning into the meaning of fasting. Before Islam, fasting meant the suffering of some privation in times of mourning and sorrow; in Islam, it becomes an institution for the improvement of the moral spiritual character of man. . . . The object is that man may learn how he can shun evil. . . . Abstention from food is but a step to make men realize—if he can, in obedience to divine injunctions, abstain

from food and drink which are otherwise lawful
for him—how much more expedient it is that he
abstain from evil. . . . Fasting is actually like a sort
of training of man's faculties, for as every faculty
. . . requires training to attain its full force, the
faculty of submission to the Divine Will should
also require to be trained. Fasting is one of the
means by which this is achieved.
    —Galwash 1966. *The Religion of Islam* Vol. II.
Studies in Islam Series, 63-64

In the days before Ramadan begins, the streets are packed
with shoppers. Women prepare the special meal that is
eaten each day at dusk just as the call to prayer begins. The
first day of Ramadan, I was woken at 3 a.m. by an uncanny
sound. It lasted a long time and was recited in a high voice,
by a man who came to our street and then moved away
into other streets of the neighborhood. I heard his voice,
first faint, then louder, then faint again, as sleep left and
came again.

How utterly lovely it was, announcing the advent of the
holy month. If sound were visible, the call would have been
the unfolding of the most splendidly ornate Arabic script,
the Qur'an wrought in gold, unfurled across the black night
sky. The man's voice rose and fell, had more notes, more
trilling, than any call I'd heard. As the sound receded, a full
chorus of calls followed, exquisite sound, urging prayer in a
night otherwise utterly silent.

Its sweetness lingered over the next days, a call to the

soul, birdsong from another world, reminding Muslims to refrain from food and drink, smoking, sexual activity— almost everything that gives us mortals bodily pleasure.

Fasting in those first days, I felt light-headed, as if I were swinging in space between the slow-paced, meditative cutting of wood joints and sleep. Sometimes I was intensely aware of a clear golden sky; then I would forget.

After that first day, at about two o'clock each morning during Ramadan, a man walked through the streets of our neighborhood, beating a drum, while calling loudly to wake the sleepers, telling them to rise, prepare food and eat, before the fast began again at dawn.

During Ramadan, shops opened later in the mornings. Everyone who could do so slept later, having celebrated during the long nights of activity, stimulated by the food and drink finally allowed to flood their systems. For the first time that year, as I headed for work at the usual time, I found 'Am Muhammad's tea shop closed, the corrugated metal door pulled down and padlocked. Sugarless, tea-less, cigarette-less, food-less, people moved about at first as if they were in a collective dream.

There was a strange silence, as people spoke less and looked inward, giving the atmosphere the strange, otherworldly aspect that fasting creates, with occasional spurts of anger or irritability. Mostly, I sensed a subdued gentleness, a quiet devoid of tension, an open state in which the winds of the spirit world were free to blow in and out with a rhythm and a meaning not easily understood by a non-Muslim.

Then, in late afternoon and early evening, before
the sun went down, you could see café chairs inhabited
by desolate souls—no tea, nor coffee, smoking neither
cigarettes nor the "hubbly-bubbly." It was a city of ghosts.
Tables and chairs were set out in the streets as restaurants
prepared to serve those who could pay and to give free
meals to those who could not. Just before dusk, except
for the cooks and waiters and women in their kitchens
flitting about, readying the evening meal, there was the
most remarkable silence in every neighborhood. As the
call to prayer echoed across the vast city, the only audible
sounds in the first moments afterward were the tinkling
of spoons against bowls and plates as everyone ate—the
first date, the first spoonful of broth, the first sip of water.
Millions upon millions of people, in Arab countries and all
throughout the Muslim world and beyond, wherever on
the planet Muslims were living, everyone eating as their
portion of the earth turned from the sun.

After the sunset meal, the city burst back into life with
the most remarkable display of energy. Later I experienced
the month of Ramadan in Syria and the West Bank, but I
never found anything to match the number of celebrants,
the lighted beauty of the Islamic architecture, and, above
all, the joyful spirit that graces Cairo's streets each night of
the holy month.

People pack the buses and travel to other parts of the
city to see relatives. They meet friends in coffeehouses,
where they talk and smoke and laugh. Excited bands of
children light the special Ramadan lanterns with the

colored glass they've been given and carry them glowing through their neighborhoods. Masses of people wander the streets, talking and laughing among the lights and festive crowds.

Invited one evening early in the month to break the fast with *M'alim* Hassan's family, I asked the meaning of Ramadan.

"It's a celebration of the time," I was told, "when the Qur'an was imparted to the Prophet Muhammad. It teaches those who have, what it's like not to have. It instructs a Muslim to give 2.5 percent of all that has been earned or received."

"Why do you fast? You are not a Muslim," I was often asked. I struggled to explain that in fasting I hoped to acquire some of the consciousness they sought—of others' need, and of my responsibility to give, just as in coming to Egypt I wanted to learn all I could, in whatever ways I was able, about things I and others in my country didn't know.

But I didn't continue fasting for the whole month, not that Ramadan or any other. In later years, this was due in part to a chronic physical illness, but as my years in Arab countries passed, and each Ramadan I began fasting, only to retreat, I decided that the key must lie in religion—in Islam. Much as I respected and honored the religion, its adherents, and its traditions, there were some aspects, like fasting, I would not be able to experience unless I entered Islam so deeply that I, too, would be lifted up and carried by belief like the Muslims I knew.

∽

One day during Ramadan, Halim took me to a street in
the section of the market in the Old City where the tentmakers can be found. The men sit cross-legged on the
floors of the tents they've erected to serve as their little
shops, and with needle and thread appliqué by hand bits
of cloth onto cotton fabric. Some of the items they make
are huge: these are the colorful, patterned tents erected
in the streets for gatherings after funerals. Beside the
men are piles of smaller finished pieces that Egyptians
and tourists buy to use as pillow covers or wall hangings.
The material is worked into geometric designs like those
I'd seen in Cairo's mosques and houses, carved or inlaid
in wood or stone.

"The geometry," said Halim, "is a secret, and I do not
know if you are prepared to know it. It's about energy. It is
a secret that hurts the teller to tell the unprepared."

∽

On the first morning after Ramadan, I was awakened by
a great chanting from the mosque. Again, and again, and
again, the men recited from next door, in a crescendo:
"*Allaho akbar, Allaho akbar . . . le ile ilAllah*"—"God is
greatest, God is greatest . . . there is but one God. . . ."

Going outside, I saw three little girls playing up the
gusty street, calling to one another, voices blown by the
wind and caught in the men's chorus, wearing small
gallabiyyas, pigtails flapping.

The night before, the smaller children clustered round the light outside the green-painted corner store, moths around a flame, telling me and each other, "Tomorrow's the feast! Tomorrow's the feast!"

The recitation: "*Allaho akbar . . . le ile ilAllah.*"

The men's voices moved on and on, in a steady chant. Meanwhile, another, higher voice recited a higher counterpoint. The noise was like thunder, punctuated by sharp cracks—firecrackers—in the sandy streets outside. Gray dawn.

At 6:25 a.m. the sermon ended as abruptly as it had begun, with *salaam aleikom, rahmat Allah* . . . Now all was still. Just a rooster crowing away in the neighborhood and a chicken clucking outside my window.

It was all male, this swelling of voices from the mosque. In an evening that deeply altered my relationship with Halim, I brought this up. We were walking, as usual, but this time with Pat, an American woman I'd met who had lived for many years in Egypt. I don't like to think that the reason I brought up feminist questions on that walk was only because there was for once another woman with me as I walked with Halim. I wasn't conscious at the time of the stridency with which I addressed him.

"Women can go inside the mosques whenever they want," Halim answered, as the three of us walked that night. "But they are not a part of the ritual; they pray in curtained areas shut off from the splendor of the mosque."

I objected. "And that caused one of them to excel the other," I quoted from the Qur'an, painfully, not liking to make the challenge to this man who was becoming a friend, but wanting an explanation.

"Islam is very complicated. I don't recommend Islam to anyone," Halim said. "If you don't like it, don't have anything to do with it."

"But I want to," I protested.

"Why?"

"Because anyone who wants to live in Egypt or this part of the world must come to terms with Islam," I answered, and shortly after, realized it was more than that. For so long Islam had served as a "shell" for a teaching I admired very much, and I was rebelling at being in any way associated with a religion in which a lower status of women was sanctified, as if it had come, direct, from the voice of God.

"These objections are all to social aspects of Islam," Halim pointed out. "They relate to the culture, not the religion."

"Yes, but religion embodies these social factors, and, in the case of Islam, deliberately and even more forcefully than in other religions. How far can one go along with religion—with the Dutch Reformed Church in South Africa, for instance, saying, 'Oh, well, the policies of that church that endorse racism are only cultural, not religious'?"

I was frustrated, angry, at what I judged to be an irresponsible stance.

"Are you saying Islam is racist?" Halim asked.

"No, sexist!" I answered. But I was aware that I would have spoken more gently, more carefully, had the other American woman not been present. Only later did I realize that, puffed up by the presence of an assumed feminist "ally," I had adopted the shrill, accusatory tone in which I sometimes argued in the United States.

I ought not to have been surprised when Halim responded that he was feeling physically hurt, that he didn't want to be in the position of defending Islam, and ended the argument. I, too, felt physically pained, by the raw feeling between us.

Later, recalling the conversation, Halim said that the anger that leapt out at him that night had shown a side of me he had never known. Ah! Well, I could have told him. A quick, angry, ranting reaction was an all-too-common response of mine.

I was left not only with shame at my own behavior, but also with an outsider's uncomfortable sense that there was much I didn't understand. As Pat and I agreed later that night, despite the role Islam apparently describes for Egyptian women, they nevertheless possess a dignity, a charisma, a strength, and, to all appearances, a sense of their own worth that I had not found in any culture, and certainly not in my own.

It was similar to the dignity and proud sense of self that I had found at various points in my life to be characteristic of many women from countries across the world—although singularly missing in the Euro-ethnic middle-class women with whom I had grown up in the United States. What might explain this inversion in a woman's positive sense of herself and her own worth, making it greatest in countries where the West considered women most oppressed? I felt like a blind anthropologist, persisting in trying to interpret a world about which she had very little information. What emotions, what prejudices, were standing in my way?

∽

Cairo ambled back to work after Ramadan and the three-day *'eid*, or holiday. I began to feel I'd become a part of that world, that Cairo's rhythm had become my own. I straggled back to the shop a day after the *'eid* had ended to find that *M'alim* Hassan had not yet returned to work either. The corrugated metal doors were still pulled down across the entrance to Ibrahim's tea shop; the morning streets were still broad, clean, and deserted, buses (relatively) uncrowded. Patiently, I waited, reading the book I always had with me, but there was no sign of my master or of his two sons.

Finally I went looking for *M'alim* Hassan and was surprised to catch him smoking a *shisha* (water pipe) in his friend Sha'aban's shop. He made the "wait a little" sign, gently moving up and down his thumb and two fingers pressed together.

"*'Eid*," he said, meaning, of course, "The holiday lingers. Be patient, work will come."

I was only too happy to wait for work to start again, and took myself off to other parts of the city. Later in the day, I loved seeing the cafés fill again as if people were once more comfortable after the hard time, and when I saw a table without a cup of tea on it or a water pipe beside it, I felt like urging, *Help yourselves!*

15: LEAVE-TAKING

One day, just as the year in Egypt was coming to a close, Halim told me that all Hassan Fathy's projects had been approved.

The first project, a large building of "indigenous material"—in this case, stone—would be constructed near Alexandria, probably with several outbuildings nearby. Twelve people from "all over" would constitute the Institute. Like symphony directors, master architects would oversee an array of craftsmen from other parts of Africa—masons, carpenters, glaziers, potters, glassmakers, stonemasons . . . each one teaching apprentices, or "companions"—since everyone would associate socially, as well as in the work.

There would be a second site, an experimental desert community, to serve as a research center for the American University in Cairo, and Hassan *Bey* had been approached about building a cooperative village community in an oasis. There would be a village on the shores of the lake south of Aswan for Nubians displaced by the construction of the Aswan Dam. In addition, both Hassan Fathy and Halim envisioned the Institute as turning out architectural plans for future buildings; publishing books, articles, and magazines; and being involved in teaching.

Plans for all the projects had either been drawn or were in the process of being drawn. Now all that remained was to raise the necessary funds and to find members of the crew. It was to be the birth of the "ongoing seminar" of which Hassan Fathy had dreamed. Hassan *Bey* was well aware, Halim said, that he had little time. He would be glad, Halim said, if he could write two or three more books and see one of the Institute buildings built before he died. Halim was concerned that "Fathy is the Institute," that, as with Frank Lloyd Wright, when the man died, his work would too.

Only a short time later, I was told the projects were *not* beginning. There was some hitch. To work it out would take time.

ᔓ

I couldn't make up my mind whether to return to the United States. I appealed to Hassan Fathy one night in Ramadan when he, Halim, another friend, and I were out together, breaking the fast in a restaurant strung with white lights.

"Shall I return to America?" I asked. I cringe now to remember how much of what I asked Hassan Fathy was about myself. "Where will I learn most, become a better person?"

"Well, there's no doubt you will be learning something here other than what you learn in the United States," Halim said obliquely.

"The apprentice way requires years and years of watching," Hassan Fathy murmured, "from youth to . . ." He raised his hand from small to high, the way a child grows. That was all he said.

"Search for the origins of the quest in yourself," Halim had told me, "and you will know what is essential to you."

And: "Don't think so much."

For three nights I slept little, stiff from excitement at the thought of change, anxiety at the knowledge that I must make a choice. On the fourth morning I woke with a disconcerting but distinct sense that the night before, when I had stayed up until 4 a.m., the decision had been made. Feelings and reasons still floated like straw in a windy field, but I could not catch them. The harvest was in, bundled and tied. The process was finished: I would return to the United States.

I loved Egypt. I knew that living there, I had been deeply influenced, and I knew that I still wanted to know which of the country's strands had most spoken to me: Was it the Egyptian? the Arab? the Muslim? I knew that I would return one day to Egypt and that I would explore other Muslim Arab cultures to learn what it was that so attracted me. But I was not yet ready to commit myself completely to that world.

I had begun a construction company with my friends back home, and had left immediately afterward. I did want to keep the doors open to my sisters in the United States, to my country there; and that, I knew, meant keeping up my end, watering the plants if I wanted them to grow. I also suspected—and later this proved true—that I, ever the loner, keeping my distance from most other human beings, had much to learn about love and intimacy. I thought I would learn these best in a country in which I was not by definition an outsider, and in which I would have the community of other lesbians.

"Decide what you want to do," Halim had advised all along. "That's the question—not 'Egypt or America?'"

∽

One night soon after buying my ticket to the US, I went to Hassan *Bey*. He and Omar were working, and I sat awhile until they finished.

"Now I see it!" Omar said of a connection Hassan *Bey* had just shown him. "All you had to do was to say it once— and I see it!"

"Design is a matter of sensitivity," Hassan Fathy replied. "Aesthetics is a science; so the dictionary defines it. It is not a matter of taste, not a matter of 'I like this,' or 'I don't like this,' although one speaks this way. Beauty is not subjective; it is objective: it can be known. It is something that one learns to perceive."

Omar kept on working in the little room, and I had time alone with Hassan *Bey*. I told him I was going back to America for a while and that I wanted him to know that the opportunity he had given me would not be wasted, that I valued it more than I could tell him. He seemed to appreciate that. Such a keen, warm look in those clear eyes!

"I know what they will say to me in America," I said. "They'll say, 'What beautiful doors! But why don't we use machines to make them? Then we could make many more.'"

"It's a question of quantity and quality," he replied. "If you use machines, you can have many doors. But when you decide to do that, weigh the many doors against the quality of the lives of a thousand craftsmen, employed creatively. The harder the task you set yourself, the greater that which it draws out of you. When you use your machines, weigh this. Learning the art, the discipline, teaches on all levels. Look at the children of craftsmen. Bring a sociologist to study them, see how they behave. The craftsman deals with them with the same wisdom he learns from the wood. Compare the craftsman to the man who works with machines, his mind unchallenged."

And see the society that results, I thought.

In the back of my mind lurked my old question: "But, Hassan *Bey,* the handwork takes so long. Each worker produces so little quantity!" But now the question answered itself: "Yes, but look at America, with all its machines, and still the poor cannot afford anything beautiful, nor the rich either, for that matter."

"Oh!" I said. "You mean *everything* must change!" I imagined thousands upon thousands of men and women employed creatively, each challenged to his or her fullest, working with hands and mind—so many people working this way that the whole fabric of life would be changed.

"I don't cancel machines out entirely," he said. "Use them in their place, but weigh, *weigh* what you gain and lose."

"What about design, the geometric patterns always used in Islamic art: Are they essential to the woodworking, or can they be changed? I feel unfaithful thinking of changing them. Though they are not America's culture, I feel they are my culture—that they belong to everyone. Also, I sense, because the artists who used them built mosques like Sultan Hassan and Ibn Tulun, that the patterns hold a secret, though I do not know it. Is it somehow wrong to use them, without fully understanding what they mean?"

"Why did the Arabic characters develop as they did, and why did other languages develop differently, in other places?" Hassan Fathy asked me in return. "Change is normal. The highest art was developed from the fifth to the third centuries BC. With the Romans also came changes, but a decline. The Arabs, the Egyptians, because they were in the desert, naturally turned to the stars, to the study of astronomy, mathematics, geometry. If they had lived in a lush climate, their art would never have developed the way it did. Conversely," he said, "Louis XV, rococo, could never have developed in the desert. The process of change includes taking what comes from somewhere else and adapting it to one's own culture, in moving on. Now the woodwork you see there"—he indicated his lovely old chests—"in geometric design, of course, and assembled with the finest joinery—could not be taken into a room furnished in the style of Louis XV and rococo. But into a modern room, with a style of simplicity, it could."

Then his Saudi guest, an architect, arrived, and Hassan *Bey* left the room for a while. We talked, the guest and I. He told me he'd spent six years studying in Texas.

"How did you like it?" I asked, and then, after he had replied politely, I said, "Egypt has transformed my view of what human nature can be, and I attribute much of what I see here that is positive to Islam." He said he agreed. I asked where he was from—Mecca.

"Ah, a city I cannot visit," I said. "Unfortunately for me, and fortunately for you."

"Well, it's not so difficult," he said. "All you have to do is to accept Allah as the one God, and Muhammad as his prophet."

Another visitor arrived. Hassan Fathy spoke to him in Arabic, then resumed in English his conversation with me. At one point, he asked, "Do you think Mustafa and his father are good craftsmen?"

"Well," I said, my loyalty to my teacher feeling somewhat pinched, "*M'alim* Hassan is the best carpenter I've ever seen. But then, we have no 'master craftsmen' in America. I'm not the best judge. But when I see the old woodwork in the *munbar* [similar to a pulpit in Christian churches] at Sultan Hassan or Ibn Tulun, I know these are better."

"I ask you for a reason," Hassan Fathy said. "A craftsman can be poor for two reasons. He can do poor work out of a lack of skill or ignorance. Or he can do poor work because he is dishonest. A good craftsman would never skimp on materials to save money. There was a carpenter who refused to do work for Muhammad Ali [Egypt's Ottoman ruler in the early nineteenth century], who was trying to get the carpenter to flatten some *mashrabiyya* that should properly have been round. One day the carpenter got sick, and Muhammad Ali went to the carpenter's son and urged him, 'Come quickly, and do the job now, before your father gets well!'

"No craftsman," Hassan *Bey* continued, "would ever do anything that is not right, for *any* reason."

Omar said Thomas, who had recently gone home to Germany, had written that he wanted to return to Egypt. "What about his teacher in Germany?" I asked. Omar gestured toward the living room, toward Hassan Fathy.

"He's found a new one."

∽

One day in September, taking the bus from Heliopolis, one of Cairo's wealthiest districts, I underwent an atypical experience—Western clothes, grim, closed faces, the heavy package not taken from my arms, silence. It was utterly unlike any Egyptian bus I had ever ridden. In short, it was a *Western* experience, the more contradictory because of the bright, generous life flowing all around our island bus. How odd, I thought, to experience this just as I was to leave Egypt for the West. I pursued the thought that afternoon during a delightful visit with Halim's youngest brother, Muhammad, and their sister Widad; her husband, also named Muhammad; their daughter Jasmine; and Syada, the last sister I was to meet, from Kuwait. How we laughed—at me, at one another—while through the laughter rippled, as always, the lower tones of a conversation more serious:

"Has money made the Kuwaitis happy?" I asked Syada.

"No, although they build beautiful buildings there."

I described the behavior I'd seen earlier on the bus. Was this the behavior of those aspiring to affluence?

"Yes," said Muhammad, Halim's brother. "It is inevitable. Not that these Egyptians are really even affluent; their wages are pitifully low compared to the wages of the foreigners who employ them. But they have adopted the *mentality* of affluence. They are concentrating on themselves and on materialistic climbing. Egypt as we have known it," he said, "will disappear." Muhammad wanted, when his army service and his medical training were finished, to move outside Cairo, where, he said, "people are still real."

Egypt and Kuwait, the "mentality of affluence" and materialism, so like the West I knew.

But another experience, that same day, after I'd left my friends, reminded me how vast remained the differences between our two countries. This incident had to do with cigarettes. At the time, Egypt made Nefertiti, Cleopatra, Suez, and Florida cigarettes, all half the price of the Winstons and Marlboros imported from abroad. However, probably due to some glitch in local production, the city had been out of Egyptian cigarettes for weeks. First to go were the golden packs, next the small white packs, then the mini half packs, until only little pockets of places, in the area of the Citadel and in "my" neighborhood across the canal, still carried them, a rare pack here and there, until the last stage—a dearth of any affordable cigarettes at all. On the street, spotting someone with a pack, we'd ask, "Where did you get those?" And on hearing there were no more to be found, we afflicted could only groan.

Then one day, 'Am Muhammad, the tea seller, had given me a smoke from an almost empty pack of Floridas, "because there are none outside." Gratefully, I'd accepted. But the next day had come signs of an influx. First in the downtown areas, which always got them earliest, where I saw a man at Tahrir with a new pack. The next night, sure enough, the seller at the corner of Mohyi Eldin Abo el 'Ezz had a golden pack for me. That was one difference between Egypt and the US, certainly: the availability or unavailability of cigarettes, and the joy or gloom that accompanied one or the other constituted an undercurrent, a separate ebb and flow of commerce and emotion, of which the nonsmoker and the smoker of foreign cigarettes were unaware. I couldn't imagine this happening in the States.

It was the same with fruits and vegetables growing in the fields, then appearing for sale, artistically arranged in pyramids, perilously high, on pretty wooden carts pulled or driven through the streets. Spring puffs of lavender gave way to bright deep splashes of orange, these to a duller red. With the lavender, oranges were sweetest. Next, bluish-pink-and-white blossoms spiked new-flowering trees and tiny flannel-clad apricots glowed golden heaped atop the carts. Then the apricots—so soon!—replaced by plums, deep red and bright yellow, skins shiny and moist as snakeskin, and as gaily colored. And so it continued through the year. In Egypt, what there was to buy was announced by callers in the streets, a way to tell the seasons. This was not America.

But it was the incident that occurred on another bus the day I came from Heliopolis to visit with the family that spoke most eloquently of the contrast between the two cultures. If I had not been a smoker at the time, I would have had no idea why the #174 bus I was riding to Tahrir zapped to a halt, smack in the middle of a run, with no passengers waiting to get off and none waiting to get on. Only one person, the money taker, a young man, his eyes already gleaming, leapt off in a rush and vanished into a small store, while all the passengers waited patiently and (except for me) incurious in their seats. Then he reappeared, looking more than a little delighted, bearing a white pack of Cleopatra cigarettes. Behind him came the tea maker, carrying a small, round aluminum tray with two tiny glasses of the sweet black tea. A celebration! Driver and money taker drank them down and passed the glasses back, and the bus went on its way. *This* would not have happened in the West.

"Would I feel the joy of Egypt if I lived here forever, instead of just passing through?" I asked Halim's relatives.

"Easy for her," Syada said, meaning me. Always the real, honest criticism beneath the lightness.

"You know Egypt through the work, the most important thing," her brother Muhammad said. He explained that until ten days or so earlier, when Halim had told him I was working in a carpenter's shop, he had thought I was a rich tourist.

"Find what is true, as each of us must," he said, "and that can be the thread through wandering or staying at home. . . . You must show them in America the work by hand. You must be strong."

∽

Halim and I went to see Nahid, whom I'd not visited for some time. We found both her and her husband, Muhammad, along with two of their children, Heba and Ibrahim. Little Rania was sleeping. I could not get over my happiness at seeing Nahid, and to know as I was leaving Egypt that they were doing so well, Muhammad in his own business, Nahid with a degree in commerce for which she'd taken the exam in May. Heba had an English tutor and Ibrahim was rattling away to me in Arabic I understood. Nahid presented me with a good-bye gift, a lovely handblown glass vase of blue painted with Islamic design, all done by hand.

Back at the shop, I nearly cried when *M'alim* Hassan's oldest son, Muhammad, said his father had been weeping because I would be leaving soon.

I stayed some hours at work, but began to cry every time I looked at *Baba* Hassan. He made me go home to his house for lunch to say good-bye to the family there, but wouldn't go himself.

The house was all in a hubbub, with Madame preparing to leave the next day for Mecca, and the children crying, and I too as I said good-bye. Madame said to give *salaam 'aleikom kiteer* to my own mother. The year ended as it began, a stranger sending a greeting to my mother.

Back at the shop, I took down off the wall the piece of woodworking I had done within a month or so of my arrival in Cairo. It was the *mafrooka*, involving the real joinery, the highest of the woodworking art. That little piece had been the culmination of the training in geometry Mustafa had given me. It had been the most difficult thing I'd ever done.

After that, Mustafa had stopped teaching me how to draw and join wood in geometric patterns. At the time, I'd assumed he'd cut short the instruction because I had done so poorly at learning. But now looking at the work, I realized that he had taken me through all the steps. From my earliest days in the shop I had been given the teaching I'd wanted so much to learn, although at the time I had not realized its worth.

At seven or so, we all drank tea in the little courtyard at the shop. Night had come already, and electric light lit bare ground and the banana tree above. That noon, for the first time, I had eaten one of the little triangular-shaped bananas we had watched fatten slowly on the tree in the courtyard for so long. I said good-bye to Sha'aban across the alleyway, and he came in again as I was leaving.

'Atif caught me as I came into Shari'a Shakuun and shook my hand. Good-bye to *ostah* Ibrahim the ironer, to

Muhammad the tea seller again, and up to Hassan Fathy's. The news: yet another reversal of fortune. After having been funded, then not funded, the Institute had now not only been funded again, but had received an alternate offer of funding from Prince Salah of Kuwait. Building would start soon, and the woodworking, too.

"The timing is strange," I commented, rather struck by the imminence of the work I had come for a year ago.

"Yes," Halim agreed, "it's as if something has been pulled out, like a cork."

The men spoke again in Arabic, finishing business I had interrupted, and Halim, seeing me staring through the window, asked if I'd been on the roof. Ah yes! I went up, grateful for the space and night beauty of the city, minarets standing tall around me. Mohammad Ali was lit, and Sultan Hassan. I could see the dunes beyond and the rooftops stretched below.

Sadness stayed with me as Halim and I took our leave of Hassan Fathy and walked toward "the most fantastic street in Cairo," as Halim called Sharia' Muazzin.

"Is there anything that must be said now, in person? For in letters I say what I feel, but don't address the person," Halim told me. "Is there anything you have remaining you want to say to me? Say it here, in this street; its energy can absorb anything."

I hesitated, not sure it was necessary, and then turned to him, before we reached the shop of the men who do the appliqué, thanked him as best I could for all he had given me, and apologized for my harshness the night we had talked about Islam. Then he was off to the street of the tentmakers to buy a good-bye present for me.

"Don't buy a good-bye present for me, Halim. I'll be back before you know it."

His smile.

"If I don't find a good one, I won't."

That evening at the teahouse, the old woman, the fortune teller, whom we all knew and whom we addressed with the honorific *hagga*, came to sit at our table outside. When I had drunk the strong black coffee, she tipped the tiny china cup upside down on the saucer until it drained, then turned it upright again. From the chocolate-colored spidery lace left inscribed on the cup's inner walls, she read to me my fortune:

"Absolutely you will be coming back to Egypt."

When I heard these words, a calm came in. Halim had not wailed when he left Egypt; he was certain he would return. I, too, was as certain as I could be that much of my future lay outside America.

Halim gave me the present he had bought.

"The wrapping is very important," he told me. The piece of cloth was "wrapped" by being sewn closed, so that I could not see the embroidery work inside. "You are not to unwrap it until you reach America. Who would wrap it again for you? It is very beautiful," he said.

〜

The boat I took from Alexandria back to Greece was a small one, so different from the huge ship *Bashkiria*, and I was glad. I slept almost the entire three days of the Mediterranean crossing, not in a berth, but on deck. Luckily the weather was cold and windy, so I could huddle in my sleeping bag without looking too odd.

At four thirty one morning I was woken by the sailor Muhammad, off shift, bringing me a large glass of sweet black tea and wanting to talk. Forty-eight years old, a sailor for twenty years, a widower, he was the father of two children, both living with his sister in Alexandria.

"Twenty years," he said, "with only"—he pointed upward—"Allah"—and downward—"the sea." He shrugged and slapped his hands together, gesturing, "And that's all."

A dolphin leapt off the starboard stern; I saw the arc of the body and a fanned tail—fulfillment of a longtime dream.

The Greek island of Paros, where I would stop, lay on the horizon.

Europe, once again.

INTERLUDE:
THE YEARS BETWEEN

During that year in Egypt, I was uplifted by a quality that, for want of a more inclusive word, might be termed generosity. It was in Egypt I first experienced being on the receiving end of such generosity, which was practiced there not only by Egyptians—Muslims and Christians alike—but which seemed to have splashed as well upon a good proportion of foreigners who had spent much time in the country.

When people ask me what I loved about living in Arab countries, it is this quality I mention first. Not to be confused with the celebrated "Arab hospitality," the generosity I experienced went far beyond the traditional welcome of a traveler or a stranger. It manifested itself in little acts and in large ones, and its influence on my life has never ended.

Through that generosity I was offered an understanding of how I might learn, and of how much there was to be learned that I had not recognized before. Everywhere I walked, I seemed to trip over a seam of wisdom. Along with this came love, friendships, a greatly improved sense of humor, gratitude, and, perhaps, the beginnings of humility. All of these combined to bring about the transformation that occurred in me, a female citizen of the United States of America, because I was lucky enough to be welcomed into a part of the Arab world through a particular door at a particular moment in time.

For fifteen years after that first year in Egypt, I lived in the United States. During that time, I did learn something of love and intimacy, as I had hoped I would. For most of those years, I worked as a carpenter in our women's company. The best job for me in all that time came with the opportunity to hand-carve two wooden doors for a Victorian home our company was remodeling in Oakland. Although we were sometimes fortunate to be able to work for people without much money, I never did build houses of mud brick, and I never did build housing for the poor.

But the other lessons offered to me in Egypt continued to unfold. My respect for and attraction to Arab and Islamic culture deepened, and with these, proportionately, my anger at my own government's actions in Arab countries and other former European colonies in what was called the Third World. US policies toward Israel and Palestine, in particular, struck me as being unnecessary and unfair, and I began to read and speak out on the issue. I got over my fear of being labeled "anti-Semitic" (Arabs are Semites, too) when I objected to US and Israeli policies toward

Palestinians. In 1991, as US planes bombed Iraqis fleeing along the roads from Kuwait, I left the US again for the Middle East, this time for sixteen years—two years in Syria, two more in Egypt, a single year in Israel, and eleven in the West Bank, Palestine.

The story resumes as I am leaving the teachers' college near Tel Aviv where I've been teaching English to Jewish and Palestinian residents of Israel. As this second half of the narrative begins, I am finally on my way to Palestine, my ultimate destination once I had decided to return to the region I loved.

I knew very little about Palestine when I went to live there. I knew that a civilian population was living under a military occupation, made possible with US tax money, political support, and US-made arms. I wanted to understand what this meant for Palestinians.

Everything in this story is told as I experienced it over the eleven years I lived in Palestine.

PART TWO: PALESTINE

"Tomorrow there will be apricots."
(Tomorrow never comes.)
Arabic proverb

16: CLOSURE

From the teachers' college where I worked outside Tel Aviv, on a clear day I could see the Palestinian town of Qalqilya resting across the hillside on the other side of the Green Line. As in every Arab village I had seen, its dwellings lay in pleasing patterns of irregularity just off the shoulder of the hill, a welcome contrast with the regimental ordering of new towns and villages inside Israel proper and in the settlements on the flat-topped hills in the West Bank.

I'd been on my way to Palestine after earning an MA in TOEFL (Teaching English as a Foreign Language) in Egypt in 1996, but was diverted by a US government program that provided new MA graduates free of charge to developing countries. The position in Palestine had already been filled, but I was accepted by a teachers' college in Israel and knew it would be useful to spend some time trying to understand Israelis' views on Palestine. After some hard thought, I signed a one-year contract to teach Arabs and Jews studying to become English teachers at Beit

Berl College, near Kfar Saba, Israel. I never regretted that decision, and I did learn a great deal, but during the year, I used to gaze across the fields at the Palestinian village in the occupied West Bank and walk in the fields as near it as I could go. At dusk, I'd lean from the upper-story windows of the English building to hear the call to prayer.

Heartsick, lonely on a campus that emptied each night and every weekend of teachers, students, administrators, and Palestinian workers, I yearned for the life I could imagine in the Arab village. On weekends, I'd walk outside the campus in groves of orange trees, planted in perfect rows. On rare occasions, one of the other teachers would invite me home. Otherwise, late at night I'd walk the lush green campus lawns and hear the *swish, swish* of the nighttime water sprinklers, amazed at the abundance of water sparkling in curving sprays on this desert land.

At the end of the second semester, in June 1997, I did not sign on for another year. When instead I moved to the town of Ramallah to begin work at Birzeit (pronounced *Beer-zate*) University in the West Bank, with workers from the very Palestinian town I'd been so wistfully eying, I rode in an old van with my few possessions—mostly books. Minutes after we had left the campus, the battered vehicle turned off Israeli streets onto the dusty, rutted dirt roads of the lands still nominally in Palestinian control.

In 1948, the State of Israel was established on about half the land that had been predominantly Arab and Muslim from the end of the seventh century until the steady influx of Jewish colonists after 1882. After the 1967 war, when Israel had annexed East Jerusalem and taken over the Golan Heights in the north, Gaza to the west, and the West Bank of the Jordan River to the east, the State of Israel was occupying more than three-quarters of historical Palestine. Only after the Oslo Accords were signed in 1993 was the newly created Palestinian National Authority given minimal, always revocable, control over parts of Gaza and the West Bank.

The roads we were taking through the West Bank ran through open, unplanted fields. The farther we drove from the Beit Berl campus, into rougher and wilder countryside, the friendlier the men driving me became. It was as if only outside Israel did they feel free to discard the tough outer shell they wore as emotional protection inside the Jewish state.

As we crossed the checkpoint dividing the State of Israel from the lands it occupied, I was, in my ignorance, taken aback to see soldiers in jeeps coming and going from their military bases atop the hills. These bases, along with the masses of residential areas built high on the hills, fortress-like and monolithic, were the Israeli settlements I'd heard about in the news and read about in books. I had thought soldiers, jeeps, the blue and white flags, and maybe even settlements would have vanished from the West Bank after the Oslo agreement. I'd been wrong. The accord, also called the Declaration of Principles, had placed only a modicum of the occupied land under partial Palestinian control, that of Yasser Arafat's Palestinian National Authority, or PNA.

Poverty! the West Bank cried, in stark contrast with the

Israeli villages and towns of look-alike orange-tiled roofs set amid the farmed and fertile land in which I'd been living. Here, on the Palestinian side of the Green Line, it was hotter, no cooling stands of trees or expanses of grass. The sky was brighter, sunlight trapped between buildings set close together.

A large crowd of men stood at the checkpoint, workers waiting to be picked up for day labor in Israel. Shepherds, their heads shielded from sun, their noses and mouths from dust by the Arab's traditional black-and-white or red-and-white woven cotton scarves, herded flocks of sheep and goats across the road. Noisy vans, shaking and rattling, took the place of sleek, air-conditioned buses. Dust, car exhaust, and dense black smoke rising from fires burning trash in open lots thickened the air; no smooth, black-topped roads, new cars, or a government-funded garbage collection system.

Here, the land was hillier, rockier, less suited for large-scale orchards and farms. Water was clearly at a premium. There were olive trees, unmistakable with their fluttering silvery leaves, and only tiny areas suitable for growing crops. Where crops were growing, they grew on terraced hillsides in portions of land too small to be tended except by hand, each level separated from the next by small stones piled up into low, uneven walls texturing the landscape.

✎

Just outside Ramallah, we passed something that might have been a "town" set in a little basin between two hillsides, composed of houses built of concrete, tin, pieces of wood, strips of cloth, and crowded so closely together that they reminded me of the favelas I'd seen as a child on the hills of Rio de Janeiro. Tents had given way to more or less permanent structures as their inhabitants had gradually accepted the futility of anticipating change. This was a refugee camp for Palestinians displaced from their homes. It was a place of crowdedness, of twisted narrow dirt lanes and makeshift dwellings. Human beings were packed together tight as chickens in a dusty bag.

At last we reached the West Bank town of Ramallah. Like the rest of the West Bank through which we had just driven, the town was poorer than Jewish Israeli towns or settlements. Roads were made of dirt or asphalt so studded with potholes that cars and vans jolted, rather than rode, over them. Sidewalks were rubbled or nonexistent, lanes narrower and more crowded, public spaces barren and untended. Houses and stores were smaller and simpler. Layers of dust powdered the leaves on spindly trees.

Within a short time, I was standing in the apartment I had arranged to rent temporarily, surrounded by the boxes of books I had brought with me, in a world completely different from the one I'd just left. Six years after I'd set out for Palestine, I'd arrived.

∾

Birzeit University, where I was to teach, had arguably the best academic reputation among the seven Palestinian institutions of higher learning existing at the time in the

West Bank and Gaza. Several times during the year I had spent teaching in Israel, I had traveled to the West Bank, and on one of these visits I had been interviewed and hired to teach English to undergraduates in the Department of Languages and Translation the coming fall. Birzeit University was the one educational institution I had heard of long before I arrived in the Middle East. Practically every writer whose book I had read or any person I'd heard speak about Palestine in the US had been connected with the university.

The summer I arrived, I was to work not on the main campus, but at the university's Center for Continuing Education in Ramallah, where I'd teach business English to women working as secretaries in one of the Palestinian "government" ministries. In the fall I would teach on the main university campus just outside Ramallah.

The morning after my arrival, I walked into the center of town, to a pretty brick building where I was introduced to the striking but formidable Haifa Baramke—Mrs. Baramke to all—and to the other Palestinians working in the Center for Continuing Education. A colleague passed me when I was sitting on the floor, as I tend to do, sorting some papers.

"That's our culture, not yours!" he teased, referring to the traditional Arab custom of sitting on the floor rather than on a chair.

"Well, it's mine, too!" I smiled back, thinking of the years I had spent crouching on the ground or on the floor when I worked as a carpenter.

I quickly found that Palestinians responded to me with both interest and friendliness. Unlike many Egyptians a decade earlier, who responded to strangers like old friends from the start, Palestinians reminded me more of Syrians. They took a few moments to evaluate a stranger encountered casually on the street or in a taxi before leaping to extend a welcome. Their acceptance, having been earned, was the more appreciated.

When my eyes adjusted more to the new landscape, I saw Ramallah as a place of beauty. Of those first weeks and months in Palestine, I recall bright light, terraced hills and narrow roads winding among them, old stone houses and new buildings sparkling white, stones and dust. I remember having many questions that I never asked; there was so much I didn't know.

One day I saw a woman carefully plucking broad, dust-filmed leaves one by one, by the side of the road, from a plant I did not recognize. To sell? To cook, filled with rice and meat? Sheep grazed nearby, their buff coats the color of the withered pasture they were grazing. Their shepherd, an old man, watched over them. Where was their resting place? Where was the shepherd's home?

The apartment I was renting stood across the street from a little farm. Just past that, with a fancy villa between them, was an empty field where a herd of sheep and a few goats often grazed. A little valley lay between the road and the high new buildings rising all along the high side.

The first days I was there, I walked out in my neighborhood. I was happy to see that I could descend the hillside and walk along dirt paths. I loved that the city of Ramallah dropped off so quickly into open land. One morning I walked until I came to a quarry. Was this the source of the materials that cement trucks were trundling along the road? The city then was growing; I guessed that soon the little farms would go, to be replaced by new commercial or apartment buildings like those farther along the road toward town. But for the time being, Ramallah was a lovely mixture of town and rural life. In the meantime, I would appreciate the country feel of this place that slipped so quickly from houses and buildings into pastures for goats and sheep. At night, the air was clear enough so that I could see stars and a large full moon after it rose above the hill and hung in the sky.

I felt safe in my apartment and in my neighborhood, but I didn't want to live permanently in a newly built-up, relatively well-off area, giving an impression of wealth I did not have. As someone entering a new culture, I knew that I had a choice, to some extent and for a limited amount of time, where in the social scale to place myself. I didn't want to separate myself even further from women I wanted to know.

Still, beneath the city's cosmopolitan facade, many people were in financial trouble. The owner of the little store across the street from my apartment building told me that he had brought his life savings back to Ramallah, his hometown, after working abroad many years. He had hoped to invest in the new economy, he said, but now he was desperate.

"Do you know how much I've made today?" he asked me. "One hundred shekels"—about $25 at the time.

The current economic situation was just as bad as it had been when he'd left, he told me, due to the frequent "closures" imposed on the West Bank and Gaza by the Israeli military. He described the different types of closures.

"Internal closures" meant that Palestinians living in one part of the West Bank were unable to travel to another part of the West Bank, and that Gazans were forbidden to move from one area to another within Gaza. An "external closure" could mean that no Palestinian from the West Bank or Gaza was allowed into Israel, and that Gaza was completely cut off from the West Bank. A combination of the first and second kinds, along with the sealing of the "international" crossings between the West Bank and Jordan and between Gaza and Egypt, constituted "complete closure."

Any of the different types of closure might be imposed on Palestinians in the Occupied Territories at any time. So when I met him, at a time Palestinians were living under a complete closure, the store owner was unable to obtain the canned and packaged products from Israel he needed to sell to his customers in the West Bank. How was he to support his family?

In time, I learned that all the relatively prosperous-looking tall new buildings I saw in Ramallah and other growing areas—three new malls were being planned in Ramallah alone—were owned by a few people. Meanwhile, the majority of Ramallah residents, many of whom had come to Ramallah because they couldn't earn a living in other parts of the West Bank, were unable to find places they could afford to rent. Generations of extended families lived crammed together in small spaces, all sharing one kitchen and one bathroom, because they could not pay more. Those who were building malls and living in villas lived very different lives from the herder of goats pasturing out my window, or the man I'd seen recently driving his donkey cart up the hill towards the center of town.

The term "closure" took on substantive meaning when, having prepared the course I was to give, I headed off up the hill toward the Center for Continuing Education for my first day of teaching, only to find no students. There were no secretaries for me to teach—none from Nablus, in the north; none from Al Khalil, or Hebron, in the south. They and the others, who lived in villages outside Ramallah, had learned via the primary communication system in Palestine—word of mouth—that we were "closed." Everyone, except those who lived inside the town of Ramallah, was blocked from coming. The secretaries I was to teach were not allowed to leave their cities. All over Palestine, people were kept from going to their jobs. Most of ordinary life—educational, economic, and social—was brought to a halt.

"How is it, being locked up tight as a drum?" asked Terry, a Jewish Israeli-American activist friend on the other side of the Green Line, repeating the words I'd used to describe the closure.

"Well," I said, "it's fine for those of us who have enough

money to live on and who aren't really locked up. We're not trapped: foreigners are allowed to pass through checkpoints when Palestinians are not."

While for me, being new in town, being "closed" was, in its novelty, rather exciting, for Palestinians it was neither new nor exciting. Masses of people were cut off from their families, from medical care, from their sources of income. One of the foreigners living in the house across the street told me that a family she knew in Bethlehem was eating only potatoes; everything else was too expensive. Others, I heard, were eating only bread and tea.

Palestinians never knew from one day to the next if they would be able to go to work or school. The owner of the auto shop didn't know if he would be able to get the parts he needed from Tel Aviv. The greengrocer didn't know if he'd be able to get fresh produce from outlying farms. Drivers of the shared taxis, the only means of public transportation in the West Bank and Gaza, sat idle all day, ferrying no passengers, earning nothing. When drivers did find enough passengers to make it worthwhile to go somewhere, the Israeli military forbade them from using the main roads. Instead, they bounced their old cars across rutted pastures and back roads, driving miles outside their usual routes. Taxi fares doubled, then tripled, making it impossible for many people to go anywhere at all.

One evening, the owner of the corner store asked me, "Do you know how much money I lost today? Twenty-nine thousand dollars." That day he and his brothers had sold the shop at a loss. Soon he would either be in debt, or he and his extended family would lose the apartment he had been renting for $1,000 per month.

"I hate it," Kim said one day when I wandered over to the house she rented for a visit. Ramallah was small enough that you could easily walk from one end of it to another. Kim, also from the United States, worked at Birzeit University. "Day after day, you wake up and say, 'Will I have work today?' And after a few days or a few weeks of the answer being 'No,' and you've done all the work you can at home, depression sets in."

Each day, faithfully, I went into the center of town to see if the closure had been lifted. Each day, I would find that it had not and would go back home. As the days passed and my faith in the possibility of a normal life shrank, I began going across the street and using a pay phone outside the little store to call the department, instead of walking into town to learn our fate. At first, I welcomed the rest and solitude, to the point that when I went to make the call, I found myself hoping, in my habitually eremitic way, that no classes would be held that day.

I didn't live in a small house crammed with people. I was not a mother worrying about how to feed my children or a wage earner whose dignity, and temper too, perhaps, were suffering because I couldn't support my family.

Easy as life was for me, I too began to fret as the days of closure rolled on. In one form or another— whether sealed from Israel and external markets or from one another—the Occupied Palestinian Territories had been experiencing closure since 1993. In May and June of 1997, Palestinians had been protesting the killing of Palestinians, the Israeli announcement of its plan to keep 40 percent of the West Bank for Israel, settler attacks on Palestinians in Hebron, the destruction of Palestinian homes and the targeting of hundreds more West Bank homes for demolition, and any number of other actions. Every time Palestinians demonstrated or an Israeli was killed, more closures were enforced. Palestinians called for strikes when the new Palestinian National Authority suspended and arrested teachers and when it was found to have abused funds. It was hard not knowing each morning whether I would teach that day, or the next, or the one after that. Should I keep myself always prepared for my lessons, live constantly in a state of readiness? Or should I forget about teaching and do something else that day? Increasingly, I roamed the streets, talking to people I met. How stopped life was by the closure; the streets were almost empty.

One morning, since I was unable to teach at the Continuing Education Center, I decided to try to reach Birzeit University to see if any of the other teachers were up on campus and what, if anything, was going on. Normally, I later learned, the ride along the winding Birzeit Road, through hills studded with olive groves growing on terraces separated by low stone walls, took about twenty minutes. That day it took two hours. Our shared taxi made it some distance before it came to an enormous pile of dirt that blocked the entire road. The Israeli army had bulldozers, which were able easily to swipe up a load of earth and dump it across a road.

Without a word from anyone—everyone but me knew the drill—the cab stopped, its doors opened, and the other passengers got out and began climbing over the great earth mound. I followed them, climbing up over the roadblock, tricky with stones, uneven and rough, clods of earth sticking to my shoes. On the other side of the mound, in a little open area, sat the taxi drivers who worked on that side of the blockade. They were waiting for us to arrive so they could ferry us onward to the next obstacle.

In this way I learned that although we were "closed," there were sometimes ways around a closure, at least an internal one. Having the roads closed meant that getting somewhere took longer, cost more, and was hard on the vehicles and on everyone else as well—but it was possible, one way or another, to get through. We could climb over roadblocks, drive through open fields, and switch taxis when one car was blocked from going further. How resourceful! I did not imagine at the time that, within a few years, even this costly and cumbersome method of working around the Israeli obstacles would no longer be possible.

Just as we reached the drivers, a jeep colored an unsavory greenish brown pulled up fast and stopped alongside the men. A soldier got out, and, while a second soldier waited in the vehicle, the first began to yell at the drivers.

This was the first time I had been anywhere near a soldier or witnessed an interaction between a soldier and a

Palestinian. The soldier was yelling at the man in Hebrew. I did not understand a word he was saying. Very likely, I thought, the Palestinians didn't either, but his meaning was clear.

One of the drivers, seated like the others on a nice-sized stone, and, like the others, not looking at the soldier, shrugged and ground his cigarette into the dirt beneath his foot.

The gesture seemed to make the soldier even angrier. He yelled louder, and his face got red.

I was surprised to see that of all the people there— the inconvenienced passengers, the drivers without a living wage, the soldier—it was the soldier who acted angry. How fitting that armies consist mostly of teenage boys: Who is more suited to the job than adolescent males, hopped up on hormones and carrying guns? I was to witness this many times during my years in Palestine—soldiers completely losing it, out of control with anger, while Palestinians stood or sat, their faces expressionless as stones, the soldiers getting more and more furious.

Thinking about the incident afterward, I had to admit that in feeling anger myself, I had been more than a witness. I had been a participant, generating more anger. Was there something useful I could do in such situations?

And the soldier—how did he justify his actions to himself? With what rational explanation did he construct the cognitive scaffolding to shore up his decision to act in such a way, day after day? I'd never considered the anger it might take—or generate—to be a soldier in an occupying army. If it's true that we feel anger when we feel powerless, then why was the armed soldier fairly bursting with anger, while the unarmed civilians sat quietly, looking grim but calm? I could imagine a Palestinian not showing anger because he'd be in more danger if he did. But why was the soldier in a rage, when he held the gun? After all, it was the Palestinians who lost their land to make way for the Jewish state.

Had the soldier been so angry because he could not make the Palestinian taxi drivers react to him? Or because he could not make the entire Palestinian population . . . go away?

Or did the display of anger mean that the soldier in fact did feel powerless, and therefore afraid? Certainly, most Jewish Israelis I'd met had indicated they were afraid.

Soon afterward, in East Jerusalem, still called the "Arab Quarter" of the Old City, despite the increased Israeli presence, a Palestinian shopkeeper sitting in his gold shop without a customer in sight suggested a reason why Israelis were afraid of Palestinians.

"Wouldn't you be afraid," he asked me, "if you had taken someone's land and then tried to live on it, with the people you had taken it from all sitting right there under your boot?"

I saw his point. Roman, Ottoman, and European colonists in Africa, Asia, and most of the Americas had for the most part established only military and political presences in their colonies. They hadn't tried to settle their entire population among the people they conquered.

Europeans who had colonized what was to become the United States of America had faced better odds because the land they had taken over was enormous, the Native American population small enough to be killed off or confined to small areas. Israel was trying to sit on a relatively small piece of land that had a native population too populous—and too visible to the rest of the world, in this day of international media—to kill quickly; and trying to keep them pacified was proving to be frustrating work.

After about ten minutes, the soldier gave up shouting at the men. He climbed back into his jeep, slammed the door, and, to my surprise, simply drove away.

I hadn't anticipated the intimacy that might exist between soldier and civilian when they came face to face. I had pictured a military occupation as a kind of mechanical thing, unpleasant, but somehow remote, impersonal. But the Palestinians' feelings were obvious, indirectly as they showed them; and the soldier, far from behaving like some sort of robot, had displayed all the volatility of which any human being is capable, particularly in situations of conflict or stress. The realization made the whole situation a little uglier—and more dangerous—than I had imagined from afar.

17: FRIENDS

When I finally did arrive at the university that day, things were quiet. Taisir, then head of the Department of Languages and Translation and one of three men who had interviewed me for the job, greeted me, to my surprise, with a kiss on both cheeks. Since most students and teachers could not reach the campus due to the closure, the summer semester hadn't ended, and the beginning of the fall semester would be delayed, perhaps by ten days, two weeks, or more.

There were only a few teachers in the department preparing their classes. But the friends I met that day, and on other visits to the university in the weeks before the fall semester began, turned out to be among the best friends I made during the years I lived in Palestine.

First I met Pat Kana'ana, an American teacher just a little older than I was. At last, someone my age! I was delighted to find that she was married to Sharif Kana'ana, whose name showed that his people had been living on the land since the time of the Canaanites. Sharif also taught at Birzeit University, and years before, in the US, I had read and admired the book of Palestinian folktales he had compiled. Could I meet him? Yes! Pat and I shared a bond in that we had both lived and worked in Native American communities, she as the daughter of a teacher in South Dakota, where she had been raised, and I in Arizona. Kind and generous, interesting and funny, both Pat and Sharif became real friends to me over the years.

"Come, drop by! Don't be a stranger!" they would say. Many of us did and were always warmly welcomed. In some of the worst times to come, I would visit to sip a little of the calm that always seemed to surround them both, snatch a gem from Sharif's understanding of Palestine, and, with luck, glean a joke or two he had recently picked up on the street to add to his treasure trove of Palestinian humor.

Taisir introduced me to another instructor in the department, a woman named Muna, who would become one of the best friends I've made anywhere I've lived. Direct, friendly, generous with her time and her knowledge of the university and of Palestine, she helped me tremendously.

While living in the US, Muna had been active in working for the rights of Palestinians and other people in the US and abroad. "But after the Declaration of Principles setting up an interim Palestinian Authority was signed in 1993," she said, "the whole movement fell apart. You couldn't say a word about anything. You couldn't say anything critical of Israel. No one wanted to believe that the problem was not solved, or that Israel was not doing its best to implement some agreement. But no one had read the agreement, which in fact held so little. The Oslo Accords never promised a future Palestinian state."

This was how I learned that the much-lauded Oslo agreement had never included an Israeli commitment to working toward the creation of a Palestinian state, even though most of the world believed it had. The same kind of misinformation was to plague other supposed agreements between Israeli and Palestinian leaders: no one who had not been present could know for sure what had happened or what the real terms or outcome of the negotiations had been. The media in Israel and the US routinely hold the Palestinian side responsible for the lack of progress.

One matter on which Muna could reassure me—in a fashion, at least—was the matter of my work permit. Everyone who visits or lives in the Occupied Territories has to be issued some form of permission by the Israeli government, which controls every crossing in and out. The Palestinian Authority has no right to issue IDs, work permits, travel permits, or visas; and so far, the university had not been able to obtain papers for me.

By means of a Kafkaesque system, complicated and ever-changing, designed to limit and reduce the Palestinian population in the Occupied Territories, the Israeli government denies Palestinians who have lived abroad for certain periods of time the right to return to the West Bank or Gaza, unless they were able to obtain certification before they left. Since Muna lived outside the country for twenty-nine years, and beforehand was not able to obtain the required certification, she is denied residency in her homeland. So is her mother. Both are considered foreigners by the Israeli government, and are not allowed to vote in Palestinian elections or be counted in the census. They must enter Palestine on their US passports, as if they were complete strangers, just like me. They must leave Palestine every three months and travel to another country, then reenter Israel and the Occupied Territories on a new visa, as any non-Palestinian must.

Muna sounded philosophical about the whole matter. In the end, her reassurance consisted of letting me know that if I could not get a visa, I would be in good company: my position was no different from that of many Palestinians. "You'll just be illegal like the rest of us," she said.

But she was more upset about the situation than her words conveyed. By means of chameleon-like mutations in the laws, the Israeli government continuously tightens restrictions on Palestinians' ability to move into and out of Palestine, as well as from place to place within and between the West Bank, Gaza, and East Jerusalem. Many Palestinians are stopped if they try to leave Palestine, forbidden to cross borders in any direction. This is especially true in Gaza, where 1.82 million people are confined in about 140 square miles, without clean water, sufficient health care, educational opportunities, and the whole spectrum of vital services, making the population density there one of the highest in the world, averaging more than 13,000 persons living in each square mile. Far from having any "right to return" to the lands they lost to the State of

Israel, many of the approximately 5.2 million Palestinians living in the diaspora find they are not even able to visit, much less live in, what remains of Palestine, even to see family members. For everyone I knew, the situation was highly stressful. Families were divided, plans thwarted, careers interrupted or lost.

"Palestinians who left in 1948 when Jews took the land by force and declared the Israeli state may never be allowed to come back. I am here on an American passport," Muna said. "Do you see the irony? Do you see the irony of this?"

I did. I was almost never to see Muna so upset as when she spoke of Palestinians' "illegality" in their own land.

∽

After the first eventful visit to Birzeit University's main campus outside Ramallah, near Birzeit Village, I returned to Ramallah, where I took up my wait for the closure to end and my classes to begin at the Continuing Education Center. One day, as I walked into town, I saw so much more activity than in previous days—more people about, more vehicles moving in the streets, and spirits seeming higher—that I thought we were no longer locked up. But when I stopped into the Center for Continuing Education, Mrs. Baramke told me that the roads were still closed. Still, the change was so remarkable that I thought it must have an explanation. In the copy shop, I asked Muhammad: Why were spirits lighter?

Palestinians had held a demonstration the night before, which had remained peaceful since no Israeli jeeps had

appeared, he told me, and the internal closure separating
different areas in the West Bank had been lifted somewhat.
He implied no connection between the two happenings;
the ways of the Israeli military were often unfathomable.
But at least I learned that closures weren't necessarily
all or nothing; they could be in force some places, lifted
or partially lifted elsewhere. In addition to being lifted,
closures might lighten or dribble away. But there were still
no students at the Continuing Education Center for me to
teach. And the main campus of Birzeit University, up the
hill, also remained closed.

§

All this time, I was looking for a place to live. This
involved walking up and down the streets of Ramallah
and asking people if they knew of a place I might rent.
One day, I turned up a road I'd not taken before, a short
walk away from the *manara*, the traffic circle in the center
of Ramallah from which six roads originated in a most
confusing way. The road is near one of Ramallah's two
hospitals, neither of which was in the best of shape, since
Israel has not spent money on hospitals, schools, roads,
sewers, telephone lines, or any other infrastructure in the
Occupied Territories since capturing the land in 1967.
In front of a little gate, which opened onto a walkway
leading to a garden and a two-story house, a woman was
sweeping.

Feeling foolish, as I always did asking strangers on the
street if they knew of a place I might live, I repeated the

request I'd been making in Ramallah neighborhoods for almost two weeks.

"*Marhaba!*" I greeted her in Arabic. "I'm looking for a small place to rent where I can live alone."

How lucky I was that day! The woman smiled and responded immediately.

"Yes, I know of a new place that's just being built. I'll call the owners to see if you can meet them, and if you call me back, I'll let you know."

Nawal was to become and remain a good friend and neighbor to me until she joined her two grown children in Jordan during the Second Intifada. She seemed about my age, fifty-two, but it was hard to tell.

My original landlord found someone to move into the place I had been staying since I had arrived ten days earlier. Fortuitously, the new apartment I was to live in, the home Nawal had found for me, was just about finished.

My new home was a little living space newly added on to a large house, where my new landlord and landlady lived with their two teenage daughters and a young son. The new addition, which included an alcove equipped with a sink and hot plate, along with a tiny bathroom, was up off the ground, its small porch reached via a stairway that led from the backyard to both the family's living space and my own. The room was clean and freshly painted, a light space. When I moved in, leaves on the fruit trees in the garden fluttered a bright new green against the window bars, which were painted white and curved in a graceful design. Its distance from the ground gave the little room the feeling of a tree house, and I loved it. Each cool morning, I would sit in my white plastic chair at the matching table in the corner where two windows met, drink tea, warm myself in the sun, and feel grateful for my new home.

The rent for this apartment in Ramallah, $300 a month, would eat away a sizeable portion of my salary, but it was safe, looked out over the family garden, and was close to the center of town. I would perhaps come to know the family who lived in the house, and my new friend Nawal, who had introduced us, lived practically across the street.

Two days after I moved in, the closure was lifted, and I began to teach the secretaries through Mrs. Baramke's Continuing Education Center in Ramallah. At Birzeit University, up the hill on the main campus, the summer semester, still unfinished, ground on, and the fall semester was further postponed.

ᔓ

I began to feel as if I could go on forever the way I was, teaching each day, then chatting with my landlady or visiting Nawal, walking through town to make little purchases—milk, apricots, bread, toilet paper made in Ramallah—talking to shopkeepers and to other customers in the shops. I looked in stores for furniture and bought a bookcase of bamboo, made in Ramallah, and a used Bedouin rug in East Jerusalem. Everywhere, people talked to me. Shopkeepers, I found, often had traveled, worked in other fields. Some spoke other languages, and many were well educated.

From the first day I walked into their little newspaper shop and bookstore, Abu Khalid and his younger brother Taisir (not to be confused with the head of the Department of Languages and Translation at the university) befriended me. During all the years I lived in Palestine they helped with everything from directions, to translations of newspaper headlines, to explanations of things I did not understand. They taught me Palestinian ways and culture.

On one occasion, they offered me information that caused me to return to a policeman outside and apologize for reacting unkindly to his calling me "Mama," which I had just learned he'd surely meant as a title of respect in view of my advanced age. They did their best to teach me words in Arabic and kept my huge sacks of books in their tiny space while I did other errands in town. Courtly and generous, always friendly, they were a pleasure to meet each day.

A tiny sandwich shop in the middle of town with the incongruous name "Mickey Mouse Submarine"—"Mickey Mouse" for short—turned out to be a good place to meet people. This was especially true if I sat on one of the high stools at the counter downstairs near the cooks, the juice maker, and the sandwich preparers, instead of sitting by myself at a table in the more formal restaurant upstairs. The young men who worked in the shop were friendly and joked with me.

One day one of them introduced me to his father, who had recently come from Chicago, where he had first worked as a journalist. By the time I met him, he had bought and was operating a supermarket. As the years went on, I learned all their names, watched the young ones grow and take on more responsibility, and saw one of the sons open a second Mickey Mouse the next town over. It was while I was in Mickey Mouse, enjoying one of their great curried chicken sandwiches, that I first had the pleasure of meeting Moussa, head of Arabic teaching in the Palestine and Arabic Studies Program (PAS) at Birzeit University. As an instructor at the university, I was allowed to take courses without charge, and PAS was known to have one of the best Arabic language programs in the region. Moussa would be my Arabic teacher, and I would come to respect and like him very much. The day we met, he told me that he and another teacher at the university had developed all their own Arabic teaching materials. The tests to ascertain the language levels of new students would be given the following Thursday.

In that shop, as in many others, I entered a stranger and left as a friend. I was something of an oddity, traveling to Palestine at my age and planning to stay indefinitely, since most foreigners were in their twenties or thirties and were known to stay just a year or two, then return to their own countries. I was unusual also in that I spoke Arabic fairly well, since foreign women who spoke Arabic tended to be married to Palestinian men, and that, of course, was not my situation. When people learned that, contrary to expectation, not only did I not work for a foreign-funded NGO, but that I worked for this Palestinian university they respected, the change that came over them was perceptible.

Even so, they wanted to see if I understood how bad things were, and why.

One day in a hardware store I found a red-handled four-way screwdriver—the very item I had been looking for without much hope, and just like the one I had at home.

"I never expected to find this screwdriver here!" I told the shopkeeper.

"Yes," came the reply. "Israel gets everything first, right along with the US. It's the—what is it? The fifty-third state? We can never remember how many there are. Are there fifty-two?" I wasn't sure either.

As we spoke, the man expressed anger at Israel for its occupation of Palestinian lands, and at the US for enabling the occupation by providing financial, military, and political support for Israel.

"I don't blame the US or Israel. I blame the Palestinians who agreed to give away three-quarters of our land. If you had a plate of something, would you allow me to cut you off a quarter of it—a little piece—and to take all the rest? These are not real Palestinians who do that."

When I first arrived in Palestine, I was taken aback each time I heard Palestinians express criticism of their leadership. I felt sad that they, who deserved to be so proud of their culture, spirit, and endurance, were saying this to me. And I worried that saying these things could land them in jail, or worse. I respected the many Palestinians who spoke up, despite the fact that Palestinians who had expressed similar criticisms had ended up in jail.

Meanwhile, my landlady, the doctor's wife, and I met

in our mutual hallway every so often and got to know each other a bit. Her name was Randa. Her English was excellent, as it was with most adults in Palestine. When I commented on this, she explained that she had attended Birzeit University when English, rather than Arabic, had been the language primarily used.

One day when Randa popped her head into my room, she saw my new rug and asked, "Did you buy it? A rug like that is so expensive!"

"Four hundred and fifty shekels [about $125 at the time]," I said, and she was amazed.

"I can hardly believe it! They usually cost a fortune!" she exclaimed.

"Not now," I told her, and I described how the merchant had pressed the rug on me, lowering and lowering the price. "Save it for someone who can pay you what it's worth," I'd said at one point, only to have him answer:

"Do you know how much I've made today? One hundred shekels."

"I'd like to go with you one day," Randa said. I assured her I would be happy to go with her.

"I only saw one other rug at that shop," I said, "but in any shop I think you could have whatever you wanted. The merchants in East Jerusalem have no business. Otherwise, I would never have been able to afford such a beautiful Bedouin rug."

I told Randa about a brass tray another merchant had pressed into my hands and about other merchants who had told me they were going out of business. I remembered what I had been told by a Jewish teaching colleague of mine in Israel the previous year. I'd found her attitude toward Palestine unusual for an Israeli Jew.

"By occupying East Jerusalem, closing it to Palestinians from the West Bank and Gaza, and charging such high taxes for Palestinian merchants to do business there, Israel is driving the Palestinian merchants out. In desperation, they sell—and leave the place open to the Jewish merchants. By putting all the heavily armed soldiers in the streets of the Old City, Israel makes it a place no tourist or Israeli wants to linger, except for the Jews who go to pray, carrying their machine guns with them.

"If the country were not *macho*, if this ethic were not pervasive and ingrained, how would Israel keep this military machine rolling? It has to be this way. Every schoolchild pays a visit to the concentration camps left in Poland from World War II. But none of them has seen the refugee camps that our government has created and maintains all over the territory it occupies militarily, and which it continues to fence off and close in."

I felt guilt, that old substitute for action, at benefitting from the situation. Randa's eyes showed the pain she felt at the merchants' desperation.

"This is the first time I have ever bought things for an apartment," I told her, by way of excusing my purchases.

We talked awhile about foreigners' views of Palestine and the Arab world.

"When I see a movie about Arabs," she said, "I am so upset. I hate that they have these images of us."

"Yes," I agreed. "Undeveloped. Primitive."

"Sometimes when I see one of these movies, I am so upset that I can't sleep all night."

✄

Nawal continued to be a bright presence in my life. She liked people and cared about them, was straightforward and warm, an altogether good-hearted woman.

One morning after I had moved into my apartment, sitting in dappled sunlight, the shadows of leaves outside trembling on the stone floor and white-painted wall, I heard footsteps on the stairs outside my window.

I looked up to see Nawal's slender form coming up the stairs on the other side of the window glass. When I opened the door to invite her in, she held out an enormous tray of homemade cinnamon rolls. While we drank coffee and I ate an appalling number of the rolls, still warm from her oven, she asked what else I liked to eat.

"Anything," I answered, but she pressed me to name something specific. "Chicken," I said, whereupon she asked me if I liked chicken "stuffed." I was to come that day for lunch, or, rather, for the main meal of the day, which occurs anytime between about 2 and 4 p.m. for people who do not have to spend the day away from home. I did go that afternoon, and she did serve chicken stuffed with rice and spices, and I met her husband, Abu Jabr, who was welcoming and kind, and who suggested I do something I would not otherwise have considered.

"You'll pick your grocer," he said, referring to the sellers of fruits and vegetables in little specialty shops, "and establish a relationship with him. Then you will always go back to him. He will show you when a melon is ripe, and warn you that the first crop of apricots will be tastiest but most expensive." The arrangement was so different from the way I shopped in the US—at huge grocery stores, where I might never meet the same checker twice, much less know the owner of the place. But the friendships I established with the merchants in Ramallah were among the most satisfying I had while I lived there. I got to know and inquired about their families; I danced at my grocer's wedding and celebrated the birth of his first child.

Nawal worked as a hairdresser, teaching the trade to Palestinian women living in refugee camps in the West Bank. Trained in Scotland, she worked part time for the United Nations Relief and Works Agency (UNRWA), which has charge of educating and caring for some 1.4 million Palestinians officially registered as living in refugee camps in the West Bank and Gaza. Much of the time, though, she could be found at home, doing the hair of private clients, mostly relatives and friends, from residential neighborhoods in Ramallah. Her customers sat in chairs in the narrow glassed-in porch at the front of her house and talked to her, as people do with hairdressers, by the hour.

This made Nawal a veritable hub in one of Ramallah's many overlapping communication networks. She never gossiped, but she was interested in other people, and she paid attention. What was not privileged information, she could pass on. I was always welcome to drop by, always introduced to whoever was there. I loved how the stories of a community flowed through her hands and sifted into mine. I counted myself lucky to have met Nawal and to have her as my friend.

ᔡ

Another week went by before I traveled again up to Birzeit University. This time the roads were open, and I was able to bring along the boxes of English language teaching books I had brought with me from Egypt and Israel. Again I was welcomed by the department head, Taisir, with two kisses, one on each cheek. My pay would be arranged, he said, as soon as the university was able to establish that I had been employed full-time the year before.

"That's the key," Taisir told me, to my getting the next level up on the pay scale. "Thirty more JDs," he promised. These were Jordanian dinars, the currency in which we were paid by the university. "That will amount to two chickens."

I was given a choice of classes and was surprised to learn that I would be teaching only twelve hours a week. This was considered a full teaching load at the university. When I commented on the few hours of actual teaching time, I was told that when I began to experience all the difficulties involved in teaching in an area under military occupation, I would understand.

With Muna, I looked over the teaching materials I was to use in my classes. When I was critical of the book from which I was to teach English academic writing, with all its assumptions that students would be living in the USA, and references to life there, Muna suggested that I could manage student responses and "laugh at the book with them. But," she cautioned, "tell them to use the material for their own progress."

Her words reminded me of the advice Hassan Fathy had given to me so many years before: "Learn the craft, then use it for whatever purpose you choose."

"Assign them subjects to write about that will interest them," Muna suggested. "And go back over the material. They'll forget to do this. They don't have a tradition of using information as tools, only of memorizing it. Students memorize whole passages in English from their textbooks on physics or business administration or whatever when they don't understand them."

She also said students were reluctant to accept— or even to listen to—new ideas, whether about English, gender issues, or religion.

"They've been trained to accept what they have already been told, whether by their parents or their teachers," she said. "They can't allow the possibility that their English teachers taught them erroneous 'facts' of grammar, that their parents, their *imams*, and God might not be all powerful, always correct. They are so closed, at such an early age. They haven't been brought up in a tradition that helps them to say, 'I'll take this part of this book or idea and reject the rest.'" Muna said that it was the freedom to obtain information that she cherished about the United States. "There is a lot of freedom in the US to learn, and to act. Yes, the majority choose not to learn or to act. But there is the possibility.

"What you'll find hardest here," she continued, "is the skill at manipulation students have learned under the occupation. In Palestine, we use manipulation to survive. The girls are the best at it.

"And then," she added, "some of the students are just jerks."

I laughed. "I can't even imagine juxtaposing the two words, 'Palestinian' and 'jerk,'" I said.

"Don't idealize the students," Muna warned. "Becky [another teacher from the US] did, and she ended up wanting to throttle *all* her students. They are just people."

With Muna to support and counsel me, I thought, I couldn't go wrong.

18: JERUSALEM

The fall session had not yet begun at the university, so one day I traveled to Jerusalem. I would go there to mail letters or packages at the post office, since letters mailed from Ramallah reached their destinations much more slowly, if at all. Envelopes had to pass first through Israeli hands, and we couldn't mail or count on receiving packages in Palestine. When I ordered a book, I would have it sent to the post office box of a colleague who lived in Arab East Jerusalem, where service was better. The Arab-owned International Bookstore and the unfortunately named American Colony Hotel, both also in East Jerusalem, had good, although expensive, selections of new books about the Middle East.

In West Jerusalem, the Jewish part of the city, I could find brown rice, the oats and wheat germ I used to make granola, and, most valuable, I could exchange used books in English at the little bookstore on a side street off Ben Yehuda Street. And, I am embarrassed to admit, I also went to West Jerusalem to drink a latte or to eat a cone of frozen yogurt, neither of which was sold in Ramallah. Mostly, I went to sit in the sun where people were free to come and go, to move about, where people had choices of things to buy, away from the poverty and problems of occupied Palestine. Only the army jeeps and armed soldiers interrupted with the harsh reality of the West Bank, and they mostly milled about on the outskirts of the mall, so as not to discourage the festive spirit. This part of the city was a world apart from Ramallah, with its dust-filled air and unwatered parks, and I was never easy at the contrast between the two. Most Palestinians were forbidden from entering any part of Jerusalem at all.

To get there, you had to have the proper identification and then take a shared car or van from the center of Ramallah and pass through the Kalandia checkpoint established to separate Abu Dis, the Palestinian area closest to Jerusalem, from the rest of Palestinian East Jerusalem, which Israel had annexed after the War of 1967.

On this day, at the checkpoint, a soldier ordered a young man out of the front seat of our van. A second soldier swung open the van's sliding door, stuck his head inside, and stared at the rest of us.

"Identity cards!" he barked, using the Arabic word *huwiya*. This was one of the few words I ever heard an Israeli soldier speak in Arabic. Mostly, they just spoke Hebrew, and it was the responsibility of Arabic speakers to understand them.

I was startled when an elderly Palestinian man

responded instantly, booming an enthusiastic greeting in Hebrew.

"*Shalom!*"

The soldier ignored him.

"*Huwiya!*" the soldier commanded again, this time even less pleasantly than the first.

Wordlessly, we all passed up our cards. Most of the other passengers, I noticed, didn't look at the soldier, as if by not looking at him, they could wish him away. Only the old man offered no identification. Glaring at him, the soldier waited, tense, scowling. Before the soldier had a chance to say another word, however, the old man reached up a hand and tugged at the gray hairs of his beard. An instant later, he had reached inside his own mouth and swiftly removed something. He held his hand out to the soldier.

"Here is my identity card!" he said, this time in Arabic, but with all his previous enthusiasm. On his open palm, stretched toward the soldier, were his dentures, tops and bottoms.

"Here!" he said again, stretching his hand further toward the soldier. "*These* are my identity card."

While the rest of us stifled our laughter, the soldier stood speechless. A moment later, without a word, he turned away and slammed the door. Our van went on its way.

For the remainder of the ride, the old man regaled the two men sitting nearest him with stories of similar escapes, but of course we all eavesdropped with pleasure. He had made our day. At the end of the ride, when we all got off near the Damascus Gate, the old man bought bottled drinks for the two other passengers he had been talking to, as well as the driver. He asked me where I was going and offered me a cup of coffee at his coffeehouse—no pay. I thanked him and declined until another day.

West Bank vehicles all had to stop a block or so from Damascus Gate, the main Palestinian entrance to the Old City of Jerusalem, although the places where they were allowed to park changed several times in the years I was there. If you walked across the street and paused in front of the Damascus Gate and looked down the great stairway that led to the city walls, you would see down at the bottom, just outside the arched stone entrance, a sight that for me epitomized Palestine.

On the bare stones lining the left side of the entrance to the city, middle- to old-aged Palestinian women, each wearing a *thobe*, the gorgeous long dress hand-embroidered in traditional design, sat in a line, side by side.

All day long, every day, these women sat, wrinkled faces and calloused hands mute testament to the hardship of their lives, talking together under the eyes and guns of armed Israeli soldiers. Many days, if they had looked up, they would have seen the bottoms of the boots of the soldier who lounged in the opening in the wall above the gate, his feet hanging down. The women sat in front of the small piles of mint, greens, and lemons they had planted in the countryside and tended, harvested, and carried in big straw baskets to the city to sell.

Some days soldiers would kick over the little piles of produce and drive the women away, but they always came back.

They were a striking sight, these women. They were tough and patient, clad in black dresses bright with colors they had worked themselves. They did what they could, endured what they had to, so that they and their families could continue to survive. To me they were the flowers of Palestine.

To reach modern, well-tended West Jerusalem, you continued past the Damascus Gate, past the women and the soldiers with their guns. You walked alongside the outer city wall, winding around and up the hill to your left. At the top, you turned right onto Jaffa Road, which led to Zion Square and the bottom end of the pedestrian mall on Ben Yehuda Street. With no cars allowed, Ben Yehuda was a kind of outdoor eatery, café, shopping center, park, and gathering place, all in one.

Here, sitting at outdoor tables, facing the raised planter boxes and stores alight with jewelry and the latest clothing fashions, there was almost always a crowd of well-dressed Israelis, young and old, strolling, eating ice cream, drinking coffee, shopping. The brick-paved walkway was wide and open to the sky, with crafts laid out for sale in stalls down the center. There was something deeply troubling to me about the evident ease with which these Israeli Jews enjoyed themselves, to all appearances unconcerned with the existence minutes away of a poor and captive population for which their government was responsible. I never sat at their tables or in their restaurants. Still, there I was, someone who had chosen to make my life with Palestinians, enjoying myself in a place they could not go.

Ambivalence notwithstanding, from time to time I did go into the Jewish part of the city. On that day in early September, having bought a bagel and cream cheese, another item unavailable in occupied Palestine, I was sitting on the curb under an overpass just outside Zion Square, writing a letter to my parents, when I heard a tremendous explosion. *BOOM!* I heard, and then *BOOM!* and *BOOM!* again.

The blasts were so loud and sounded so close that I looked up to see if the buildings above me were about to collapse. It seemed they were not, but within seconds, people around me had begun screaming and running in all directions. The air was alive with panic.

"Oh, fuck!" a man exclaimed in English. I could see smoke—or was it the dust from a crumpled building?—filling the space within the mall. Soldiers rushed about with their guns. Sirens screamed. All around me, people began talking in various languages on their cell phones. Others gathered in small groups, talking, asking each other what had happened, tears in their eyes.

A bomb. Certainly it had been a bomb, probably detonated by a suicide bomber, most likely a Palestinian civilian, walking in the mall, blowing up himself and Israeli civilians with him. The whole world knew of them, these people who had come to believe that the most useful thing they could do with their lives would be to kill themselves in the process of killing other people.

I knew better than to go toward the scene. There would be nothing I could do to help; the harm had been done and help was there and on the way. People began coming out of the mall area, women with men's arms around them, women with their arms around other women. Crying.

As I turned to leave the area, heading back toward East Jerusalem and home, I passed a woman I had spoken to earlier in her basket shop.

"I'd already closed and left the shop, but I had to come back for my husband's satchel, which was full of checks, invoices, and other paperwork that would have taken time to recover if they were stolen," she explained. "But everything is here."

Then, in a bitter non sequitur: "They will never stop until the last Jew has been driven into the sea." The "they" went pointedly unnamed. "You live with them, but you don't know them like I do. I was born here. I've lived here all my life."

"You've lived here all your life and never known one good Palestinian?" I asked.

The woman paused. "Well, there were friends in Bethlehem, Christians, whom we used to see," she said. "And our neighbors next door."

"Remember them," I suggested. "Palestinians do not benefit from this. Everyone loses. Those who do this are few."

"Not as few as you imagine," she answered. "We can't

walk in the streets. We don't go to their neighborhoods and throw bombs at them. That is not our way."

In view of the situation, I refrained from reminding her that in their efforts to acquire the land, Jewish terrorist gangs had done exactly the same thing in the years preceding the establishment of the State of Israel. They had set off bombs in Arab markets, killing Palestinians as they shopped. They had attacked and killed Palestinians in their villages, driven them out and destroyed the homes they left behind. They had bombed the King David Hotel in Jerusalem and blown up a ship of Jewish refugees in the Haifa harbor. Had she never heard?

Throughout the tumult in the streets, I felt calm, almost numb. It was as if I had entered some other dimension. I didn't feel particularly grateful that I had escaped with my life. I felt instead a sense that the next time I took a step, I might not find the earth underneath my feet. Soon we would learn that this had been a suicide bombing in which four Israelis, including three teenagers, along with three bombers, had been killed. Those who loved them would find their own lives changed forever. In response, the West Bank would be closed again, and Palestinians would be unable to go to work, to school, to visit their relatives, to get medical care. More Palestinians would go hungry. Frustration and anger would grow on both sides of the Green Line. Israeli soldiers would kill more Palestinians. A few more Palestinians would turn themselves into living bombs, and the entire Palestinian population would suffer even more at the hands of the Israeli army. Distance between the two peoples would expand, and hatred deepen. The cycle would continue.

Rather than feeling the humility I'd felt in the face of destruction caused by natural forces, I felt sick, aware at a new level of the ugliness that human beings inflict on one another. Seeing the bodies wheeled to the ambulances, sensing all around me the panic and the feelings of helplessness and horror, had brought me closer to a personal experience of violence than any newspaper article or TV newscast had done.

∽

Back in the West Bank, we were unsure whether the university would be able to open on September 15, given the bombing. Then Birzeit students announced they were going to strike because tuition had been raised. A few days later, we were told that representatives from the Ministry of Education would meet with student representatives. Next a rumor circulated that the ministry, responsible for all Palestinian educational institutions except private schools and universities, wanted all the public universities to open on the same day. Finally, we heard that the ministry didn't even have the funds to open the universities.

It was about that time that I was introduced to another Palestinian teacher in our department. Her name was Lamis, and along with Pat and Muna, she was to become another good friend. Lamis included me sometimes when others might not have thought of it. She would make Arabic coffee in the department's closet-size kitchen and invite me to drink it with her and the others.

At times grim, gloomy, or cynical, always sensitive, quick, and smart, Lamis was to me unpredictable, and many times her wry humor took me by surprise.

Her name, Lamis informed me early in our acquaintance, meant "soft to the touch." When she first imparted that piece of information, she took me by the arm and made as if to take me off to the Women's Studies Center where she knew there was an Arabic-English dictionary. I had to go to class, but I believed her.

"Soft to the touch!" I exclaimed the next time I saw her. "We should have a test."

"We should have a meeting," she countered.

But Becky, always rational, asked, "Are you evaluating softness on the outside or on the inside?"

"Ah," I said; and, thinking about it later, I decided it must be Lamis who was softest on the inside, for who but a person needing the most protection would have so crusty an exterior? She might be wearing the toughest skin to cover the kindest heart.

∽

One afternoon, still before our fall semester had begun, Taisir greeted me as I wandered into the department office with the words, "*Ah, ya bint halal!*" which I had just learned meant, "Oh, you've come at the very moment you were needed!" and asked me to teach three classes instead of the two originally scheduled.

That was fine, and I agreed. But I was anxious about the fact that classes were about to begin, and I did not yet have the textbooks I was to use. Due to the delays, none of us had yet been supplied with books for our students. Everyone else seemed to be taking it in stride.

At the first department faculty meeting, I asked, "How long will the semester be? How many weeks will we have to teach the material on the syllabus?"

The answer was a collective laugh.

"It always depends on the Israeli military," Taisir explained.

From my colleagues, I learned that the Israeli military had closed Birzeit University for a total of four years during what was called the First Intifada, or uprising. But education is valued as much by Palestinians as by Jews. What Israelis tried to close, Palestinians struggled to keep open. During those years, Birzeit professors taught students in community gathering places or in their own homes, despite the fact that they were arrested when they were found with schoolbooks or other teaching materials in their possession.

～

The fall semester on the main campus at Birzeit University finally did begin in mid-September. I met my students, and "real" life began.

But "real" life in Palestine, I quickly learned, was unlike any other life I had known. Israel continued to confiscate land in the West Bank, including in East Jerusalem.

Political negotiations were floundering. There was dissent within the Palestinian population: Palestinian teachers went on strike to protest the arrest of some teachers by the PNA. In my classes, students were obviously upset, preoccupied, unable to concentrate. Everyone told me it was life as usual.

Ten days after classes began, there was an assassination attempt in Jordan. The Israeli secret police, the Mossad, had attempted to kill Khaled Meshaal, the political leader of Hamas opposed to Yasser Arafat's Fateh Party.

"You will never be bored in Palestine," Taisir chirped to me, as he was to do with each major event. But another side to that was exhaustion.

A common answer in Arabic to the question "How are you?" was the response, "Living." Just barely, was the implication.

∽

"Did you know we have a martyr, miss?" a student of mine asked one morning in late October. A martyr, I already knew, was any Palestinian who had been killed by Israelis.

Israeli authorities had announced that one of the men who had carried out the suicide bombing the day I was in Jerusalem had been a twenty-four-year-old student at Birzeit University.

A few minutes later the grating tones of a loudspeaker crackled across the campus.

"What are they saying?" I asked, for to me the words were unclear.

"It is a call to cancel all classes and exams for two hours," a student answered.

Only as we left class did I realize the connection between the two events. Outside, students and faculty gathered in the outdoor courtyards between the buildings for the next two hours, while verses from the Qur'an were recited over the loudspeaker. I would hear the particular intonation of these same verses countless times in the eleven years I lived in Palestine—at the university, in towns, in cemeteries, and in people's homes—each time a Palestinian, child or adult, man or woman, from the Birzeit or Ramallah areas was killed by an Israeli.

19: "THERE IS PAIN ENOUGH"

As life in Palestine ground on, I was having my own troubles. In the second semester, an entire class of my students proved problematic. I had never had much difficulty controlling my classes before. But one group of students, new to the university and therefore weakest in English, I found almost impossible to teach.

They would ask questions and then not listen to the answers. One would speak, and the others wouldn't listen. They talked among themselves so loudly and continuously that I was unable to cover the material. It didn't seem to me that students were being willfully rude. It was as if, rather, they simply couldn't concentrate. And I couldn't get them to.

I started thinking of the days I taught that class as "nightmare days." Often I became angry with the students, and then hated myself for turning into a witch. At home, I would go over their homework assignments, appalled at the sloppiness, the questions left unanswered, the illegibility of the handwriting, the apparent laziness. Some of them didn't bring their own books to class, or brought books into which they had copied the answers of another student. No one came for help in office hours.

Why was I having so much trouble with such nice people? What, I asked myself, was I doing wrong?

I was baffled by the behavior of these students who came from a tradition of such respect for education. Their inattention, I knew, involved far more than a playful attitude. The problem went much deeper, and it was both theirs and mine. Helping them reach the level they were expected to achieve—even had they paid perfect attention—began to seem an impossible task, given the educational tools they were lacking when they entered the university.

I took my problems to Muna: "My students in this class aren't at the level I am supposed to be teaching them."

"Teach them less, then," Muna advised, "and make sure they know it well." But she also said, "All they need is a piece of paper. After that, it will be who they know that will help them find and keep a job. It's who they know that will determine their lives. No one will look to see if they actually know anything, and no one will care how they got the diploma. The underlying understanding is that life is not fair—so cheat, beg the teacher for a passing grade, do what you need to survive."

Old educational practices were also at work. With the closures, teachers in primary and secondary schools hadn't been able to enroll in courses that would have advanced their skills or challenged entrenched teaching philosophy and methods. The first year or two I was there, teachers from all parts of Palestine came together in annual meetings of the Palestinian Association of Teachers of English as a Foreign Language (PATEFL). One year we all gathered at Al-Quds University in East Jerusalem, another year at Hebron University. At these conferences, I participated in Palestinian-led professional development workshops, the academic level of which equaled any I had attended at the American University in Cairo or at the teachers' college in Israel.

But as Israeli restrictions on Palestinian movement tightened, teachers could no longer leave their own areas to meet and learn from one another. Nor were they allowed to leave Palestine for training elsewhere in the Arab world or beyond.

"The students come from a tradition of intimidation in their schools," Muna told me. The same was true of students I had taught at American schools in Egypt and Syria. "They come to Birzeit and are treated differently, without intimidation, and then don't know what the limits are. We must show them."

If I had taught in schools in the US, I wouldn't have been so surprised. In the US then, as now, some students were bringing guns to school or selling drugs. Discipline problems were horrendous. Great numbers of students didn't see that they had much chance in life; why, then, should they care about studying?

But I had never taught in the US, only small classes in special language schools in Egypt and Syria, and the larger classes of Palestinian and Jewish Israelis who were about to begin their own careers as English teachers. I had never had experience keeping large numbers of at-risk students interested and involved. I could see that the easy informality that characterized university-level instruction in the US, combined with my own tendency to idealize and my need to be liked, could lead to students' misunderstanding the seriousness of the work we were asking them to do.

Muna informed me also that all our students had missed years of schooling.

"They didn't go to school—the schools were closed," she told me. "The bravest, highest actions were against Israeli authority, but eventually 'authority' extended to include their own parents. They'd go throw stones and come home and not listen to what their parents said. Why should they respect their parents? Their parents had no power over the military occupation. Young kids could stop cars and make old men get out. They could burn tires in front of houses and write all over the walls of buildings in downtown Ramallah, throw trash everywhere. Kids destroyed libraries, and then weren't allowed in. To this day, Birzeit University has a hard time letting students have access to the books, and for a long time, it didn't."

I was teaching the children of the Intifada. *I must seem like an Israeli soldier to them in a way*, I thought. *Push the limits, and watch me get frustrated, then furious.* Students—like kids anywhere—could relish experiencing their own power, watching the authority figure spin and dance in fury, as helpless as soldiers who screamed at taxi drivers.

"Don't show them you are upset," Muna warned me, "or they'll make a game of it." She told me that the current generation of students was the least politicized since Palestine's beginnings. All their lives, she said, young Palestinians had heard the rhetoric about Palestinian resistance and a Palestinian state. But they had watched their parents struggle and fail to end the occupation. They had seen the economy shrivel and political repression increase. Now, students might well be asking, "Why think about it anymore? What's the point?"

What was so difficult? What made life so hard? Mostly it was the killing and destruction—and the knowledge that these were occurring daily. In terms of their own lives, students knew that, due to the economic and political situation in Palestine, they could not count on getting jobs using their academic skills, or any jobs at all, after they graduated. Pat introduced me to a bright graduate from the university's Engineering Department who was working in a *shawarma* shop in Ramallah.

On another level, what made life stressful was the unpredictability, the start and stop of life.

"It's not that things are so bad here for me," Muna told me as we were eating in the cafeteria one day. "[Due to the lack of news coverage] people in Ramallah sometimes say they can't even tell what is going on in other places in Palestine. Often we don't know what people are suffering in other parts of the West Bank or Gaza.

"Certainly, compared to others, I have no problems. I'm not hungry, and my house still stands. It's just that I can't count on anything; I can't be assured that I will be able to carry anything out. Everything is stopped. What I could accomplish before in four hours now takes two weeks, as people are held up, cannot come, cannot be counted on."

Life in Palestine didn't foster sustained effort. On the contrary, all of us who lived there had to become accustomed to erratic expenditures of energy. I wondered if this was part of the problem my students were having.

"The closures make us lazy, miss," one student told me. No wonder students missed class every chance they could. Perhaps they initiated strikes because unplanned changes and chaos had become the only rhythms they knew. Talent is stifled, and effort cannot flow freely, I realized, when there is no momentum to carry you through the hard times. If happiness is related to using one's talents to the fullest in a field one loves, there is no way Palestinian students could be happy.

Many students also had financial problems. The 350 students from Gaza who were currently enrolled at Birzeit University had to pay to live away from their families because the roads between Gaza and the West Bank were so often closed. As the economic situation worsened, more school-age children were kept home. Many who do attend school don't have money for books, eyeglasses, or clothes.

The university gives scholarships, and the Institute of Women's Studies helps through their Hala Atalla Educational Fund, but these can assist only a few. Because of the limited resources of Palestinian universities and the fact that students, for financial or political reasons, aren't able to leave Palestine to study abroad, many dedicated students are studying subjects that will prepare them for careers they do not want—assuming they'll be able to find jobs. One of my brightest and hardest-working students was studying engineering, although her dream was to pursue a career as a dentist.

Students were continually arrested by Israeli soldiers. Others, who spent years in prison and returned as adults in their twenties and thirties to finish their degrees, brought with them physical and emotional problems they acquired from torture and incarceration.

One day a student of mine, whom I will call Mu'tasim, left class abruptly, saying things I couldn't understand. Neither, it seemed, could the other students. Since it was nearly time for a ten-minute break, I called the break and went after him, concerned. In the hallway I found him distraught.

"You know," he said, "how short a time a neuron takes to fire, to cross the neural gap? It takes one millionth of a second—shorter than this"—he snapped his fingers.

"My state," he said, "is to be suspended forever in the interval. What should take a second never happens at all. I watch the choices come and go, and I can do nothing. I am paralyzed."

Mu'tasim had missed years by being in prison. By the time he was released, his father had been killed, his fiancée had married someone else, and Israelis had taken his house.

At night, he could not sleep. "I am not a criminal!" he cried. "They made me one!"

The following day in class, I asked another student, Hassan, to work with Mu'tasim. Afterward, I asked Hassan how it had gone. He said that Mu'tasim had been terribly negative. "He had a hard time during the Intifada. I think maybe he feels guilty for what they made him do."

✑

Meanwhile, the students' families, in addition to dealing with all the usual difficulties of life—sickness and chronic health problems, cancer, strokes; infirmities of elderly parents at home, the usual problems with money and relationships and children—suffer multiple layers of enormous additional hardship created by the Israeli military occupation. Their children's problems and disappointments are their elders' problems too.

Like Mu'tasim, every Palestinian I know has either been in prison or knows someone else who either has been or is still in prison. Imprisonment, or the threat of it; torture, or the threat of it; and pressure to inform on family members or friends—these, I found, were central pillars of the occupation.

A middle-aged teacher in our department told me one day of her own imprisonment for participating in nonviolent political activity. The whole time she was in prison, the Israeli military, or perhaps military intelligence, hounded her younger brother, who lived in the West Bank. They followed him and threatened that they would rape his sister in prison if he did not inform against other Palestinians. They would reward him, they said, if he could provide names of others involved in political activity.

The boy refused. The agents kept following him. Everywhere, he was watched. From time to time someone would approach him and tell him of the terrible things they would do to his sister if he refused to work with them against other Palestinians.

At last my colleague was released from prison. Her brother never had become a collaborator, and she would never have wanted him to be one. But the boy, although he had not had to pay the spiritual price of becoming a traitor to his people, paid a price of another kind. Living in perpetual terror, he developed the symptoms of paranoid schizophrenia, unable to separate nightmare from reality. He was certain he was always being followed, always in danger. He could never rest, could not work or love or live what passed as a normal existence in Palestine. Eventually, he took his own life.

When she told me this story, my colleague had just learned that her teenage daughter, who had traveled to Jordan, was being held there and interrogated. The daughter was not involved politically, but her mother was desperate, calling everyone she knew in Jordan to try to get help. She was afraid that her daughter, if subjected to too much pressure, would crack emotionally and lose her way as her brother had.

More Palestinians than I can count have told me of times they spent in Israeli prisons. One young man, a member of Fateh, the party of Yasser Arafat and the Palestinian National Authority, told me that he had been placed in a wooden box the size and shape of a coffin and made to lie there, with the lid closed, for days at a time. Another prisoner had been threatened by an interrogator: "You will leave prison either crazy or paralyzed."

Children are imprisoned and tortured for throwing stones at soldiers or their vehicles. Prisoners are held for years under an Israeli legal provision known as "administrative detention," which means they can be imprisoned without being charged and without trial for a period of time that can be extended indefinitely.

During the years I taught, students of mine would suddenly vanish. Sometimes they would reappear, and sometimes they would not. Those who loved them lived with the strain of knowing a family member was in prison. Families traveled long distances to visit and worried always, hoping for news.

Ongoing loss of land, of housing, of greenhouses and fields devoted to agriculture was and still is a daily fact of life under the occupation. Not only do Israelis occupy the lands they took in the War of 1967, they keep taking more. By the time the Arab-Israeli War ended in 1949, Israel encompassed 50 percent of the lands formerly called Palestine. By the time I arrived in Palestine, even the 23 percent of ancient Palestine still being bargained over was shrinking and subject to Israeli military intrusions and invasions.

Palestinians historically were farmers, but by degrees

the agricultural land on which they depended for growing food and earning a living has been taken and replaced by Jewish settlements, connected with Jewish-only roads, which cut through the farmers' lands. In Gaza, vast areas of planted orange and olive trees have been uprooted to clear spaces between Palestinian homes and Jewish settlements or military checkpoints. Houses in Gaza, the West Bank, and East Jerusalem are demolished when the Israeli government decides to build on the land or to punish a household for something a family member has done.

One day I saw an old man in a long robe and Arab headdress standing over a toppled tree, a severed branch in his hand, his neighbors holding him back from trying to stop the soldiers. He was weeping. Behind him lay the felled remains of an orchard of olive trees.

I had been a suburban resident of a country of immigrants. In many US communities, adulthood is marked by a child's leaving home. My parents had moved many times, both within and outside the United States. As a result, I had never known the grief a group of people can feel with the loss of land and a way of life that had been connected with that land for hundreds of years before. It had never occurred to me that someone could love an olive tree. Now I was confronted with scenes of old men stretching their arms out in desperation as Israeli bulldozers uprooted fields of vegetables, orange orchards, and, most precious of all, the olive trees they and their fathers and grandfathers had tended for generations.

Water, which I'd seen used in Israel to fill swimming

pools and keep grass green, is sometimes not available at all in the West Bank and Gaza. Israel needs increasing amounts of water to grow food in fields and greenhouses and to supply the hundreds of thousands of Jewish immigrants the government has flown into Israel from Russia, Ethiopia, and other countries. This is a desert land, which had never supported millions of people. Many summers when I lived in the West Bank, water was turned on only once or twice a week—and we never knew when this would be. Otherwise, families have only the water they can save in the tanks that sit on the tops of their houses. When Israeli soldiers shoot holes in the water tanks, West Bank communities have no water at all.

In Gaza, the water is not healthy to drink. "Oh, please, take this bottled water," I was urged in a UN office in Gaza when I turned to the tap. But where could Gazans get clean water? The Palestinian lands hold plenty of water in underground aquifers, but Israel maintains control of the flow and volume of the water to be used by Palestinians. Palestinians are not allowed to dig wells deep enough to access what they need. Instead, Israel pumps water from the aquifers underneath the West Bank and sells it back to Palestinians at prices many of them cannot afford, while the average Israeli uses four times as much water as each Palestinian.

Restrictions on movement apply even to the dead. One of the most painful stories I was told was about Lamis's older brother Khalil, who had been studying in Greece but had not responded when his mother sent him a birthday card. A second brother went to look for him, to make sure he was all right. Khalil was found in his room, already decomposed, a skeleton, having died of an aneurism.

"There is pain enough," I said to Lamis, "without adding more. Without this extra pain."

"My brother retrieved the body so that Khalil's remains could be buried at home, in Palestine. He succeeded in getting the coffin to Jordan. But when the coffin arrived at the bridge [the Allenby Bridge, between Jordan and the West Bank], the Israeli military wouldn't let him carry it across the border.

"They will not let you bring a body home. You can ask and beg," Lamis said, "and you can cry. The answer remains no."

"They will not let you bring a coffin with a dead body into the country?" I asked in disbelief.

"No," she said. "Did you know?" I had not.

"For ten days, my brother waited at the border with Khalil's body. At last someone gave permission. And then, of course, the soldiers opened the coffin."

"What?" I exclaimed, although I had heard quite well what she had said.

"Yes, they always do that. They are afraid there will be a bomb. The body must be transferred to another coffin before the Israelis will allow it through the checkpoint.

"They made my brothers and my uncle pick up Khalil's body, which by that time was a mixture of embalmed flesh and bone. With their hands, they scooped the remains of my brother's body into the second coffin. And brought him home.

"You said there is pain enough," Lamis said, "and there is, without the extra pain the occupation adds."

∽

During the eleven years I lived in the West Bank, Palestinians suffered increasingly from a lack of adequate health care. Palestinians have no resources with which to build or to renovate hospitals, like Ramallah Hospital, next door to my home. Israel ignores the international law that not only places a limitation on how long land can be occupied, but that also holds the occupying power responsible for the welfare of the population living on the occupied land. Palestinians with serious health problems try to go to the better-equipped hospitals in Jordan, but most are either prevented from traveling by the Israeli authorities or cannot afford to go.

As the years went on, Israelis refused to allow even the very ill to pass through checkpoints to reach a hospital or clinic. I saw more than one invalid being carried on a stretcher by medics on foot across a checkpoint. Even pregnant women about to give birth were prevented from passing through. So many babies were born at checkpoints that they could have had their own support group, assuming, of course, they could ever have gathered together in one place. Some eighty mothers and babies died at checkpoints during the Israeli siege of the West Bank in 2002. Regular inoculations became impossible, and doctors worried that Palestinians would begin suffering from childhood diseases such as measles, which had long been wiped out, but which had returned during the closures of 1991 with the first Gulf War.

For Palestinians, the most ordinary action can become a humiliating experience. Grace, our department secretary, and I were talking one morning after she had returned from visiting family in the United States. This was years before 9/11, after which, of course, Arabo- and Islamophobia became national diseases in the US. I don't know if the airline officials even knew Grace was a Christian. But she was an Arab, and she was Palestinian.

She fumed as she described the trip and swore never to fly Tower Air again. They had treated her like a criminal, she said. They had made her board the plane in New York half an hour before the other passengers, and made her sit there until all the others had boarded. They had taken her purse, and refused to return it to her during the entire flight, until the plane landed. Next time, she said, she'd pay the extra $300 to fly another airline.

Lack of income is widespread and a constant problem. Birzeit employees, even those who earn the least, including the male guards and the women who clean, often go unpaid. All over Palestine, there are times when teachers and other public employees at all levels are not paid at all or face delays of uncertain lengths in payment of their salaries. At one point, Israel decided to hold back the taxes it owed the Palestinian Authority, and Palestinians were left dependent on aid from other countries. Through all the years I taught in Palestine, we all went weeks on half pay or with no pay at all. Although at Birzeit University our pay was always eventually made up, instructors at other Palestinian universities were not so lucky. Teachers at Al-Quds University in Jerusalem, I was told at one point, had not been paid for the previous five months.

As the school year progressed, I began noticing that the people I knew had an extraordinary number of physical health problems. People had headaches, backaches, difficulty breathing, irregular heartbeat, chronic diseases, and other conditions with no cure. One morning, as Muhammad finished teaching and returned to his office, he looked more tired than ever. From my office, directly across the hall from his, I could see that he was having difficulty breathing.

"Muhammad," I said sternly. "Muhammad. Why can't you get enough air?"

"I can!" he answered, laughing.

"You can't!" I said.

"I can!"

"I think it's all this union business," I said. By that time Muhammad was head of the teachers' and employees' union at the university. "On top of all else you do," I said, "coordinate, teach . . ." I didn't mention the work he did with Fateh or the fact that he taught in two places.

"And I'm a father," he said.

As for the union, things were worse than he, as union leader, or the union itself could fix, he said.

"It's awful," he said. "I went to the ministry today. There is *no money*, and there is *no plan*. The employees are coming to me. They haven't been paid and"—he flicked a paper toward me—"this says there will be no salaries this month. And there won't be. They want to strike Monday. How can we strike Monday when every day after that there is no money to pay them?" He had great shadows under his eyes, and his face was gray.

"It's getting worse, isn't it?" I asked.

"Yes," he said, "it is." Then, more sad than bitter, he said, "Since King Hussein died, the US has given Jordan $300 million. If you get into the US boat, and go where it wants you to go, you float. If you disagree in any way, you sink."

Even I, whose family and friends were not in danger of arrest, imprisonment, or death; who owned no house or land or business in danger of being annexed, occupied, or destroyed, was beginning to feel the strain. From the time I was forty years old, I had suffered from chronic fatigue immune dysfunction syndrome (CFIDS), but since I'd given up carpentry, I had always been able to hide the fact from my co-workers. Now the suffering I was witnessing was taking its toll on my health. I could no longer pretend to be in good health, but it hardly mattered: everyone else was as exhausted as I.

20: TEARS, LAUGHTER, AND BUSINESS AS USUAL

One day I came into the department to find that Taisir had abandoned his usual jeans and striped shirt for slacks, a jacket, and a tie. He had worked with Americans in Saudi Arabia for some years, and I figured that was where he had picked up the habit of wearing jeans, along with a Texas drawl he would come out with at unexpected moments. I complimented him on his spiffy new look and asked him why he was all dressed up.

"I wear my best when we're not being paid," he said. "Then, when we are being paid, I go back to my jeans."

I was intrigued. My tendency was the opposite.

When Taisir was not getting paid, he admitted, he was gripped by a desire to spend more, not less. Walking in the street the week before, his wife had mentioned that she wanted to buy long underwear for the children. Meanwhile, "my kids were asking for chocolate this and chocolate that" from the store. To all requests he had acceded. This tendency, unlike the first, was one I knew well.

"How do people survive?" I asked.

"There's not a Palestinian family that doesn't have a sack of rice and a sack of flour put away," Taisir told me. "When those are gone, they borrow from relatives."

I learned that after families use up all their own resources, they buy on credit at the neighborhood store, until even this source dries up. Even when they were receiving full pay, many teachers in our department, as well as in other schools and universities throughout the Occupied Territories, worked more than one job to make ends meet. When things got desperate, the Union of University Teachers and Employees would strike. Eventually, the university would raise student fees in order to pay its bills, whereupon students would strike to protest the increased tuition. When there were strikes, payment of salaries would be delayed that much longer. Muna told me that in the cafeteria at lunchtime, some students could afford to buy only a piece of bread filled with fried potatoes. Others ate nothing at all.

My colleagues arrived at the university each morning with deep circles under their eyes. Sometimes faculty and students were able to drive or ride to the university. Other days, we walked up the long road through the hills under a hot sun or in rain and mud and cold, with soldiers making sure no one tried to move the solid blocks of stone or heaps of earth that obstructed the way.

◢

One of the most important facts about the Israeli-Palestinian conflict is that the years I have been describing were not exceptional. For the first few years I lived in Palestine, and for years before that, nothing particularly noteworthy, in terms of news reported in the Western press, was happening in Palestine. Certain events were noted, such as the tension that developed between younger members of Fateh, President Arafat's own political party, and the Palestinian National Authority, the body created under the Oslo Accords and headed by Arafat. In 1998 the Israeli High Court legalized torture by ruling in favor of the use of force against Palestinian detainees by interrogators, and a year later essentially delegalized it when it outlawed interrogation methods used by the Shin Bet, the Israeli internal security service. Later came the break between Fateh and Hamas, the conservative religious party nurtured and armed by Israel at its inception in order to bring about precisely the kind of division that did result within the Palestinian population. That got the world's attention: Europe and the US promptly withdrew all funding from any effort associated with Hamas. The withdrawal of settlers and soldiers from inside the Gaza Strip attracted attention, and so did the death of Arafat. But for the most part, with no major Israeli invasions of Palestinian territories, and no major Palestinian uprising, it was "business as usual," and there was no news deemed worthy to tell. By the time I arrived, even the First Intifada had, in the eyes of the media, become a bore.

The genius of the occupation, I came to see, is that the noose is tightened in such infinitesimal increments that the movement is virtually invisible to the rest of the world. Slowly, inexorably, throughout the eleven years I lived there, the Israeli army demolished Palestinian houses one by one, and, one by one, erected multitudes of barriers and checkpoints throughout the West Bank. In 1997, then-President Benjamin Netanyahu rejected anything more than a 9 percent Israeli withdrawal from the West Bank, while Palestinians protested the continuing loss of their agricultural and village lands to Israeli roads built exclusively for settlers and other Jewish Israelis. The Wye River Memorandum was agreed to, broken, revised, and signed again. Palestinian youth and adults demonstrated and were shot. Palestinian children threw stones, or did not throw stones, and were shot. From time to time, Israeli soldiers and Palestinian police exchanged fire. Some Hamas leaders were released from Israeli prisons; others were assassinated.

Thus mainstream newspapers, which by definition report the "new," find only the same tired kinds of incidents to report day after day. Another house demolished, more stones thrown, a few Palestinian civilians killed, another olive grove uprooted—after years of witnessing and reporting the same happenings over and over again, journalists had "nothing to report." Unwilling to pay journalists to undertake in-depth reporting or to write longer articles containing news analysis, editors in the US could not countenance printing the same happenings day after day. It was easier to designate anyone who resisted the military occupation—with a stone, a peaceful demonstration, a bomb—with the label "terrorist" provided by the Israeli authorities. Israeli repression of any act of resistance was justified in the name of "Israel's right to defend itself," along with a sprinkling of pointed references to the Holocaust and to Israel's unpopularity with its neighbors.

I tried to understand: What did Palestinians have to do with the Holocaust? What had Israel done to be a good neighbor to Arab countries? How can a nation have the "right" to "defend itself" from a civilian population it holds captive under a military occupation defined as illegal under international law? How had this come to seem rational? It was upside down. Alice in Wonderland. The Emperor's New Clothes.

But, whether the world notices or not, the iron clamp steadily tightens, and Palestinians feel the quality of their lives worsen as Israel imposes more closures, stifles more business and educational opportunities, and divides Palestinians from one another and from the rest of the world, all in the name of Israeli "security." Israeli settlers continue to obey the call issued in 2001 by Ariel Sharon, their political heavyweight: "Everybody has to move, run and grab as many hilltops as they can to enlarge the settlements because everything we take now will stay ours. Everything we don't grab will go to them." Palestinians can only watch their land gradually shrinking away as it is annexed or confiscated or classified as "a closed military area," only to sprout more Jewish-only settlements. After the Oslo Accord was signed, Palestinians watched as, in the name of the Oslo Accord, the West Bank was divided into Areas A, B, and C, with Area A designated as under Palestinian control, Area B under joint Israeli-Palestinian control, and Area C completely controlled by Israel.

"They are teaching us the alphabet!" ran the joke. Since then, Palestinians have watched through the years as Israel has sucked all these areas back under Israeli control.

At one point I was told by a reporter from a British newspaper that Israeli soldiers and settlers were killing so many Palestinians that newspapers would print news of the deaths only if more than six Palestinian civilians were killed in a single day. Since Israel has more powerful—and more vocal—supporters throughout the world than Palestinians do, the death of even one Israeli, although much rarer, unfailingly makes the news.

Two other kinds of events are always reported, in addition to any Israeli death. One is any Palestinian suicide bombing or rocket fired into Israel from Gaza, whether or not an Israeli is killed. The other involves any negotiations that take place between the Israeli and Palestinian leadership, and there have been many: Oslo I and Oslo II, the Hebron Protocol, the Wye River Memorandum, the *Sharm el-Sheikh* Memorandum, the Camp David and Taba summits, the initiation of the "Road Map" at the Annapolis Conference. Each time negotiations between Israel and Palestine give a hint of progress, whatever has been accomplished will be undone. Whether provoked by Israel or by a few Palestinian individuals, some sort of trouble occurs, the agreement is put aside, and land confiscations, killings, house demolitions, and all the other occupation trademarks continue. In any case, Palestinians have nothing left to negotiate, having made their major concession in 1993 with Arafat's letter recognizing Israel's "right to exist in peace and security." Each time they sit down at the bargaining table, they can only concede even more land and water rights. For all the years I lived in Palestine, and in all the years since, the situation has felt infuriating—and hopeless, as long as the US funds and otherwise supports Israel in its military occupation of Palestinian lands.

∽

At first, I was amazed at the alchemy by means of which Palestinians were sometimes able to transform horror, grief, and anger into feelings they could handle. In some of the worst times, you might find more laughter and lightness than usual in the offices and hallways of our department. One day between classes, as Pat, Muna, Lamis, and I sat talking with a couple of other teachers, we found ourselves nearly hysterical with laughter. Someone suggested that our levity was connected to our not having been paid. If so, I was getting a good taste of the medicine with which we could dose ourselves in a situation that, looked at from a normal perspective, was not funny at all.

I had no idea what to expect when Taisir stopped by my office one morning to tell me a story that was going around Birzeit University.

"Once there was a lion," Taisir began, "and he always

liked to beat a little mouse. Every time the lion saw the mouse, he went *bam! bam! bam!* with his paw across the mouse's face. So the little mouse thought, and he decided to put on an American hat, the kind like a baseball hat, with stars and stripes all over it. He wore the peak in back.

"The next time the mouse saw the lion, the lion immediately hit him.

"'Put your cap on forward!' he said. So the little mouse turned his cap around and wore the peak in front.

"Now the lion had no reason to complain about the mouse. What to do? So the lion went to the fox and told him the problem.

"'Aha!' said the fox. 'Here is what you must do. Ask the mouse to bring you water. If he brings it cold, tell him you wanted hot. If he brings it hot, tell him you wanted cold. Either way, you've got him. See?'

"Satisfied with his new plan, the lion went looking for the mouse. When he found him, he told the mouse to bring him some water. The mouse asked him, 'Do you want hot water, or do you want cold?' The lion was enraged. He smacked the mouse again across its face, screaming, 'Why aren't you wearing your hat?'"

I laughed, and felt the bitterness ease.

Another day, Lamis teased Muhammad after he complained of being "broken." The three of us were in his office, and he had just told us that his wife was pregnant with an unplanned baby. Lamis raised an eyebrow.

"You are partially broken, or completely broken?" she asked. She added a phrase or two in Arabic that I could not understand, but which, from Muhammad's blush, I was startled to realize must have implied that his sexual prowess, at least, was intact. The last thing I would have expected in Arab culture was to hear a woman teasing a man about sex.

Abashed, Muhammad acknowledged his responsibility in the matter. Not long ago, he said, he had entered a room where his daughter and young son were watching cartoons on television and had seen Mickey Mouse standing in the center of a circle that he was busily cutting out all around himself. When he had completed the circle, Mickey Mouse and his little circle of land dropped down and out of sight.

"That's how I feel," Muhammad said; and for some time afterward I couldn't think of him without picturing a tiny tragicomic figure on his circle, sawing and sawing, and then—dropping down.

ᔓ

In time, there had been so many killings, closures, burials, and protests that I found it hard to keep them straight—two brothers killed in Hebron; a schoolboy killed in Birzeit and others wounded by a settler who claimed his car had been hit by stones; shots fired and grenades thrown in Hebron; a van burned; Jewish women settlers overturning stalls in the Hebron market; complete closure in Hebron; and before that, in Hebron, workers in a van that pulled ahead in line at a checkpoint, all killed by soldiers. In Gaza, Palestinians attacked the Erez checkpoint, two soldiers killed a medic, and two Palestinians were blown up in a car rigged with explosives. There was rioting in Umm al-Fahm and else-where inside Israel over land taken by the military, and riots spread north to Nazareth.

Which event had come before another? Which had happened last? One afternoon from the hospital near my apartment came sounds of a loud disagreement, men's voices raised for an hour or more.

I went in to Randa, who was using her whirring machine in the kitchen. She switched off the machine and listened.

"Oh," she said, "there was a fire in a factory in Ramallah. Some workers were hurt."

"Do you know how it started?" I asked.

"No," she said. "We try not even to think about what happens over there anymore."

I didn't want to shut out the awareness that someone was feeling pain. But how was I to hold someone else's suffering without feeling that I would crack apart? The hospital was beginning to seem like an enormous, breathing thing, alive, monstrous in its noisy expressions of fear and suffering.

Later the same day the hospital became very quiet. I looked out: the parking lot was filled with Palestinians wearing red berets—the Presidential elite? And then the high cry of a woman's anguish. The mother, I thought, whose voice always rises above the voices of everyone else. Higher, higher, went the cry, seeking comfort the woman would never find, for the death of her husband, her daughter, her son. There was no comfort for anyone.

In the US, President Clinton was on trial for having

lied about an extramarital affair. Then Clinton was in Israel, wearing a *kippa*, or yarmulke, lighting the first Hanukkah candles. Finally, Clinton visited the West Bank, where I noted he had not replaced the *kippa* he'd worn in Israel with a *kufiya*, the Arab checkered headscarf. He lectured the Palestinian people: you must share your land with Israel. No one had told him, it seemed, that Palestinians had already "shared" most of their land with Israel, and that Area A, the only area over which the Palestinian Authority had even nominal "full security and civil control," at that point comprised less than 3 percent of what remained of the West Bank. Palestinian youths burned flags and threw stones to protest Clinton's policies.

"Throwing stones!" muttered voices in the West. "How primitive! How stupid! Why do they do that?"

"If you ask them, they will say what else can we do?" remarked Taisir. Someone else asked, "When was the last time you heard of an Israeli being killed by a stone?"

By this time, I knew that anyone who tried to demonstrate peacefully was in danger of being tear-gassed, sound-bombed, blasted with powerful streams of water shot from a high-pressure hose, arrested, beaten, shot at, injured, blinded, killed, or any combinations of these.

People outside Palestine do not see the macabre ritual played out every Friday, and other days, too, at some Israeli checkpoints.

Kids hurl stones. Israeli soldiers fire guns and wound and kill the kids, even though the kids move fast, ducking behind overturned cars, throwing a stone and then rushing for cover. The Israeli soldiers, for the most part, take their time as if they are on a pleasure outing on a lazy summer's day.

The television footage we got in Palestine showed both Palestinian and Israeli participants close up. We saw the kids hurling stones, smaller children helping to find the stones and pass up the supply. Smoke rose from the tires the Palestinians set on fire to hide themselves from the soldiers. The camera would focus for long moments on the Israeli soldiers moving as if in slow motion, standing out in the open. *Bang!* A leisurely turn, back to the armored jeep. Through the jeep window, an arm is visible, inserting something into the barrel of a gun. Eventually, the gun comes up again. The soldier saunters out toward the overturned car, the kids. Aims. No hurry. Fires.

In its dreamlike pace, the Israeli portion of the scene looks as if it's occurring underwater—in contrast to the Palestinian side, all speed and flames. Sometimes one of the soldiers talks on a phone. Sometimes you can hear murmured conversations coming from inside the vehicle. Sometimes the soldiers stay inside their armored cars and just shoot out a window or a door.

Any Friday, after the noon prayer, unless the entire area was under curfew or invasion, a confrontation would take place fairly near my house at the bottom of Nablus Road, near the multistoried City Inn Hotel. Beyond the hotel, on either side, were empty fields, and straight on up the hill, at the very top, sat the Israeli military base called *beit eel*. It was to *beit eel* that Palestinians and ordinary, non-VIP foreigners had to go to request permits to travel anywhere outside the Ramallah area—to the hospital in Jerusalem, for instance, or to the Israeli airport outside Tel Aviv, in the days when Palestinians from the West Bank and Gaza were still allowed to use the airport. I went to *beit eel* often enough myself to wait for hours in long lines with Palestinians, in my case, to get a visa. It would have been suicidal to attack the military base, and I never saw a Palestinian anywhere near it except to make a request. In the years I lived there, no Palestinian ever went up the hill to throw stones.

At the bottom of the hill there was nothing but a crossroads—one road blocked off, another leading up to the military base, a third passing around the far side of the base and going on to Nablus, all meeting the road the kids came down from Ramallah. None was used except by the military and cars with special permission. Down by the City Inn, there was nothing for soldiers to protect, just an empty hotel, empty roads, and open land.

Yet every Friday, just across from the hotel, where the road from Ramallah met the other roads, you'd find one or more armored jeeps facing Ramallah, soldiers in them visible, ostensibly guarding the Israeli army base from attacks that never came. Each Friday, from the Ramallah side, Palestinian youths went down to confront the jeeps, resulting in what the press called "clashes." Palestinians were often hurt there, sometimes killed.

Curious about this weekly event, one Friday I went down to see. When I arrived, the ritual was in full swing.

As I crested the hill coming from Ramallah, I heard shots and saw, parked smack in the middle of the road, a couple of armored Israeli jeeps, windshields and side windows protected by the usual bulletproof glass. The closer I got to the City Inn, the more people were out on the sidewalks watching, in front of their homes and little yards, clusters of people, mostly men, but some women too, looking down the hill, the groups thickening along the way, until, at last, mad activity—running, shouting, rocks flying, bullets whizzing by, youths ducking, reaching, throwing again, Israeli guns popping. . . .

The center of everyone's attention was the flat ground, where the jeeps sat unmoving, lights on in the middle of the day. Just in front of them, a few yards away, an old car had been turned on its side, presumably to provide the boys a bit of shelter. Three or four youths, probably fourteen or fifteen years old, crouched on one side of the car, each standing just long enough to toss a stone at the jeep. The stones bounced off the hood and sides of the jeep, harmless to the soldiers inside. A bit farther back up toward town, black smoke rose from a burning tire, and behind this dense screen, too, youths were running back and forth, hurling rocks at the stationary jeeps of army-fatigue green. Sometimes a boy would run directly toward the fire, and then, at the very last moment before entering the flames, leap over them, high in the air, his arms flung up. He would land just the other side of the fire, then whirl away, back to relative safety behind the smoke. Not far from the center of the action, two or three girls, and even a couple of women, bent, reaching and sifting, selecting stones of the appropriate size. They put the stones into plastic buckets and passed them to runners, who in turn fed the warriors sheltering behind the car.

It was easy to see that anyone who made it through the ritual safely would be a kind of hero. He would have shown bravery in facing the enemy and carried out a symbolic act of resistance to the Israeli occupation. He would have felt the exhilaration that comes from exposure to danger.

In a life of study or work, stuck in a village or a town, cut off from mountains or the sea, unable to hike even across nearby hills and valleys, without movie theaters or computers or safe spaces in which to play, the youth might have, in flirting with death, discovered how it felt to be alive. Even as an onlooker, I could feel this high.

All up and down the sidewalk on both sides of the road, the groups of watchers tested their courage by moving closer to the upturned car, the fire, and the jeeps. Then they swelled back up the hill again in successive waves as tear gas canisters were shot in their direction or as a cluster of bullets popped apart and landed nearby. The street would be strewn with round black balls or with small black cylinders, "rubber-coated bullets" they were called. They were steel with rubber coating—steel that could kill or paralyze, maim, or blind, as well as injure in less dramatic ways. The younger kids collected the bullets as trophies. There were so many kinds, some the color of brass, thicker than a grown man's thumb and five or six inches long— these were the tank shells. Others, just an inch or two to four in length, were more delicate, copper-colored, each also ending in a pointed tip. These could be drilled, then threaded onto a piece of rawhide to wear around your neck.

I learned this when I was shown just such a necklace by a boy probably six years old whose home I visited during an Israeli invasion in the old, lower part of Ramallah. The boy's mother told her son to take off the necklace, making me a gift while simultaneously attempting to protect her son. "It's illegal to wear them," she told me. "They'll arrest him if they see it."

But today the boys playing with soldiers outside the City Inn were in no danger of arrest. The soldiers in the jeeps were not about to venture out among the crowd. They would stick the barrels of their long guns through their small jeep windows and shoot from inside, and their aim could be deadly. We heard that soldiers sometimes entertained themselves by aiming their guns at one or both of a target's eyes; they bragged of their skill to news reporters who quoted them in their stories. The sport was so widespread that four boys appeared in a front-page photograph one day in a Palestinian newspaper, sitting in a row in what looked like a doctor's office, each with a patch over the socket of his missing or injured eye.

On the Friday afternoon I went, the scene was unfolding just as described. A couple of red and white ambulances marked with the Muslim red crescent moon waited outside the soldiers' shooting range on our side of the City Inn. The spot near the ambulance was fairly sheltered from the firing, and because it was, it had around it an assortment of younger children. Up the hill, on the town side, a few boys slung stones from their slingshots, and two or three young Palestinian men with guns were taking potshots at the jeeps with their ancient puny Kalashnikovs and receiving barrages of gunfire in return from the Israelis' rapid-fire M-16s. The presence of the armed men, the "real" fighters, lent an extra edge to the battle, although none of the young boys crouching behind the car or running about on the low ground were armed with anything but stones.

The scene was grotesque, kids running and leaping over the fire, throwing stones at intervals amid clouds of black smoke, and the sound of gunfire as bullets landed on the ground all around, even going over my head and landing behind me. I stood transfixed, appalled by what was happening. None of these kids had guns! With no pretense of bravery I turned and ran away from the direction of the gunfire until I was cowering in a garage, horrified and afraid, when a student of mine from the university entered.

"Miss!" he said in surprise. "What are you doing here?" He reached out to shake my hand. A few minutes later another student of mine came in. This student was one who had been so angry at me when I failed him in a course that he hadn't spoken to me since. He also reached for my hand, and he thanked me "for caring enough" to come. Another youth, wearing a red-and-white-checked *kufiya*, found me bullets of different types so he could explain their differences. Some, he explained, were shot out from the gun in a little container that opened when it hit the ground, releasing the bullets in a spray of killing missiles.

Back up on the hill, I watched four boys crouch behind the battered old car as they threw their stones in the direction of the armored jeeps, dark spiders with bright yellow eyes, ominously still, Israeli soldiers safe inside. Two of the boys were wearing rust-red T-shirts, one a yellow shirt, and one a white one, easiest to see from where I watched on the hill behind them. After about an hour, the boy in the white T-shirt apparently decided he had had enough. He left the shelter of the overturned car, crouching at first, then straightening as he ran fast away from the jeeps, back toward the stores and houses where people stood watching. That was when they shot him—not the soldiers in the jeeps, but Israeli snipers, shooting now with a clear aim from the empty hotel's upper stories. The running figure paused, hung a moment in the air, and fell. One of the ambulances rushed to the spot. The medics, clearly labeled in their orange and white jackets, rushed to pick up the wounded youth and to carry him to the ambulance while bullets rained down among them from the snipers above. I was almost speechless with disbelief.

"Did you see that?" I demanded of the people nearest me. "He was running away, and they shot him! His back was to the soldiers! He was leaving the area!" Several boys looked at me almost sympathetically.

"Yes, of course," they said, matter-of-factly. "That's what the Israelis always do. They can't see them well behind the car, so they wait until they leave—and then they shoot." The speakers were not the slightest bit surprised.

In an article the next day, an Israeli government

spokesperson was quoted as saying that Palestinians had fired on Israeli soldiers during the demonstration, and that Israelis had not returned fire.

After the youth had been shot, the armored jeeps whipped away from their favorite post near the stone throwers and zoomed up to the Israeli base at the top of the far hill. Soon after, two tanks lumbered partway down the hill, and began coughing and booming in the direction of the Palestinians. More Israeli soldiers ran, crouching, to take up positions on the hill near the tanks. Finally, the armored jeeps returned to their positions a few meters from the car on its side, and waited for more stones to come their way. Kill someone, then send two tanks? The logic escaped me.

Later I heard the boy they had hit had been shot through the heart and was dead before he left the site.

Friends in the US asked me, "Why would you want to live in a part of the world where there is so much war?" It had seemed to me that some of us, the lucky ones, had a choice—we could live either in the place that paid the price, or in the place that reaped the benefit of the price that others paid. Within months of my arrival, I understood that the entire Palestinian population was unsafe, their homes, land, jobs, identities—their lives—all at risk. Palestinians were always in danger from Israeli soldiers and Palestinian police. Then I felt only the cold knowledge of my own inadequacy, my own powerlessness to make their lives any better.

Something else within me was shifting also. It was

becoming increasingly difficult for me to feel compassion for or connection to Israelis. Years before, an artist and a wise woman, a Hungarian Jew, who had lost her best friend to the Nazis, had said to me, "If you are to achieve anything when you go to Israel and Palestine, it will be because of who you are, not because of anything you do." At the time I had not understood how a person could achieve anything simply by *being*, instead of *doing*. But it must include the ability to hold each person in my heart as a human being. Adding my own anger or hatred to the existing emotional mix could not be useful. But now, Israelis were slipping out of my heart entirely. *My heart shrivels*, I found myself thinking, *and when I try to stretch it, it tears. I hide amid layers of myself.* I could understand the Palestinian student, a woman, who said to me, "Tell Israelis it's time for them to stop thinking only about themselves."

21: NEAR DEPARTURE, NEW BEGINNING

Balancing times of doubt were times of joy—at home, in my ramblings in town, at the university. Although many days I woke to a colorless dawn, leaves dark against my window, sometimes one pale lavender crocus in a barren yard, or a brilliant morning sky, would be enough to light a simple appreciation of what was, against the horror.

Sitting in a café, correcting papers, I saw a white horse float down the sidewalk, followed by two brown-and-white sheep trotting briskly, all guided expertly around the corner and out of sight by a small boy on a miniature bicycle. Where in the US would there be such a sight? Such unpredictability?

On some of our days off, a group of us took long hikes on pathways through the hills outside Ramallah. Once we visited a spring, from which the water ran cold and clear. Village women were washing their clothes in pools formed of rock, while boys fetched water in huge plastic jugs and hauled them up the hill to their homes on the backs of donkeys.

Gradually, my rowdier students began taking part in our class competitions and other activities, and the classes went increasingly well. Every so often Muna, Pat, and Lamis and I would sit out in the department hall at the end of classes and smoke and laugh and talk. Their friendship made any difficulty worthwhile.

Sometime in the first year I was there, I learned from Muna that the university had a Women's Studies Center, which offered courses to university undergraduates on issues relating to women and gender. I was intrigued. Relatively new, it had begun three years earlier, when I had been working in Egypt, as a Women's Studies Program. The year I arrived in Palestine, 1997, it morphed into the Women's Studies Center, and the following year, it gained more independent status as the Institute of Women's Studies. Muna told me that Lamis had been one of the center's founders and that she taught classes in the Institute as well as in our department.

"Do you work there too?" I asked Muna.

"No," she answered. "But I'd love to."

"Do you think there's any chance I could volunteer there?" I asked Lamis. Without family responsibilities, I was the only teacher in our department who had time even to think of volunteering. Lamis suggested I write a letter to the women's collective who ran the Institute, suggesting ways I might be able to contribute. In time, I heard back and was invited to work with a young librarian's assistant, tutoring her in English. I was delighted, and the connection with women's studies became a great pleasure for me.

Meanwhile, at home, Nawal, incorrigibly generous, continued delivering food to my door. There would come a knock, and in she would come, bearing an enormous plate of chicken, of rice with pine nuts, a bowl of hummus. My all-time favorite experience was entering her kitchen just as she was removing her homemade donuts from the oven. She introduced me to both her children when they visited from work and university in Jordan. Sometimes, she would lure me over to her house to watch the US TV program *The Bold and the Beautiful*, which I justified watching because some of my female students referred to it in class.

∽

In March, it snowed. Taking advantage of the shuttered stores in downtown Ramallah, bands of *shabab*—in this case, teenage boys or young men in their early twenties—roamed the streets, snowballs in hand, so that the city center became a different kind of battlefield. Black- or red-checked *kufiyas* covering their heads and masking their faces against the cold, combatants heaved snowballs at each other, ducked, ran, laughed, and shouted. With no chance that day of ending up armless, blind, crippled, or dead, the young men played like children.

Their aim, though, was terrible. When a whole group seemed to be getting the best of one taller than the rest, this tallest boy picked up an enormous piece of snow and heaved it at his attackers, only to watch it disintegrate as he sent it on its way. After a moment of surprise, I realized that of course, given their world-renowned stone-throwing backgrounds, the lighter weight and unaccustomed heft of these unfamiliar missiles meant that in this new medium, the renowned children of the Intifada might be no good at all.

∾

But the good times glittered in a fabric of drab colors. The killings continued.

One day I asked Muna what she thought the end result of the struggle would be.

"We will have a state some day," she answered, "but we will wait a hundred years. I won't see it, my children won't see it."

At work, with my colleagues, and in class, with my students, I was aware that I was becoming an angrier, shriller person. I felt as if I were emotionally thin. My right eyelid and the skin below the eye began twitching; then the skin twitched all around my eye. For days on end I had terrible headaches. People in the community were being tortured and killed; how could a mere headache cause me pain?

"What do people do with their anger?" I asked Pat.

She didn't answer. Never a big talker, she often didn't answer when I asked this sort of question. *Of course*, I thought, *it becomes depression; anger turned inward.*

❧

By the end of my second year of teaching in the Department of Languages and Translation, as summer began in 1999, I had decided to leave Palestine. Even though my classes were going better, I didn't feel I was doing good work with the undergraduates. That knowledge, along with my own chronic fatigue, compounded by war, was wrecking me emotionally and physically. I would wake sleepy and grope my way through the day, ready to sleep again by mid-afternoon or earlier. Moussa, visiting his brother in the hospital two or three times daily, spoke of seeing people sick and injured and dying each day as "a load on the soul." I began to dream that I was too weak to walk. In my sleep, I hung from bars, grabbed at streetlights, clawed at corners of buildings, unable to raise myself due to a crippling weakness in my arms and legs. I decided to stay through the summer and leave in the fall.

But as summer began, Rema approached me. "You don't know me," she began, but of course I did. She was head of the master's program in Gender, Law, and Development that the Institute of Women's Studies had established the year before. At the time, the program was the only one of its kind in Palestine and one of just two in the entire Arab world. Although we had never been introduced, Lamis had pointed Rema out to me as a member of the women's studies team, and once, I'd heard her give a talk I'd found incomprehensible, studded with words like *modernism, postmodernism, subaltern,* and *discourse of development.*

On Lamis's recommendation, Rema asked if I would teach part time in the Institute's new English-teaching program during the summer, preparing students to read articles in professional journals for the coursework they would begin in the fall. If I wanted the job, I could begin right away.

Of course I did!

Loving the new work I was asked to do and the learning that came with it, inspired and intrigued by the group of women with whom I was now working, I ended up staying and working in Palestine for nine more years. For a while I continued teaching part time in the Department of Languages and Translation, but soon I was working full time in the Institute of Women's Studies. For six years I taught; for the rest, I did research and wrote and edited reports and academic papers for Institute members.

Entering the world of women's studies was the greatest gift I could have imagined at the time. These were some of the Palestinian women who been among the pioneers of the Palestinian Women's Movement. They had participated in the First Intifada. They were strong, independent Arab feminists, who had introduced gender studies into Palestinian education and gender awareness into the PNA ministries and into development projects throughout the West Bank and Gaza. Now I was working with them—Rema, Islah, Eileen, Lamis. Others—Ilham, Rita, Lisa, and Penny—who had worked for years to create the Institute of Women's Studies, raising the necessary funds and getting permission from the university administration, were at the periphery. Shortly, we would be joined by Fadwa, another early feminist and political activist.

∽

My first job in the Institute of Women's Studies was to create a curriculum for several course levels, using as many of the concepts and as much of the terminology as I could from the readings students would be assigned in their regular master's classes. From Rema, I received only support and encouragement. On the first day of class, introducing me to my students, she said to them:

"Everything Chivvis asks you to do, you will do. If Chivvis says the sun sets in the east, you will believe it."

What an introduction! What faith! As soon as Rema had left the room, I informed my students that the sun set in the east. They all passed the test nicely.

The men and women who applied and were accepted into the MA program in its first years of operation were older than most of the undergraduates I had taught in the Department of Languages and Translation. Acceptance was limited to those with a certain grade average, and there were more applicants than places for them. They all worked at full-time jobs, and most had families, including children—factors that might have meant they had little time to study. But both men and women were working in jobs where the information offered in the MA program was relevant, even useful. Development projects in the Occupied Territories, whether sponsored by the World Bank, another government donor, or an NGO were all subject to review for their policies on gender. Were women included in the planning of the project? Would women and children benefit from the projects? Did planning take into account existing family systems and the community's social structure? The students were thirsty for knowledge, and willing to learn English to acquire that knowledge. They were a delight to teach.

A number of my students were from Gaza. Pat had told me that her students from Gaza often struggled more than others to come to the university, but that they were frequently her best students, serious and hardworking. She also said that West Bank students tended to look down upon those from Gaza, a reaction not uncommon from one side or another in a population divided under an oppressive rule.

But if my students from the West Bank looked down on their Gazan counterparts, I never saw it. I would have liked to see anyone try: my students from Gaza were smart and hardworking, and they were proud. I liked them tremendously and felt lucky to know them.

That first class of mine glowed. I see them now: 'Andalib, Nihad, Felicia, Ayman, Intisar, Samar, and the rest, some from the West Bank, some from Gaza. I had been swept up into another reality entirely. Partly because of who they were and partly because the first classes were smaller, I grew to know these students better than those who came later.

There was Samar, who had become engaged to her husband, Hilmi ("my dream"), after the first year of an eight-year prison sentence he was serving in an Israeli prison. For what, I did not know. If someone offered an explanation for his or her time in prison, I appreciated hearing it, but I felt it was intrusive to ask and possibly unwise for people to tell me what, if anything, they had done. On their wedding day, Samar and Hilmi passed their rings through the prison bars, and Samar, who had sung during the First Intifada before thousands of people at a time, sang that day for Hilmi. After that, she said, she shut herself up for seven years in her own "prison at home," because she couldn't stand to hear people pouring doubt into her ears: "You might wait for him, and when he gets out, he'll find you are not the right one for him. . . . You're wasting your time." Samar paid no attention.

I met Hilmi at the end-of-year picnic my students organized. He was just as handsome in person as he was in the pictures Samar had showed me. I knew that he had been tortured, and when we had a chance to talk, I asked him how he had found the spirit and the strength to keep going and to live afterward as a loving husband and father. He was not religious, he told me; he'd not had that belief to keep him strong. Had firsthand knowledge of the cruelty of which humans are capable shaken his confidence in human nature?

"No," he answered. "It was easy."

"Easy?"

"Not easy like eating meat." He gestured toward the chicken he was expertly barbequing. "In fact, it is the hardest thing I know. But easy in the sense that you know exactly why you are going through it and that you believe in the reason. Everything else flows from that."

From other Palestinians, both men and women, who had spent time in Israeli prisons, I had heard of the disciplined schedules they followed in order to exercise, pray, and exchange knowledge—knowledge of different kinds of work, of various political views.

"Of course," Hilmi said almost offhandedly when I asked him if this had been his experience also. "We studied and we worked together. We had a pattern for our days, a plan for self-improvement." It helped too, he said, to know that he was loved and valued by people "on the outside." The First Intifada was under way during the years he was in prison; his arrest had predated it by just a month or two.

"But it was our belief in what we were doing that was the key to my years in prison."

It was what impressed me most, all those years in Palestine—the fact that the treatment people endured did not make the great majority of them brutal and small-minded. We know that reactions to abuse can go in opposite directions, and I would ask Palestinians sometimes how they retained the best of their humanity living under a military occupation. They'd only raise their eyebrows and shake their heads. I decided it had to do with the depth of their conviction, at all levels and in every dimension. They knew they were doing no wrong in demanding the return of their land and independence from an occupying power and from the other, greater powers colluding in their subjugation.

～

In the years I spent working in the Institute of Women's Studies, I learned details of some of the so-called development schemes that the US and Europe were pressing on the rest of the world, and how they affected the Global South. As we read about "development" or "aid" projects in Africa, Asia, and the Middle East, I learned that these schemes mostly involved trying to bring poor countries, the former colonies of the nineteenth and twentieth centuries, in line with global capitalism—with the poor countries on the losing end of the competition.

Countries such as Egypt, whose population had been growing enough food to feed themselves, were encouraged to grow just one crop, like sugar, cotton, or coffee for export, and to import the processed food and manufactured goods they needed from the "developed" countries at costs the people could not afford. Wealthier donor countries still encourage poorer countries to set up special areas, called "export processing zones" (EPZs) or "free trade zones" (FTZs), where labor laws do not apply and unions are forbidden, and where workers, mostly women, work long days without benefits and for low pay.

Project donors might direct funds to male heads of families in cultures where the workload—and decision making—had formerly been shared between men and women. Or foreign donors might direct money to individual families, when traditionally the land had been communally shared. Countries were encouraged to borrow money and were then required by institutions like the International Monetary Fund and the World Bank to cut social services in order to pay back the loans. This left women to provide for the sick, the elderly, and the disabled, in addition to all the rest of the work they were already doing. Donor countries were setting the agendas for these new colonies in the "neoliberal" political climate.

Western countries, where women's issues were the current fad, were funding women's centers and campaigns against early marriage and "honor killings" in Palestine. Women I knew thought these issues were important, but at the time they were more concerned with providing their families with food and clean water and with keeping their children alive under a military occupation.

One of my students was shocked to read that 75 percent of the profits from these so-called aid projects was flowing not from the "donor" countries of the Global North to countries in the Global South, but in the opposite direction. She brought me the reading, and pointed to a paragraph.

"Is it true," she asked, "that 75 percent of direct investment supposedly going to 'developing countries' actually ends up in the hands of other industrialized countries?"

"Check the source," I suggested, "and see if you can determine whether it is trustworthy." The source was a publication of the UN-NGO Group on Women and Development.

Another subject that especially interested me—and

one that is among the most controversial to arise when I try to explain the years I chose to live in the Middle East—has to do with women's place in Islam. Westerners' assumptions on the topic often remind me of the skepticism, even hostility, I'd expressed many years before in Egypt, when I'd argued with Halim. Working with Institute faculty and my students, I learned of contemporary Muslim voices, both male and female, challenging many of what I came to see as the "trappings," but not the core, of Islam. These voices are questioning prevailing male interpretations of Islam just as Christian and Jewish women are challenging practices demeaning to women in their own religious traditions, like limiting the priesthood to males, or favoring men over women in matters pertaining to marriage and domestic rights. At the time they were adopted, early Islamic teachings about the veiling and seclusion of women in fact represented radical efforts to protect women from rape and other atrocities they were suffering. But in our time, contemporary scholars and activists argue, customs that in the seventh century AD were progressive and tolerant in spirit are being used by male interpreters of Islam to keep women subservient to men in ways that counter the spirit of Islam.

One of my first students in the Institute of Women's Studies was 'Andalib, who, incidentally, is somewhat unusual in not choosing to cover her hair despite living in Gaza, an area generally known to be more conservative than many parts of the West Bank. But then, 'Andalib (her name means "nightingale") is extraordinary in many ways.

Head of a women's center in Gaza, married to a Palestinian journalist, and already the mother of a small child, she began the MA program at Birzeit University when she was pregnant with her second child. Anyone who hasn't traveled the distance from Gaza to the West Bank and back again in a day, and waited in long lines of Palestinians, and walked in and out of Gaza through a structure resembling a cattle run, would be hard put to imagine what it might take for a pregnant, working wife and mother to travel daily to the West Bank and study for a graduate degree and return each evening to Gaza.

Although among the first to enter the MA program in Gender, Law, and Development, 'Andalib, ironically, was also one of the first to be forced to leave it, when Israel closed completely the "borders" between Gaza and the West Bank and refused Palestinians the right to travel between the two pieces of land. Any Gazan studying at Birzeit University was out of luck, and could no longer study there. This is still the situation today.

Once, when I was still able to visit Gaza, 'Andalib told me the story of a friend she encountered after one of the Israeli invasions of Gaza. This friend knew that since foreigners often stayed just a year or two in Palestine, those of us who stayed longer were sometimes asked by Palestinians we had not seen for a while, "Oh, are you still here?"

But 'Andalib's foreign friend, meeting her in Gaza, turned the question around and inquired of 'Andalib, "Are *you* still here?"

She was, and still is, in Gaza, suing the Israeli government to be allowed to finish her MA in Gender and Development at Birzeit University. The unborn child 'Andalib was carrying when I met her is now fifteen years old.

22: Uprising, Again

In January 2000, a year that would initiate a new chapter in Palestinian resistance to the occupation, a bomb exploded in Israel, injuring twenty-six Israelis. In addition to sickening the Palestinians I knew, the action ensured Israeli retaliation against the entire Palestinian population. In the same month, Israel announced plans to build a Jewish settlement in Abu Dis in East Jerusalem and interfered with renovation work Palestinians were doing on the Al-Aqsa Mosque. In February, the Israeli army forcibly removed fifteen Palestinian families, some one hundred people, from their homes in caves in the south Hebron region. In March, Israeli forces stormed the village of Taybeh, inside Israel, looking for Hamas members and killing four Palestinians in the process. In April, the Israeli organization Peace Now reported that there were at the time 7,000 settlement housing units under construction in the West Bank, and the Knesset approved $400 million for security in settlements and the construction of twelve new bypass roads on Palestinian land. In May, the Likud Party proposed amending a law to ensure that no part of Jerusalem would ever be transferred to the Palestinian Authority.

A relative in the US wrote me. "The problem with you people over there," he said, tossing me into the mix, "is that your memories are too long."

"How long would it take," countered a Palestinian acquaintance, "if the US were invaded, for Americans to forget, or at least to quietly accept, that more than three-quarters of *your* land had been taken away?"

That summer, due to strikes at the university, I held classes for West Bank students in the new home I had moved into at the invitation of Fadwa, one of the women working in the Institute of Women's Studies. After my first year in Palestine, I had left the first place I lived, across from the hospital. The doctor who owned the house told me that a relative of his wanted to move in, and since the relative was with the Palestinian Authority, the family did not feel they could refuse. I had moved to a room in the house of a Palestinian woman who, unfortunately for me, watched television nonstop in the hall just outside my room. That second house was high on a hill on Betunia Road, next door to a lovely old stone mansion that had belonged to Karim Khalaf, the Ramallah mayor whose legs had been blown off by a car bomb Israelis had planted during the First Intifada. Each morning I had pulled back the curtains from the two high, narrow windows in my room to admire the "castle," with its graceful arch and irregular stone wall, and beside it the arms of the great eucalyptus reaching to the sky. I had never lived in such lovely surroundings, but my appreciation of the beauty was outweighed, on the one hand, by my intolerance of noise and, on the other, by the prospect of living with a colleague I liked so much.

So, in my third year in Palestine, I moved to the town of Al-Bireh, which adjoins Ramallah. There I shared a house with Fadwa, from Jerusalem, and Ohaila, whose family lived in Nazareth. Both welcomed me like family. Thus began what was to be the happiest living situation in the years I lived in Palestine.

I was never lonely. Both women were activists: Fadwa with a political party and women's issues, Ohaila counseling and training women on issues of rape and abuse. I learned a tremendous amount from them both—about Palestinian feminism, about politics, about both their lives. Although Fadwa spoke perfect English, she spoke to me in Arabic so that, painful as it must have been for her, I would get better at understanding and speaking the language. Ohaila did the same. As a child, Ohaila had lived with her family in the Kalandia Refugee Camp on the edge of Ramallah, and later in Nazareth, where her family lived when I met her, but she had no wish to continue living in what had become the State of Israel. Like my colleagues Sharif and Moussa at Birzeit University, she preferred to make her home in the West Bank, despite the difficulties and the danger.

∽

On May 15, 2000, the day Palestinians commemorated the *Nakba*, or Catastrophe, of 1948, in which some 750,000

Palestinians were driven from their homes, and most of the land that had been Palestine became Israel, Palestinians in Ramallah held a general strike that led to confrontations, including an exchange of fire between Israeli soldiers and Palestinian police, in which six Palestinians were killed and more than 1,000 wounded.

One night shortly after that incident, I was home when I thought I heard shots. I had a sense, then, that something was changing below the surface of even "ordinary" life. The Palestinian Authority had begun rounding up members of the PFLP (Popular Front for the Liberation of Palestine), one of the political parties to the left of Fateh. Palestinian police arrived at the home of a female student of mine at 3:00 a.m. and arrested her. They let her go after midnight the following night, but her comrades remained in prison.

To a friend who had spent years in prison, I described what happened to me when I heard stories of imprisonment, death, or other loss.

"I take in the person's pain but do not heal," I told her. "I think after talking to me, the person goes away feeling worse than before."

"That's because you go around the pain instead of through it," she answered. "I go through it and draw it out. Like a screw turning into the heart."

In July 2000, the people of Gaza were refused permission to leave Gaza, and Palestinians from the West Bank were not allowed in. The week we were to start the summer intensive English course, I learned that none of my students from Gaza would be allowed to leave the little strip of land on which they lived to attend the university in the West Bank. More students from Gaza had entered our program in the year I had been teaching at the Institute of Women's Studies, and more still needed to be tested and to begin studying English until they could leave Gaza to attend MA classes at Birzeit University.

As a foreigner holding a US passport, I was still allowed to travel back and forth between the West Bank and Gaza, and so I began holding classes in Gaza twice a week. In the early morning I would walk into Ramallah and wait with other passengers until a seven-passenger taxi filled, and then we would make our way across lovely agricultural land that now belonged to Israel, until we reached the Erez checkpoint. This was the "border" that Palestinians had to cross in order to enter the Israeli military base and get clearance (or be denied permission) to enter the Gaza Strip.

Gaza, next door to Egypt, had been governed by Egypt before being captured and occupied by Israel in 1967. I loved Gaza, with its landscape so much like Egypt's—flat, planted with date palms and other crops in the south, dense urban life in the north, and everywhere the dialect closer to the Egyptian dialect, along with an especial irreverent humor that I also associated with Egyptians.

After being approved, with more or less delay, by soldiers on the Israeli side, I'd make my way across the checkpoint. On the other side, Palestinian police would greet me cheerfully. There were taxis to take me to wherever the class would be held that day, sometimes the Center for

Women's Affairs that 'Andalib headed, sometimes a clinic fairly near the checkpoint, and other times 'Andalib's house in Gaza City. Our location depended on what parts of Gaza the Israelis happened to be shutting off that day.

Teaching in Gaza, I saw the women at their places of work or in their homes, no longer "just students," but in their full roles as wage earners, community workers, wives, and mothers. I remember with pleasure the afternoons I spent with 'Andalib and her friend Nihad, who was also in the program, as we struggled through the academic language in the journals they were trying to read on their own in an effort to keep up with the university classes they were missing. Other times, I'd meet and test a new batch of students in the office of the Women's Affairs and Technical Committee in Gaza City.

In the afternoons, I would return the same way. While waiting in a long line of cars for the return taxi to fill, I would see Palestinians streaming off the buses that had taken them to Israel to work for housewives or building contractors. This is something that does not happen anymore: Gazans are no longer allowed to enter or leave Gaza, much less perform day labor in Israel. Along with the human cargo the buses emptied at the mouth of the cattle run came the most extraordinary mix of objects the workers had acquired in Israel. Men and women carried bicycles, blankets, sacks of fruit and vegetables, refrigerators, tires . . . in their arms, on their backs, on their heads.

∽

In the last week of September 2000, Ariel Sharon, then leader of the right-wing Israeli Likud Party, accompanied by 1,000 riot police, visited Al Haram al-Sharif in East Jerusalem, which contains Al-Aqsa Mosque, the third holiest shrine in Islam.

The following day, during demonstrations against the intrusion, which Palestinians and the rest of us viewed as unnecessary and provocative, Israeli police killed six demonstrators and wounded 220 more. They used live ammunition and rubber bullets against Palestinians who were throwing rocks but otherwise unarmed.

I was in Gaza that day, teaching our students at the Women's Technical Committee office, when we smelled smoke and heard shouting outside the windows. Looking out, we saw youths burning tires in the streets. The women, concerned that I wouldn't be able to leave Gaza if I waited, stuffed me quickly into a taxi that took me to the Erez checkpoint and back across lands farmed by Israel to Ramallah.

For the next several days, ambulances screamed, Israeli guns fired and were answered by Palestinians' older, slower guns, Israeli helicopters shot missiles that destroyed buildings, tanks surrounded West Bank cities, and unmanned reconnaissance planes droned overhead. All of us were "closed"—trapped—in our various places, Ohaila in Nazareth—which had also been declared a military zone, even though it was a city in Israel—and my students in Gaza, Nablus, Hebron, and elsewhere. None of us had any idea how long this would last.

The Second, or Al-Aqsa, Intifada, had begun.

ᔐ

From then on, Israeli actions in Palestine took an even nastier, more violent turn. US-made attack helicopters, named Apache—suggesting that one dispossessed indigenous population was bombing another—began firing on the compound where Arafat was living. US-made F-16s flew over us with ear-shattering roars and dropped their bombs. People stayed home at night as Israeli soldiers began making night incursions into Palestinian areas, killing and arresting people.

Under the Oslo Accord, the PNA had set up an armed police force so large it ranked among the world's largest in the proportion of police to citizens. Using this police force, Arafat was instructed by Israel to "quell the violence in the territories." The message came from Ehud Barak, then Israeli prime minister, who generously gave Arafat "an extension" in his "deadline" to end the resistance.

One morning I visited the *manara* to find one of the little hand-pushed carts that sold coffee and tea had a bullet hole through its glass window. I had bought tea many times from the vendor and I went over to ask him what had happened. The night before, his cousin, tending the wagon, had been shot dead by an Israeli soldier apparently aiming for someone else.

Another day I attended the funeral of a Palestinian man

who had been taken by soldiers from his small village north of Ramallah to a settlement where he had been tortured to death, burned, and mutilated, then dumped on the road for his people to find. No gunshot wound was found on his body. I saw the man's face, burnt black. The image was horrifying. I stood speechless with the other mourners as the body was laid in the ground. As was almost always the case when a Palestinian killed by Israelis was being buried, even when the funeral was attended by large numbers of family and friends, little was said. Wailing and crying came earlier, when the murder, the torture, the killing was first discovered. At the graveside, we watched; those close to the family offered comfort with quiet words and embraces, and then those of us who had come from outside the village piled back into our vans and cars and headed back to Ramallah.

How can I explain what we all did with our feelings of outrage and grief? To this day, I'm not sure. Certainly, neither I nor anyone else became inured to any of what we saw. It felt, rather, as if the experience was too profoundly upsetting to express in any way we knew. In any case, there was the grave to be dug, the stone to be placed, prayers to be said. Then it was time to return to all the tasks that, death and torture notwithstanding, had to be done. I suppose that much of what we felt was absorbed into our bodies, while our minds tried to go about life as it needed to be lived.

I know that was true for me. I began to wake at night to find every muscle in my body clenched tight. I would will myself to relax, muscle by muscle—neck, upper arm, finger, back, thigh—only to find myself a few moments later clenched again, completely rigid. Was this how it was for everyone who lived in Palestine? Did each of us sleep clenched and tight, steeled against dreams of our own fears, our own losses? Was I the last to realize the disappearance of the bridge as I walked the riverbank?

We heard that a boy in Bethlehem was asleep in bed one night when Israelis shelled his house, blowing off both his legs. Figuring it would be better to go as a whole than to lose myself in parts, from then on I slept with my knees pressed tight against my chest, my legs as closely tucked to my torso as I could get them.

At the university, life limped on. October, then November, passed with no students from Nablus, Hebron, or any of the other areas outside Ramallah, and certainly not Gaza. I could teach a couple of students by traveling to their homes in Bethlehem, and I could teach a few others by teaching a small group at a women's center in Jerusalem, but I was never again allowed into Gaza. 'Andalib and Nihad and my other students from Gaza were never allowed back into the West Bank to continue their studies at Birzeit University.

People's spirits were grim. Still, humor came through. At one point, after Rema had returned from a vacation with her sister in the Caribbean, I heard they had been attacked by a barracuda.

"Is this true?" I asked Rema. "You and your sister were attacked by a barracuda?"

"Yes," she said.

"So what did you do?" I asked. Rema said she had fended it off by making faces.

"I said to myself, 'I lived through the 1967 war. I lived through the [First] Intifada. I'm sure not going to be done in by some fish!'"

On a day in November, walking into Ramallah, I noticed that every one of the ironers' store windows had been blown out when an Israeli plane had bombed the Palestinian police station across the street. I must have been staring so hard at the police station the times I'd passed that I had never noticed the damage to the shop.

"Good heavens!" I said to the man at the counter. His twin brother worked there too; I'd found that out one day by asking him if he and his brother were "garlic," the Arabic word that remotely resembles the Arabic word "twins." I'd received a polite and straight-faced "Yes."

"When did this happen?" I asked, of the broken windows. "I never noticed."

"It's so we can greet people better," he answered. He stuck his right hand out past the remaining shards of glass in one shattered window opening, and his left hand through the broken-glass-studded metal frame of another, and made the motion of shaking hands. I handed the shirts in through the second window, nearest where the ironers were working.

"Very convenient for us," I said to them. "God willing, you are also happy with the situation?" They laughed as if I had made a very good joke.

Another day I met Sharif on the street. In addition to being someone who dresses especially well in times of trouble (which was, by then, all the time), Sharif usually had a trove of the most recent jokes and rumors of his people. To this anthropologist, psychologist, and writer, rumors serve as significant indicators of what is going on inside people's minds, adding dimensions to what is happening on the physical plane. Jokes, Sharif believes, show either what people hope for or what they fear. With official news channels limited as they are, word of mouth gets special credence and Palestinians spin narratives rich and varied as a patchwork quilt. If for one day I stayed home in an empty house and saw no one, I felt completely out of touch. Sharif, I learned, felt the same, only of course he could understand all of any joke anyone told, whereas I inevitably missed the punch line. Knowing he was out on this cloudy morning plucking at wisps of conversations flying by on the air, I greeted him and asked, as I usually did, if he had any new jokes to pass along.

"We are in a dry spell now," he said, "except for a couple of jokes that appeared at the very beginning of the Intifada." One of these was a Khalili joke.

Al Khalil is the Arabic name for Hebron, and there is an entire class of jokes in Palestine that are called Khalili. In these, the person from Hebron is slow, as in not very bright, and talks a little oddly, even though Khalilis are perfectly intelligent and quick, and have a reputation of being extremely hardworking. Even Khalilis tell Khalili jokes, usually beginning, "I am Khalili."

To understand the joke Sharif told that day, one had to know, as all Palestinians did, that a remarkable percentage—as high as ten percent—of Palestinian casualties during the previous two months were turning out to be brain-dead. When we spoke, rumor had it that in Hebron alone, seventy people had been hurt by soldiers or settlers in such a way as to render them brain-dead.

In Sharif's joke, a Khalili went to the checkpoint, got wounded, and was taken to the hospital. Waking up at last, he looked around the hospital room and asked the doctors: "Am I brain-dead?"

What interested Sharif about the joke was that the phenomenon of being "brain-dead"—which until a couple of months before would have been a medical term unfamiliar to most Palestinians, and certainly not a joking matter—had become so ordinary that the phrase was common parlance, and jokes made about it were understandable to everyone on the Palestinian street.

On the Israeli side, a particularly baroque word configuration was the government term "present absentees." These were Palestinians who were called "present" because they never left Palestine but also "absentees" because they were evicted from their homes and lands in 1948 or afterward.

Another significant phenomenon of which Palestinians took note was the divergence in language used by the two sides in the conflict to describe various events or objects. For instance, the enormous housing bloc Israel was constructing to separate Bethlehem and the rest of the West Bank from

Jerusalem was called by Palestinians "an illegal Israeli settlement on occupied land," but was referred to by the Israeli government and press as "a suburb of Jerusalem." In addition, Palestinians call the land just west of the Jordan River "the West Bank," and consider it part of Palestine; religious Jews call the same area "Judea and Samaria" and cite the Torah, the Jewish account of the Jews' early history, as evidence that their God gave the land to the Jews.

One of the most important differences lies in the ways the two sides describe the Palestinian actions that began in September after Sharon's visit to Al Haram al-Sharif, for the most prevalent terms are those that determine the way most of the world sees the situation. The actions collectively are referred to in the Palestinian media as an "intifada," or "uprising," as in "an uprising against repression." But Israeli media always refer to the situation as "war," making it sound more like a battle between two opposing armies. A number of us who were engaged in writing letters to the media invited Graham Usher, then Middle East correspondent for the *Economist*, to address us at Birzeit University to give us advice on approaching the media. "The events called by some 'intifada,' or 'uprising,' and by others 'war,' is in fact a war," he said. "They constitute a media war, a battle over language and a battle over who sets the agenda. The Israelis don't censor the media; rather, they are very good at creating an atmosphere of self-censorship, so that writers censor themselves. Do we talk about Israelis being shot at, or do we talk about Palestinians driving an occupying power from their land?"

෴

Gaza was always low on food and other supplies. On the news I heard that people in Gaza were running out of money for food and that the gas stations in Gaza were running out of petrol. Now, with all the killings and closures, parts of the West Bank, as well, began running out of food. One night two of the university guards, having worked on campus for ten days straight because they couldn't get to their homes in the villages around Birzeit, told me that their villages were running out of flour, rice, and sugar.

Israel began to lay mines around the Palestinian districts. Palestinians attempting to remove a roadblock the Israelis had put up discovered four anti-personnel land mines inside a Palestinian village. A week earlier, a land mine had blown up a ten-year-old boy in the Balata Refugee Camp in Nablus as he was on his way to the bakery.

෴

One morning, walking through Al-Bireh, and into the main circle, the *manara*, in Ramallah, I saw the bank was closed. That was odd, for a Tuesday. Looking up the street, I saw the rows of narrow, folding, iron shop doors still closed and locked—a sure sign of a strike of some kind. From the mosque came a somber recitation of the Qur'an, normally a sign that a Palestinian had been killed. But as far as I knew, no one from Ramallah or Al-Bireh had been killed in the bombardments of the night before. Others had been killed, in other places, and more houses near settlements in Gaza and the West Bank had been destroyed, and people hurt, but there had been no mention in the morning paper of any killing the night before so close to home.

Past the rosy, massive marble lions, newly installed around the central column in the center of the *manara*, Bilal was standing outside his locked news and stationery shop, selling the day's papers.

"Bilal," I asked, "who died?" It was beginning to rain again, lightly.

"Ah," he said, "it is because of the negotiations."

And then, of course, I realized. Arafat was in Washington for yet another round of negotiations with the Israeli government. But with so much land already lost, and with Israel unwilling to remove settlements or to allow Palestinians control over their own borders, people knew that anything Arafat agreed to could only bring more loss.

As Taisir might have put it, "What can be the outcome when the lion sits down with the mouse?"

Hence the signs of mourning.

It always baffled me that so many well-meaning Israelis did not see the absurdity of wishing that Palestinians would just keep quiet and do nothing, as more and more land was taken from them.

"Tell them we want peace!" a Jewish Israeli administrator at Beit Berl College implored me as I left to live in the West Bank. She had been kind to me in my time at the college, and I knew she meant well. But I also knew that what she meant was: "Tell the Palestinian people to keep quiet and not object or attack us," with the unstated implication: "while we do what we want." From New Jersey, a friend of mine wrote: "Why is it so hard for people to discern the difference between provocative violence and defensive violence? I wonder how the grandfathers of these re-settlers might have reacted to a headline in the January 1943 issue of some imaginary paper: 'Terrorist Jews from Warsaw Ghetto Launch Brutal Armed Attack. Many Germans Killed or Wounded.'"

How could anyone think that "peace" meant someone's lying still with the attacker's foot on her neck? With "peace" a code word for "submission," it was not surprising to me that Palestinians were using that word less and the word "justice" more.

Meanwhile, at the university, I got some training as a librarian so that I could work in our Institute of Women's Studies library. This was partly because our librarian, who lived in Jerusalem, was unable to reach the university due to closures, and partly because I was unable to enter Gaza to teach my students there.

One day the library received a message from our book distributor in Amman, Jordan:

We hope you all are well at Birzeit University.

We would like to mention to you that we have been notified by our shipper in the UK that all shipments to Palestine have been stopped. This is due to the fact that Israeli authorities are dumping all shipments to Palestine in an open-air storage area, and are refusing to clear them, while charging storage fees.

Royal Jordanian [Airlines] tried to bring shipments to

'Amman, and then send them across by truck, but this was stopped by Israeli authorities as well.

We have managed to send some books with passengers, but on a very small scale. The bulk of orders will have to wait until there is a change in the situation.

With our best regards . . .

Around that time, a young man whom I will call Fu'ad stopped by my office in the Institute of Women's Studies one day to help me with a computer problem. Bespectacled and soft-spoken, he looked like a quiet academic type. White-faced, thin, Fu'ad carried himself stiffly, as if he were in physical pain, although he must have been only in his early twenties.

Ignoring the chair I cleared for him, he stood, his drafting tool a slender wooden cross in his hand. When he was finished fixing my computer, he stayed to chat.

He told me that he had once spent two months in an Israeli prison. The reason the soldiers took him was that he was standing at the gate of his house when stone throwers ran by. The stone throwers escaped—and there, conveniently, was Fu'ad. One of the soldiers told him to come over and pick up one of the black masks that a stone thrower had left behind. Fu'ad did.

"Now get in the van," the soldier ordered.

Fu'ad did that too, and so began sixty days of beatings, being put in the sun for days on end, having to wear on his head one of the vomit-drenched sacks for which Israeli prisons are known, being interrogated, having a toenail pulled out with a pair of pliers. . . . During the interrogations,

Fu'ad told the soldiers to ask the spy he knew they had planted in his neighborhood whether he had been involved or not. The spy, whom everyone in the community knew to be a spy, had run by with the others, Fu'ad said, and had even spoken to Fu'ad.

"Ask him; he knows I did nothing," Fu'ad said.

After sixty days of this, Fu'ad was told he could leave the prison. They told him they had known from the start he had not been involved in the stone throwing.

"We just wanted to make sure that you never would be," they told him.

To that, Fu'ad answered: "Now you can know that I will be. One day I will be, I promise you." The soldier to whom he was talking then kicked him, literally, out the prison gates.

Twice, later, soldiers came to Fu'ad's home in the middle of the night.

"Thirty or so soldiers, on the roof, on the stairs . . . Thirty soldiers—for me!" Fu'ad said. He is shorter and slighter than I am and looks a lot more delicate.

Each time the soldiers came, the commander spoke to Fu'ad. The first time, about a year after he had been released from prison, the commander said, "We remember your words."

"I still mean them," Fu'ad said. "You have already done everything to me that you can do. The only thing you have left to do is kill me."

The second time, about a year after that, they came, again in the night, days after his wife had given birth to their first baby. The soldiers took pictures of the baby, of Fu'ad's wife, of Fu'ad and his family together.

"We remember your words," the commander said.

"I still mean them," said Fu'ad. Then the soldiers left. As far as I know he has not yet seen them since.

"It is not the time to talk," Fu'ad said a couple of times during his story.

I wasn't sure what he meant.

When he had finished his story, he added, in the Arab way: "I have bothered you." I assured him he hadn't. Before he left, he said, "There is too much pain. Everything I see, everything I hear—it is too much pain."

23: Dancing with Soldiers

While I was in Palestine, my father became seriously ill, and I began returning to the US for visits twice a year. I would stay with good friends in Berkeley and see friends there, make a quick trip north to friends in Mendocino County, and then spend time with my parents at their home in Arizona. More than once as it came time for me to leave the States again and return to Palestine, my spirits flagged and I waffled. I was exhausted, and the idea of returning to Palestine and war seemed overwhelming. The San Francisco Bay Area, in particular, seemed a place of bliss with its cool nights and clear air, its quiet streets, its abundance of food and water. The absence of soldiers.

But in the end, I always decided to go back. I cared too much, was too deeply involved, and felt too *alive* in the challenges Palestine offered to give up my life there. Each time I returned, the streets and buildings of Ramallah looked older, dustier, in worse repair, as if they and the atmosphere had been painted grayer in my time away.

Once, upon coming back from a visit to the US, I found that what Palestinians called "the situation," or "it," had gotten perceptibly worse in the three weeks I had been gone. Although it was barely past six o'clock in the evening the night I flew into Tel Aviv, there was no public transportation at all on the road between East Jerusalem, which Israel had annexed, and the rest of the West Bank. For the first time ever, I had to take a private taxi from East Jerusalem to my home in Al-Bireh. Some checkpoints had been added, others moved from one place to another. As we approached a second checkpoint, the inevitable Israeli soldier loomed out of the dark to wave us away, motioning that we should turn the car around and go back the way we had come. This meant we had to take the long way around—even though, when we reemerged, we would still be in the soldier's sight. Up the dark hill we traveled, along the narrow, rutted roads, rejoined the main road in plain sight of the same soldier who had waved us away, and continued on our way.

At home that night, Nablus Road, the main thoroughfare between the two major towns of Ramallah and Nablus in the north, ordinarily a cacophony of light and sound, with cars and trucks moving busily all through the night, was silent as death. Not a vehicle moved. The same enormous eighteen-wheeler that had been parked along the road for months before I left was parked there still; no business for that driver, for that company, in the weeks I had been away.

The noose had been drawn tighter still around the towns and villages of the West Bank, and the news in Gaza was just as grim. The economic stranglehold was doing its ugly job.

The next evening, Lamis called to welcome me back; I was amazed she could make the effort.

"We feel guilty," she said. "We drag around and do a tenth of what we are able."

"And the students?" I asked. "How are they?"

"I had five," she answered. "Rema had five—out of twenty-five. After the bomb went off in Netanya, they just can't get here. Islah says hers are fine, although she only had eight to start. But those who are here are not thinking; they are not working."

"And Eileen's?"

"Eileen says hers are dead bodies. How is your mother?" Always, first concern was the mother.

It was not until I repeated this conversation years later and heard my friend remark on Lamis's reference to "dead bodies" that these words struck me as an interesting choice to employ under these circumstances.

The next day, in the light, when I could see the eyes of people I knew on the streets and in the shops, receive their greetings and absorb their humorous shrugs when I asked them how they were, my spirits lifted, as they invariably did each time I returned to Palestine. To be in the midst of this situation, and to know not only how it felt at the time, but to be able to imagine all the future repercussions, and still to laugh, and move about—that people could do this each day won my admiration.

I asked my students how they were doing. At first, they seemed almost taken aback by the question. This was life, wasn't it? What was I asking?

"We're used to it," they said at first. But then answers came.

"I feel as if I am losing control of whole parts of my life," said Shahnaz. "I miss the women I work with in the camp in Bethlehem. I miss the men and women I work with in Nablus. I worked hard for the whole last year on those projects, and now I can't get to them. I am afraid I am going to lose them."

"We're in a huge prison," said Muhammad, another student. "And we can't get out."

Sharif told me that a friend of his, who lived even nearer to the Psagot settlement than I did, and who therefore heard the nightly tank assaults with yet more deafening clarity, had a trick to get his children to go to sleep each night. He would turn on the television as loud as it would go, showing the most violent US film he could find. Then he told the children that everything they heard was coming from the TV.

The front pages of the Palestinian newspapers carried photographs almost daily of women holding up their hands in a futile effort to halt the bulldozers in the act of demolishing their homes. Or photographs of women standing beside the ruins of their homes, both arms stretched wide to the sky, calling on God to witness the destruction, their loss. In the background, children picked through the ruins for broken furniture and kitchen pots. On television you heard their screams and cries. The planted fields of Gaza became a wasteland.

There was so much death. I was reminded how we used to say when thinness became the fashion, "Inside every fat person is a thin person wanting to get out." Instead, I felt like one of the Russian painted dolls, each a nest of many dolls, packed one within the other, each smaller than the one containing it, until the last—the solid, smallest doll. When I looked or listened inside myself, I would find not a thin person wanting to get out, but the tiniest, most hidden doll, screaming to be heard.

At one point, my students were reading about Fordism, the assembly-line production system that keeps workers doing the same thing, over and over, year in and year out, as each puts together one part of a machine—the first, a Ford car. In class, I mentioned how in Palestine, with no huge factories and where all companies and organizations were new and relatively small, there might be more room for creativity and individual initiative than in many jobs in the United States.

"Well, I certainly do the same thing over and over," Muhammad, countered. Studying to be a journalist, he was working in the Palestinian Authority's Ministry of Information, and he chafed at the way the news was delivered.

"Each day we write: 'So many killed, so many wounded, so many eyes shot out, so many funerals held, so many olive trees and houses bulldozed, so many dunams of land swept [razed by Israeli bulldozers, often armored] or confiscated.'"

"So Muhammad *does* have Fordism," quipped Shahnaz.

∽

Everywhere I went, Palestine was in distress: Hebron, in the south; Bethlehem, Jericho, Nablus, and other more central cities; the Golan Heights, on the Syrian border, in the north. Towns in the desert, in the Negev where the nomadic Bedouin were forced to settle. A miserable Bedouin encampment high up on a barren, dusty hill overlooking a freeway. Inside Israel, more than four hundred Palestinian villages from which Palestinians had been expelled by force or terror in 1948, still in ruins or inhabited by Israeli Jews. Even in all this, Gaza stood out, with one of the highest population densities on the planet. Its refugee camps, where children walked barefoot amid the dust between walls of makeshift homes, so close together cars cannot pass, and where sewage runs in the streets, huddled in stunning contrast with the Mediterranean's azure beauty just beyond.

Refugee camps throughout the West Bank and Gaza—Balata in Nablus, Dheisheh in Bethlehem, Khan Younis and Jabalya in Gaza, Al Am'ari in Ramallah—are not hard to distinguish from other towns and villages in Palestine. Despite the fact that the dwellings are not tents, as you might expect from the word "camp," and though their appearance does not indicate the transitory nature one associates with a camp—many had by then existed for more than sixty years—a camp is unmistakably a camp. Houses are smaller, closer together, poorer-looking. Streets are narrower, with few cars and few roads wide enough to hold them.

There are fewer stores in the dense cluster of living spaces. There are more people of all ages, and especially more children, in the streets than in other neighborhoods. The air is dustier, more polluted; the streets, even if they are paved somewhere underneath, are often covered with sandy sediment, as if the very environment is trying to cover up the camps to put them out of mind. In a camp one does not find the sparkling contrast of color that characterizes other parts of Palestine—silvery green of olive tree, deeper fig or grape-leaf green, rosy pointed rooftops atop golden stone. . . . There are fewer trees, flowers, and growing vegetables. No roses in May, no crimson poppies in March or April. A camp, with little room for the prized Palestinian garden, looks all one tone—a dusty beige. The rooftops are flat—the traditional, cheapest style, useful for hanging clothes. The buildings are mostly concrete, uniformly smooth, washed to a pale gray. Ribbed metal sheets, plastic, or even scraps of cloth are used to shelter chickens, sheep, and goats.

All the years I lived in Palestine, Palestinians were participating in peaceful protests that called for an end to the military occupation. They demonstrated against the demolition of their homes, the arrest of civilians for political activity or for no reason at all, the torture of adult and children prisoners, and restrictions on movement, as well as the killings of unarmed civilians and "targeted assassinations" of anyone Israel decided might be planning armed resistance. Farmers unable to work their fields because of attacks by Israeli settlers or confiscation of their lands by the Israeli military demonstrated against the loss of their lands and destruction of their crops and olive trees. Villagers held community workdays to replace waterlines destroyed by Israeli tanks. As their portion of Palestine shrank, Palestinians demonstrated against the building of new settlements and new bypass roads for settler use on West Bank land.

In northern Israel, Syrians caught on the wrong side of the border when Israel seized the Golan Heights still live in towns with no access to relatives and friends in Syria. On a Friday, you can see parents and grandparents holding up small children on the Syrian side of the "no-man's-land," calling with handheld loudspeakers to family members living in towns in the annexed Golan Heights. Faintly, their voices waft across the divide from the Syrian city of Quneitra, where Syrians picnic among the ruins of the houses that were their homes until Israel destroyed the city in 1967.

In time, Palestinians began holding peaceful demonstrations across the West Bank. They protested construction of the enormous structure by means of which Israel is cementing the encirclement of Palestinian areas. This structure is an elaborate system of fences, trenches, patrol roads, barbed wire, and concrete slabs, and, in places, a twenty-six-foot-high concrete wall that Palestinians call "the Racial Segregation Wall," or "the Apartheid Wall." The wall, called by Israel a "security fence," takes the place of the soldiers, piles of dirt, concrete dividers and the smaller trenches and checkpoints used up to then to corral Palestinians and to separate them from Jewish-inhabited areas. The wall dips well into Palestinian lands outside the "Green Line" considered by near-unanimous international agreement to demarcate the State of Israel. It snakes around Palestinian farmers' lands and aquifers, including them in the expanding Israeli state. Palestinians, farmers working their lands, children attending school, must pass through guarded gates at times determined by Israel. When the wall is completed, it will render permanent all the various means Israel has used to separate communities of Palestinians from one another and from the land and other resources Israel continues to confiscate from the West Bank.

For years, foreigners collectively referred to as "internationals" living in Palestine have joined with Palestinians to demonstrate against all the human rights violations. Although I took part in demonstrations to open the road to the university, it was not until May 2001 that I began to participate regularly in actions against settlement building and construction of the wall, sometimes in other towns or villages. A group of us set up tents and slept for a few days in a field across from the Palestinian police headquarters when we heard it would be bombed. Palestinian families invited us to come and sleep in their houses in Beit Jala and Hebron, hoping our Western presences would serve as "human shields" from attack by settlers and soldiers.

We stayed the night in Hebron—to me, the most unpleasant and dangerous of the regions under the Israeli military occupation. There, Jewish settlers occupy areas right in the middle of the city, many inhabiting the upper stories above the now-closed Palestinian market, where they throw their garbage down onto the Palestinians living below. In the mornings we walked Palestinian children to school to guard them from stones thrown by settlers. Sometimes Palestinians from inside Israel came to demonstrate in the West Bank, and, increasingly, Israeli Jews came too.

Neighbors and others gathered to help families rebuild houses destroyed, sometimes more than once, by Israeli army bulldozers, enormous beasts cleverly clad in armor. One sunny Friday morning, a group of Israeli and foreign volunteers met on a grassy knoll where the same Palestinian home had been destroyed three different times as the Israeli state attempted to take the land to enable expansion of the Hebrew University in Jerusalem. Led by the owner of the house, family members and volunteers, organized by Jeff Halper, American-born co-founder of the Israeli Committee Against House Demolitions, set about rebuilding the house for the fourth time.

Once, a call came for supporters to visit a Palestinian family whose members had participated in a demonstration against the building of a new settlement on village land. From the Palestinian home, we could see the settlement, just across the valley. To punish the family and to prevent further demonstrations from the villagers, Israeli soldiers had taken over the family home—while the family tried to continue living in it. Soldiers occupied the basement of the house, along with the upper story, where the eldest son and his new bride were to have moved. Village children laughed and called to the single red-faced Israeli soldier who prowled the ground below.

One morning on a day off, Palestinians were joined by internationals living in the West Bank and a couple of busloads of Israeli Jews to demonstrate against a settlement built on village farmland. The little grove of trees in the center of the village was calm as people arrived and greeted one another quietly, waiting for the mayor of the village to signal that the demonstration might begin. A few women sat talking amongst themselves on the stairways of houses framing the village center; unlike women in many villages, these women were not joining the demonstration that day. Children, of course, were omnipresent; they could not be kept away. Young boys milled about excitedly, anxious for the demonstration to begin.

Then a couple of kids up on a roof called urgently to the others and pointed down the hill. I joined the children on the rooftop, and my heart sank when I saw, on the road that ran through the valley between the village and the hill settlement, a long line of army jeeps and soldiers. More frightening was the sight of settlers armed with clubs and guns, striding down the hill from the settlement. Other settlers joined them in cars, coming along the road toward the military vehicles. Soldiers were always bad news. But settlers, who tended to be full of rage, and who carried guns and used them, too, were uncontrollable, not answerable to any military authority, and hence more dangerous still.

That day, as we waited for the group to get together, I was afraid, and so I made myself go in front as we all headed down the hill. Meanwhile, some of us did our best to get the kids to stay behind us as we descended. Unsuccessfully, as usual, the adults instructed them not to throw stones.

As we walked slowly down the dirt road, the soldiers began shouting at us in Hebrew. Even to those of us who did not understand Hebrew, the message was clear: "Stop where you are! Stay away!"

We kept walking. Settlers began yelling at us. Soldiers raised their guns in our direction. We walked right up to them, whereupon they began shoving us, shouting, waving their guns, and arresting people. Arik Ascherman, American-born Israeli Reform rabbi and co-founder of Rabbis for Human Rights, handed me the keys to his car as he was being pushed into an Israeli military vehicle, asking me to give them to his wife. Then a burly blond soldier appeared and advanced toward me, so I began backing up the hill. He wasn't moving fast enough through the roots and underbrush to reach me, so I kept backing away, darting one way and another, as he chased me up the hill. All the time, partly through nervousness, I kept up a steady patter of words directed his way.

"Wouldn't you like some water?" I asked. "Why do you keep Palestinians from their land? You look like my youngest brother, a nice guy. . . . Don't you think Palestinians have the right to farm their land?" Skittering back and forth, he moving forward, I backward, we danced our way up the hill, until he finally gave up and went back down.

Because there were so many Jewish Israelis among us, it was a better day than most. As long as Jews were present, no one shot at us. But after soldiers had disbursed the crowd, back down on the road we had left, one of them shot and wounded a Palestinian youth. Unaware of this, the rest of us foreigners climbed into the Israeli bus and followed those who had been arrested up to the settlement to see if we could get them released. It was then I turned around in my seat and realized that one of the Israelis among us was Tanya Reinhardt, activist, academic, and author, whose writings—and whose courage—I greatly admired. Like her former teacher, Noam Chomsky, she was a linguist and a longtime critic of Israeli policy toward Palestinians.

She was tall, lean, and unassuming. For all the steel she showed in confronting her own government and people, I felt from her a vulnerability and a gentleness that surprised and touched me. I asked what she thought the Israeli government wanted out of all this and was taken aback when she answered, "a regional war." Israel was already making war on the entire Palestinian civilian population; now it wanted war with its other Arab neighbors too? But I had no time to ask for an explanation: Tanya looked dangerously flushed, and almost immediately she left with her friend, apologizing for being affected by the sun. In 2006, she left Israel. I felt I'd lost a kindred spirit when I learned she died in New York a few months later.

There were also times when it was possible to speak to

Israeli soldiers in somewhat calmer situations. A few were willing to talk when I passed them leaflets printed in Hebrew. I could not read them but had it on good authority that these pamphlets were calls from the Jewish Israeli organization Yesh Gvul (There Is a Limit), urging soldiers to become conscientious objectors rather than participate in the military occupation of the Occupied Palestinian Territories.

Soldiers were relatively approachable, too, at checkpoints in those days, although they became much less accessible in the more sophisticated checkpoints later guarded by metal, concrete, and bulletproof glass. One rainy evening, just at dusk, sitting in a *service* a half mile or so before the Kalandia checkpoint in Ramallah, I saw two Israeli military jeeps parked by the side of the road. In the distance, in the field beyond the road, partly hidden by the jeeps, Israeli soldiers were taking their places in the fading light.

"Three, four, five . . ." Another passenger in the *service* counted them aloud as we all stared. Planting themselves by rock boulders, their army fatigues and helmets the color of the darkening field, the soldiers soon would not be visible at all. When the children came out from the refugee camp, unknowing, to throw a stone or two, the boulders would grow dark arms, holding guns, and shoot them.

One rainy morning at the same checkpoint, I arrived to find that soldiers had blocked the higher, drier lane, leaving open only the lower lane, by then virtually a river, through which the cars, out of necessity, passed at a crawl. Elderly Palestinian women in their long embroidered dresses, without raincoats or rain boots, waded across the checkpoint. Among the vehicles was an ambulance, crawling like the rest. Getting out of the *service* I was in, I ploughed through the water to the ambulance and asked the driver if he was trying to get to a hospital. Yes, he said, so I walked up to one of the soldiers at the checkpoint, pointed to the ambulance, and asked if it could go through the checkpoint without waiting any longer.

Finally one of the soldiers said yes, the ambulance could cross the center divider and pass through the checkpoint on the other side of the road, where no cars were being allowed to pass. As turned out quite often in my efforts to help, by the time I got back to tell the driver, the ambulance was almost at the checkpoint, and soon after, went straight on through.

I returned to the soldiers and asked one of them politely if I could move the orange plastic barriers to one side so that the cars could move along at a more normal speed on the higher ground.

"I need to watch them," the young soldier explained to me.

"But you're not watching them," I said, as politely as I could.

"I am."

"But you're not! In fact, for the past fifteen minutes, you've been looking at me," I answered, again politely.

"I'm a soldier," the soldier said.

"Yes," I said, sorry to haul out the timeworn image, "but Hitler's army was filled with soldiers. What is the sense in this?" I gestured to the road, the waiting line of cars.

"Should a soldier always do what someone else says? Now we look at World War II and we say no."

"That was different," the young man said.

"No," I said, "it wasn't. Not at all. It was just the same."

Changing tacks, the soldier asked me, "Where are you from?"

"The United States of America," I said.

"Aha!" he said. "What about Vietnam?"

"Yes," I said, "exactly. It was wrong. It was a crime. We should never have been there. Just like you."

Uncomfortable suddenly, the soldier tried to back out of the argument. He was much younger than I was, and English was not his first language, and so, except for the gun, I had him at a disadvantage.

"No," he backtracked. "Vietnam wasn't the same at all."

At that point, I lifted one of the orange plastic roadblocks to clear the second lane. Two soldiers shoved me away. As I waded through the rain the way I'd come, a driver waiting in the line called out to me: "Thank you for your solidarity!"

A few months later, I could no longer get by with that kind of intervention. Increasingly, soldiers became separated from the people they controlled, ensconced in new, fortified concrete checkpoint structures. As tensions grew, they became far less likely to engage in conversations, except ones they initiated:

"*Huwiya!*"

"*No!*"

"*Go back!*"

24: "I'll Die with a Gun or without One"

Meanwhile, the Israeli military was destroying on a regular basis the road linking Ramallah to Birzeit University, the village of Birzeit, and some twenty other villages. In the daytime, Palestinians filled in the road with dirt; at night, Israeli machinery tore it up again.

One day two tanks were parked up on the hillside, behind a house. I walked up the hill to get a better look at the tanks, after asking permission from the group of young Palestinian men standing on the veranda of the house. By the time I came back down, the woman of the house had made coffee, which she brought out on a tray and served me in a little cup, then sat and drank with me. People were flowing up and down the road on foot. One woman, who had been brought by car, had to be carried by stretcher the length of the ruined road, until she finally reached an ambulance and was taken away to the hospital. Some young boys, no older than junior high school age, threw stones at the Israeli armored jeep that had parked itself in the middle of the road. When the boys did that, the armored vehicle zoomed up toward them and shot at them, sometimes bullets, sometimes tear gas.

Adults trying to use the road scolded the children as if they were their own: "No stone throwing!" they called. "Are you out of your minds? There are people walking here!" The boys would stop for a while, then start again.

At the Ramallah end of the road, older boys were shoveling a pile of dirt, filling in a hole the Israeli bulldozer had made. Since there was only one armored car, it had to rush from one end of the blocked-off section, to shoot at the boys filling in the trench, to the other end, to be a target for the stones the younger boys were throwing and then to shoot at them. Since the armored car was running up and down monopolizing the center of the road, we all had to walk by it to pass. I selected a quiet moment to pass around the back of the vehicle. The rear doors were open, and through them, as I passed, I saw two soldiers, one eating from a rather large tub of yogurt. It must have been break time.

"Want some yogurt?" he called in English. Sensing that the offer was not heartfelt, I did not respond, whereupon the other soldier drew his revolver and pointed it at my head. I had seen him do that to a young woman who had passed near him just before me. I looked at him, then away, thinking the disgust I felt for his behavior was probably showing on my face and might be just the inducement his trigger finger needed. I turned away, furious. With my light-colored hair and non-Semitic features, I was pretty sure he wouldn't shoot me. Killing foreigners was bad press. But the young woman? Palestinians were shot every day. What did it do to a person to know any moment might be her last?

On this particular day, there were many more of us, including journalists and photographers, as Birzeit University had extended an open invitation to the community to come and demonstrate against the closure. Speeches were made by famous people, among them Hanan 'Ashrawi, perched up on one of the mounds, but their voices could hardly be heard. Then, in the distance, moving along the road from the direction of Ramallah, we could see a miniature bulldozer, called a bobcat, coming our way. A Palestinian contractor must have bought it to use in a construction project in hope of better times. The young man driving might have been a member of his crew.

As the bobcat shoved the first blockade from the road, it was greeted with mighty cheers and adorned, on the spot, with posters and Palestinian flags. Then, to more cheers, and carrying the boys who had jumped on top or crammed themselves inside the tiny cab with the driver, the intrepid machine made its way on down and then up the winding road to the next, larger blockade. Down off the steep hillside, a man walked his horse, plowing the flat red land, back and forth.

The armored car elected not to take on the newcomer, and for a few moments, it was a quiet, bucolic scene. Then,

Israeli soldiers in the tanks up the hill began firing canister after canister of tear gas at the bobcat and at those of us standing nearby. Valiantly, the little bulldozer kept trying to fill in the trench, but the driver's eyes were streaming tears from the gas trapped in his plastic-covered cab. All our eyes were doing the same. Someone offered me the usual antidote, a piece of onion, and a young woman hopped out of an ambulance and offered around new, high-tech anti-tear gas devices consisting of pieces of cotton soaked in perfume.

By then, in defeat, the baby bulldozer had turned around and was heading back toward Ramallah, a thin streak of tear gas billowing up from it like smoke. But a good start had been made, and the boys continued clearing the road by hand, until, at last, another ambulance, first in the line of vehicles, could get through, and made its way down the road, up the other side, over another damaged part of the road, and on into Ramallah. Other vehicles followed. We knew the opening was temporary, but still it was a rare good sight to see the vehicles moving continuously along the road, unblocked now, their passage marked only by occasional puffs of tear gas landing near them.

The problem, of course, was not one road, but the entire network of them. Even if we could pass through each blockade, over or around it, the journey to the university took so long the effort would be meaningless. Earlier, in town, someone had pointed to the jewelry store across the street.

"You see that store?" he asked me. "The man who

works there comes each day from Nablus. He gets here at about ten in the morning, and at one o'clock in the afternoon, it's time for him to start home again. The rest of his time is spent getting here and getting home. The cost is exorbitant. If each *service* driver charges enough to feed his family, to go the shorter distances from one roadblock to another, the passenger ends up paying at least double. No one can afford it. So you will all go to the demonstration, and the tanks will eventually fire, and a couple of kids will get killed, and that will be the end of that.

"When we see this," he said, "and we see that even a person who has never thrown a stone can get killed on his way home from school, it makes us think, 'Well, I'll die with a gun or without one, either way. I might as well get a gun.'"

Some young Palestinian men did obtain guns—and began using them on Israeli soldiers when they could reach them. Guns had poured into the Occupied Territories with the creation of the oversized police force engendered by the Oslo Accords, with the expectation that the Palestinian Authority would use them to keep the Palestinian people in line. If Israeli soldiers were going to pull out of even small parts of the Occupied Territories, the thinking went, some armed force would have to take their place.

Just how these guns ended up in the hands of some of the young men of the Second Intifada is not generally known. Some of the young men shooting at Israeli soldiers were probably "security" men in civilian clothing who were already armed. One story was that Israel allowed Arafat to arm civilian supporters to help protect him from assorted enemies and dissidents. There were also rumors of covert operations involving the clandestine smuggling of arms from inside Israel.

This made the Second Intifada very different from the first, when Palestinian youth had done no more than throw stones. The First Intifada had involved widespread and rigorous community organizing at the grassroots level, as Palestinians tried to provide for themselves the products and services they were denied and, in doing so, to lessen their dependence on the Israeli economy. But the appearance during the Second Intifada of youth militias willing to use guns against Israelis troubled Palestinians who were older and wiser than the youths using the guns.

"Great," Rema said one day. "Arm all these guys and then what will we have—a generation of thugs?"

To the extent that the Second Intifada was an armed effort, it was not a popular uprising at all. Palestinians had already tried every nonviolent means of resistance to the occupation during the First Intifada—demonstrating, and organizing their own schools, social services, and businesses. I had assumed a second intifada would mean another great community organizing effort.

"Why aren't most people doing anything?" I asked Fadwa and her friends. They just looked at me. They had not initiated this intifada. Picking off individual Israeli soldiers with guns was not the way they wanted to go about trying to make a better life for their people. Nor did they have the heart to start all over again trying to build an economic and social service structure parallel to the Israeli one on which they were dependent.

With the First Intifada, Palestinians had been hopeful. But that uprising had ended with the Oslo Accords, after which the situation had only grown worse for Palestinians. Now there was no hope to be had. So while the *shabab* fired their guns at the soldiers guarding the enormous new settlement construction in Gilo, outside Bethlehem, their elders worried, and continued doing the best they could in their own lives.

৶

Meanwhile, the Ramallah-Birzeit Road was gone again. The afternoon after the bobcat had opened the road, Israeli armored bulldozers had come and torn up all our work. Littered on the ground were two types of tear gas canisters, and bullets, also of two types—steel with the hard thin coating of rubber, and cartridges from the "live" ammunition. Along with these was an empty bucket labeled in red letters TEAR GAS CANISTERS UN 1700 and the word TOXIC, all in English, along with a nice rendering of a skull and crossbones next to the words DANGER: FLAMMABLE. Also on the bucket, in addition to a Tel Aviv address for the Israeli Department of Defense, was written FEDERAL LABORATO-RIES, INC., AN ARMOUR HOLDINGS, INC., COMPANY, 1855 SOUTH LOOP, CASPER, WY. But we'd already known what country was supplying many of the weapons, as well as most of the funds, Israel was using to maintain the occupation.

Because of the US-made F-16s and helicopters, along

with the $3 billion the US was giving Israel each year, I was sometimes asked by strangers, "Do you see what America has done?"

Ashamed, I could answer only, "Yes. I see what America has done." Belonging as I did to two worlds—one suffering, the other enabling, even supporting, the suffering—I did not feel consoled when Palestinians assured me, "It's not you who is responsible. It's your government." Still, I felt, if not guilty, at least responsible. I lived in a democracy, didn't I? So if "we the people" were not responsible, then who was? It took me years more to conclude that a nation that selected its leaders on the basis of how much money they could raise was not a democracy at all.

In the end, tanks, armored cars, and armed soldiers had closed the road from Ramallah to Birzeit so many times that only those who absolutely had to traveled it at all. Even if people were allowed to pass along the road, they were arrested, humiliated, and hassled to the extent that they were no longer willing to try. I stopped trying to teach at the university and instead taught my students wherever I could find them.

I taught at a girls' secondary school, the Friends' Boys' School, or at the British Council in Ramallah. For students who could reach Jerusalem, I still taught at a women's center there, and I was still teaching a few others in their homes in Beit Jala, near Bethlehem. Gaza I could never reach, and I could hardly stand to talk to my students there. If hearing their voices had not been such a joy, I wouldn't have been able to make myself call at all.

"Do you have enough to eat?" I asked them. "Do you have cooking gas?" One student, who lived in the refugee camp in the southern Gaza Strip, told me once when I called that she and her family had left their home and gone to stay with her brother, whose house was somewhat farther—for the moment, at least—from the areas that were usually bombed.

"We are bombed every day, Chivvis," she said to me.

"And every night?" I asked.

"And every night." This was the student who, with her friends, used to dress up like an old woman in order to be able to deliver food to areas that were completely cut off.

"Are you still doing that?" I asked her. No, they had had to stop. There was too much shooting; they could no longer get through.

☙

After the summer break, when I returned from visiting my parents in the United States, I heard from a friend who had participated in a number of peaceful demonstrations in my absence: "First it was tear gas and mostly rubber bullets. Now it's just live fire." She told me stories of tear gassings and shootings, of soldiers' increased brutality at nonviolent protests toward Palestinians, internationals, and Israeli activists, and of students and employees walking over the mountains to evade the "flying checkpoints" that had sprung up while they had been at work or in school.

Yata, a village near Hebron, was sealed off by the Israeli military while Israeli soldiers forced some thousand

Palestinians to leave their homes, dozens of which they then demolished. Villagers' wells were filled in with dirt in the rural area between Yata and Jibna, and the entire area was declared a "military zone," giving Israeli soldiers carte blanche to destroy or oust anything or anyone within it. Land mines were placed and exploded on a farmer's land, which was then declared a "military outpost" closed to Palestinians. Palestinian children were beaten unconscious by guards in Israeli prisons.

Settlers, too, were bolder in their attacks on Palestinians and their lands. Israeli occupants of the settlements built in the West Bank burned farmers' fields in two villages outside Nablus, while soldiers prevented firefighters and ambulances from entering the area. Settlers shattered windows of homes with stones while Palestinians were trapped inside under curfew. I heard the stories from my friends, then found the documentation in news accounts written by people who were there. It was worse than anything I had imagined, worse than any other time I had returned. The road downhill seemed steeper now.

"If they succeed in getting rid of Arafat," said a Palestinian colleague of mine, "we will see massacres, the like of which we have never seen before. And yet how many can they kill—five thousand, ten thousand, fifty thousand? And if even one Palestinian is left, that one will become more, and when that happens, the whole struggle will begin again. This way solves nothing. And next time, unlike now, Palestinians will want the whole thing—not just the

West Bank, Gaza, and East Jerusalem. Next time, they will be fighting for it all."

∽

On September 11, 2001, the US was attacked. I learned of it when a colleague came into my office one evening when we were both working late. On my computer, he and I watched as the New York towers puffed smoke and fell, over and over again.

I was astounded. Since before its founding, the nation that would become the United States of America had attacked other peoples and other countries, but never before had I seen my country attacked. And the means was so dramatic. Someone had planned well to capture the attention of the world.

Certainly, the lives of the thousands who died that day were no cause for rejoicing. I learned that among them many were working class, and many others who'd had no power to abuse, and my sympathies were with them. But at the time, watching the towers fall, stand, and fall again, as if the cameras themselves were stuck with surprise, I fervently hoped the event would enable United States citizens to recognize what our country inflicts on others. I hoped that Americans would finally learn the terrible price they had to pay for all the unjust wars—social, economic, political, ideological—their government, armed forces, and corporations were fighting across the globe. *Perhaps, I thought, Americans and their government will learn that there is a limit to the bullying and killing they can do. Perhaps*

*they will decide there is a better way to live among the other
nations in the world than with arrogance and greed.*

I could not have been more mistaken. Within the
month, the US began bombing Afghanistan, and after that,
ugly anti-Muslim, anti-Arab rhetoric became only more
rabid, threats uglier, war technology more inventive.

The US invasion of Afghanistan touched us, too, in
Palestine. Word went round that Israel would probably
take advantage of the fact that US attention was focused
elsewhere to crack down even harder on Palestinians. This
rumor came true.

The 2002 New Year began badly. I arrived at the airport
in Tel Aviv after spending the Christmas break with my
mother. Up to then, I had had no problem using the airport,
which was, of course, totally under Israeli control. But this
time, as I attempted to pass through immigration, I was
told that I would not be able to enter Israel.

"I don't want to go to Israel, only to Palestine," I assured
the soldiers, but it did no good. The only airport in Israel or
Palestine—since Israel had destroyed the new Palestinian
airport in Gaza—had been declared off-limits to residents
of the West Bank or Gaza.

Israel had not announced the new ruling before
beginning to enforce it. Anyone trying to enter Israel was
being put on a return flight to whatever country he or she
had just left, and told to return to Gaza through Egypt
and to the West Bank through Jordan. The airlines had to
absorb the cost of returning all the travelers to the country
they had just left, while Palestinian travelers had to pay for

one-way flights from those countries to Egypt or Jordan.

Those of us who had to wait for flights out of Israel were confined at the airport in two little rooms, one for women, one for men, both serving as temporary jails. When I entered the women's cell, I found 'Afaf, the sister of my student 'Andalib from Gaza. She had just flown in from Stockholm and was being held until the next flight out.

By now it was the middle of the night. I was told I could make one telephone call, and only to the US Embassy, from a phone in the office of the jail. But when the soldier wasn't looking, I dialed Muna's number instead and spoke to her as if I were leaving a message at the US Embassy. Muna understood. She called Rema, who called the well-known champion of Palestinian legal rights, Lea Tsemel, who then called me via another cellmate's cell phone when I was back in the jail. Lea already ranked as a hero of mine; she is one of a handful of Jewish Israeli men and women I met who have dedicated their lives to working for Palestinians' rights despite threats and harassment from Jews who despise them for the work they are doing. Since I had thoughtlessly tried to enter Israel on a Thursday, Lea had to wait until offices opened again on Sunday, after Shabbat, the Jewish weekend, to make arrangements for my release.

'Afaf, whose company I had been enjoying, was not so lucky. Early the next morning, she was put on a plane and flown back to Stockholm. From there she had to pay her own way to fly to Egypt and enter Gaza through Rafah. The other woman left as well. I was alone in the cell when a short, red-haired female soldier paid me a visit and informed me that if I refused to get on a plane back to Toronto, where my plane had stopped en route to Israel, I would be put in an Israeli prison. She began to describe it, but I must have looked interested, because she threatened me instead with having to pay for a policeman to fly from the US to accompany me back to the United States. That did scare me.

In the end, Lea Tsemel saved me by arguing that Birzeit University required my English teaching skills. But this did not happen before I was actually put on a plane, then taken off again because I had a migraine and was vomiting, and was declared "too sick to fly" by an Air Canada pilot to whom I will be grateful for the rest of my life. After three nights in the jail, an officer opened the door, handed me my knapsack, and, without offering reason or apology, announced that I was free to go. After that, Israeli immigration officers made moves to hold me each time I passed their way, and I had to ask Lea to help me every time I wanted to leave or reenter Palestine.

From time to time during those first years I lived in Palestine, one or another of us would say, "Well, it can't get any worse than this." But by the end of the first week in March 2002, we had stopped saying that, and we never have again.

25: THE SPRING INVASIONS, 2002

During March and April 2002, as people had feared, while the world was watching US warplanes pound Afghanistan, Israel began attacking cities, towns, and refugee camps in Gaza and the West Bank with F-16 fighter jets, helicopters, and tanks. In Ramallah and Al-Bireh, we heard the rumors before the tanks came. They entered Ramallah on March 12, and immediately, the entire population was placed under curfew. Stores were made to close. No Palestinian walked or drove along the streets. Enormous, ugly, dark-colored tanks ground up and down Ramallah's hills, leaving deep tread marks in the asphalt. With them came large armored vehicles that looked to me like little tanks, called "half tracks," just as ugly but with a smaller gun on top, along with a fleet of faster-moving armored jeeps. Israeli soldiers broke into houses and apartment buildings in Ramallah and its environs, packing forty or more residents into a single room for days, often without use of a toilet. Meanwhile, the same thing was taking place all over the West Bank and Gaza. The troops invaded an area, pulled out—"redeployed," the media called it—only to go right back in again. Meanwhile, Israeli troops were assassinating Palestinian activists and civilians in missile attacks and raids, both in daytime and overnight; and Palestinian suicide bombers, fighters, and a lone sniper killed Israeli soldiers and civilians in attacks on checkpoints, a hotel, and a restaurant.

The refugee camps, we all knew, were in the worst danger—tightly packed, harder to escape from, and easier to surround and besiege. The army always targeted the camps, figuring, I suppose, that those who had lost the most and now had least to lose would be most likely to resist invasion. Al Am'ari was the camp I was most familiar with, since it was close to home. An Irish activist had told me earlier that week that she and a young Palestinian woman had been able to drag wounded men from the camp to the closest ambulances outside. For foreigners, this seemed a logical task. So I walked out of my house and headed for Al Am'ari, gambling on all the superficialities for protection— my age and gender, the dishwater-brown hair I had always hated. The year I had lived in Israel, I had regularly been mistaken as Jewish; I could pass.

Anger, I discovered, bested fear. For the first three days of the invasion, I walked past the tanks, the armored personnel carriers, the armored jeeps, beneath the guns of the snipers on our rooftops and in houses Israeli soldiers had taken over. No one even shot at me. One of my strategies was to avoid looking at the Israeli military vehicles as I approached them or as they approached me. If I didn't even see them, how could I do them harm? Also, if I didn't look, I wouldn't see if a bullet or a shell came at me. I tried to look benign.

In Al Am'ari there were substantial clusters of children in the streets. With housing so crowded in a refugee camp, it's virtually impossible to keep children indoors if something exciting is taking place. And something exciting was, if not happening, then at least anticipated: the Israeli military often warned it would invade, but then, instead of carrying out the threat right away, soldiers would wait, then pounce when no one was expecting it. The morning I was in the camp, though there had been warnings, there were no shootings or house invasions. Later, when I was not standing around to lend a hand, there were many dead and wounded. I was never in the right place at the right time.

Much later, I was in the camp when Israeli armored personnel carriers drove through the streets, ordering, in what was even to my ears pretty poor Arabic, all Palestinian males between the ages of sixteen and forty-five to gather at the United Nations school, one of a number of UN buildings the Israeli military took over in various refugee camps during these invasions. Children in the camp showed me where some two hundred men were sitting on concrete stairs across the street from the school. A soldier up on the broken school gate pointed a gun at the men, while several other soldiers hid behind sandbags stacked up on a wall painted with children's drawings in bright colors—pointed mountains with sunbursts peeking between them and childish renderings of the Dome of the Rock.

Upon being called, each of the Palestinian men, after opening his jacket to show he had no gun or suicide belt, walked past the colored drawings and disappeared. Not a one, I was told, had reappeared since the men had started vanishing into the schoolyard, and no sounds could be heard from within. Several of the younger men on the far edge of the group got up from the steps at opportune moments and faded off into one of the streets leading away from the school and out of the camp.

As I walked back through the camp, women approached me, anxious, asking, "Are they beating them?"

"I don't think so. There is no sound."

Hours later I went back to the school, approaching it from behind, to see if I could spot the prisoners. On the other side of a chain-link fence, I could see them all sitting in the concrete courtyard in back of the school.

"*Salaam 'aleikom!* [Peace be with you!]"

The men looked my way. So did the soldiers guarding them, so I knew I had little time.

"The world knows!" I called to the men to hearten them. "The whole world is watching!"

This, of course, was a blatant lie, or, at best, wishful thinking, but I wanted to bring a little cheer. A soldier started quickly toward me, lifting his gun, and I ducked away.

The television was on in the house soldiers were in the

act of raiding when I entered. It was the final day of the World Cup—Brazil, Palestine's favorite, against Germany—and the Palestinian residents of the house and I, despite the soldiers' presence, kept finding our attention reverting to the screen. Even the soldiers seemed less involved in their ransacking than they might have been, although they'd avert their eyes from the TV and continue tossing aside the family's belongings when any of us saw them looking. After the game, I returned to the school where I had last seen the Palestinian prisoners sitting in the yard.

"I can tell you the result of the World Cup," I shouted over the fence to the soldiers inside the schoolyard. Five or six helmeted heads swiveled my way. "I'll tell you who won if you'll release the prisoners," I called to them. No one took me up on it. Their loss: the winner was Brazil.

From the camp, I called Rita on my cell phone. Rita, Muna's sister and head of the Institute of Community and Public Health at the university, was the one-woman volunteer emergency medical switchboard and general assistance coordinator, operating three phones continuously from her home. "Rita," I said, "I'm no use here. There's no one wounded. Got any other ideas?"

"The Red Crescent Maternity Hospital near your house has been fired on," she said, "and no one is being allowed in or out."

But by the time I got to the ward, there was no shooting and no one was trying to go anywhere. If I were to be of any use, I would have to go where the shooting was. I headed across town again, in the direction of the shooting I could hear, only to be hailed by two young men in the upper window of a hotel. Invited in, I was fed bean soup and warm fresh bread and lemonade, compliments of the hotel management. The two men told me that they had seen a man bleed to death that morning just down the road because Israelis would not let the ambulance get close enough to pick him up.

∽

And so it went for the rest of the spring and summer, good intentions, empty gestures. The most challenging mission involved walking through the *manara* past several Palestinians taking potshots with their Kalashnikovs at rooftop snipers, past the tanks and into the hospital for medicine I'd believed was vital, but which turned out to be for a skin rash, and the hospital didn't even have any. By then Rita had extended her medical service to providing non-emergency medicines for people with chronic conditions. Call a number, and in good time, an ambulance would arrive with the needed supplies.

"She went in!" I heard one of the groups of Palestinian fighters call out as I passed the tank. Someone, perhaps the same person, called again as I came back down the hill from the hospital. "And now she's coming back!" Relieved to have my back to the tanks and to be returning to what looked more like the "Palestinian side," I spread my hands in a gesture of greeting, and the men all cheered.

The next days I opted for milder duty, wandering down Nablus Road in my neighborhood past the tanks, and meeting my neighbors stuck in their houses. Bread, milk for babies, medicine for someone with a heart condition, for someone else with diabetes, small things I could find and carry back easily. Some of the houses and apartment buildings I visited had no water; some had no electricity. Some had neither. Tanks had cut electrical lines, broken water mains. Water gushed, un-collected, out of buildings. The baker near my house asked me to accompany him to deliver bread to the hotel where some sixty journalists were staying. Another neighbor gave me his van to go pick up bread (now that the bakery had opened), and some electric cable for a temporary hookup. He tried to send his children with me to show me the way, but I told him that the color of my hair might not be safe enough to protect the children, especially since it would be difficult to discern through the windows of a van. Everyone seemed certain hair color would get us through. They seemed to be acting in accordance with the words of the Prophet I'd first heard quoted in Egypt: "First tie your camel, then trust in God."

Those who could keep busy during the invasion had the best of it. When I passed the few resistance fighters, their spirits seemed good, even in the middle of the night, and their friendliness and courtesy staunch as ever. It was afterward—visiting the graveyard where so many had been buried; walking through the ruined streets of Qadoora Camp, strewn with cars burnt out or tanked flat for the fun of it; hearing of days of no water, no food, and no money to buy any; visiting the homes Israeli soldiers had occupied and looted and wrecked; passing downed power lines and broken water mains—that I began to grasp more fully what had taken place. Toilets had been stuffed with paper by the soldiers, overflowed, and then been declared off-limits to everyone. That might include fourteen, twenty-four, forty-three Palestinians crowded for days into a single room in a house or an apartment building. Mirrors and furniture had been shot up inside the houses, bathroom fixtures senselessly pulled from the walls. Drawers inside the Ministry of Culture had been filled with soldiers' feces.

Every day we heard shooting, the grinding tank-walk, the crash of their shells. One evening, my housemate, Ohaila, offered a rendition of the sounds of our life.

First, she made a muffled little sound: *"Pock! Pock!"* I recognized the Kalashnikovs, which, as we knew, made hardly any sound and could barely hit anything.

Next, she shouted, which she had never done before and never in my presence did again: *"Ratatatatataatatat!"* Of course—the stronger, faster Israeli guns.

Then she roared: *"Bam! Bam!"* for the big guns mounted on the tanks.

For a moment, Ohaila made no noise at all. Perfect silence. Finally, in a tiny, high voice, she wailed: *"Wah-uh-wha-uh-wah-uh!"*

With luck, the Palestinian ambulance, which made us laugh.

∽

During the spring invasions, I had some bizarre encounters with soldiers. One night I sang loudly in English as I walked down the hill toward the *manara* in Ramallah, partly to cheer myself up and partly to make it clear to any Israeli soldier who might be nearby that I was not approaching stealthily with intent to harm. Although the Israelis did kill several developmentally challenged Palestinians in the course of the invasions, I hoped they would figure that anyone singing in English in the middle of the night would at least have no gun.

Sure enough, they were there.

"We'll shoot!" soldiers shouted at me from the center of the *manara*. "Go back. Do not come any further! We will shoot!"

I kept walking, waving a dingy white rag in one hand, signal that I would do them no harm. I had lost my long white scarf in an ambulance. When at last I reached the soldiers, one of them, presumably the one in charge, came toward me. He reached out his right hand in my direction. Assuming he wanted to take away my little flag, I handed it to him. But his hand bypassed the cloth, and instead, shook mine.

Was he trying to compliment what he viewed as courage? It wasn't courage; it was anger. Congratulate me on the fact I had not got shot? The decision had been his. Whatever his motive, I had no success getting him to free the six Palestinian men he had lined up against the wall.

On another day, soldiers were still in the center of Ramallah, but Palestinians were allowed out of their houses long enough to buy supplies before the curfew was called again. Angry because soldiers had set a coil of barbed wire and a bucket blocking people's way to the stores, I kicked the wire aside and lifted the bucket. A short but hefty soldier growled and came my way. He came quite close, lifted his gun, and pointed it at me. He was looking at me with an expression I'd never before seen in anyone's eyes and hope I'll never see again. I had read about it, though, and it was instantly identifiable. It was the look someone gives you when he is thinking of killing you and has the means to do so. I moved away fast, leaving the wire and the overturned bucket in the middle of the street.

A few days later, in another part of Ramallah, as I was trying awkwardly while walking to attach my limp white cloth to a long stick, to make it more visible from a distance, I saw the soldier who'd given me the look coming down the road on the opposite side. Not a promising encounter. But to my amazement, he approached me, reached out, and twisted the cloth firmly onto the stick. When he'd tied the rag, we both turned and walked away. Neither of us said a word.

$\backsim$

After some days or weeks of walking about on my own, I heard that volunteers from the Union of Palestinian Medical Relief Committees (UPMRC), headed by Mustafa Barghouti, who among other roles, was Rita's husband, and so also my friend Muna's brother-in-law, were delivering medicine and food by ambulance. People would call in to the office, volunteers would take their orders for medicine, clothing, and food, boys downstairs would load up the ambulance, and off they'd go. A doctor would go if he was needed; three doctors were taking turns in the makeshift clinic night and day.

I knew of Mustafa but had never met him. He was well-known for his role in Palestinian politics, as well as for the services the UPMRC provided. The foreign press frequently interviewed him or called upon him for comment. In addition, he looked a little stern. So it was with some trepidation that I approached him the day he happened to be in the apartment being used as storeroom and clinic and requested permission to drive an ambulance.

For a day or two Mustafa said no: "Too dangerous." But we both knew that Israelis would be less likely to shoot at an ambulance driven by a foreigner than at one driven by a Palestinian. In the end, he agreed, and so began my short but happy career as an ambulance driver.

A group of us would load the ambulance with supplies donated by aid organizations and Palestinians from inside Israel, including medicines and baby milk, and drive off to the bakery to pick up fresh bread, then go on our rounds, stopping to deliver and to take orders when people called to us. We all wore white vests identifying us as medics, with the prominent yellow logo of the UPMRC.

When I wasn't working, Lamis welcomed me at her house to rest and eat and sleep, since her house was much closer than mine to the center of town and the UPMRC building. It was comforting to be with a friend, too, since Ohaila was with her family in Nazareth.

One night there was a call that a building in town

was being hit with tank fire, and that thirty Palestinians had been killed. After having to put a little pressure on Mustafa, I was allowed to drive an ambulance to the site with Karim, a driver and medic, by my side. We heard shooting as we pulled up to the street where the tank sat. Israeli soldiers were milling around. One soldier came down and warned us in Arabic to drive no further. By that time I was doing what I always did, announcing on the ambulance loudspeaker as loudly as I could, repeating over and over, "We are foreigners [even though I was the only one]. We have come to pick up the wounded Palestinians. We do not have guns. We will not shoot you. We have come to pick up the wounded Palestinians."

We waited two hours. From time to time the same soldier who had approached us when we arrived came down to talk to us. I asked him if he was Syrian, because of his accent, but he told us he was a Jew from Lebanon. We talked about the occupation, and the soldier said, "At least we are not animals like you; we don't murder people in shopping malls."

We waited, still prevented from picking up anyone. When we asked about the wounded, the Israelis said, "We are taking them." At one point, we heard a call in Arabic: "Come out one at a time!" But we still weren't allowed to approach the men or go into the building. We could see people being herded into the army trucks that stood up the hill.

Finally, at about 1:30 in the morning, Israeli soldiers searched the ambulance and said we could pick up two bodies. But since we had been sitting there for two hours with the ambulance lights flashing, the battery was dead, and the Arabic-speaking soldier had to jump-start us with cables. At last we drove up the street to a little courtyard outside the entrance to the building. Two forms, covered with blankets, lay on the ground. Seeing only two bodies, Karim wanted to call the hospital. UPMRC had been informed by an Israeli officer that thirty people had been killed. The whole city had heard the explosion and people were frantic. But the soldiers wouldn't let Karim call. "Why not?" he asked, and the Arabic-speaking soldier said, "We want people to think we killed thirty."

"Pick them up! Take them away!" one soldier ordered, gesturing to the bodies. He told us they had checked one of the bodies, but not the other, and said, "Be careful."

Why?

"One of the bodies has no head."

Karim pulled back the blanket on the bundle they said they'd checked. The man lying there was slight, and his skin was very white. He was wearing only his underwear. He looked about twenty years old. His body felt light as we lifted him into the ambulance. Then we turned to the other blanket-covered form. Karim nodded to me and I bent, despite my better judgment, to uncover the man. His head was on his shoulders, although part of it was smashed in and his brains were on the pavement. The soldier had been trying to scare me, entertaining himself in the process. The dead man looked about sixty years old and was wearing an old tracksuit and slippers. We learned later that he'd come down the stairs of the apartment building, his hands raised, and stood next to the door. Neighbors said the soldiers had shouted at him to strip off his clothes, but that he did not understand Hebrew and apparently thought they were telling him to come forward. They shot him at close range in the chest and head.

We placed him on the stretcher, but then, to my embarrassment, although I tried as hard as I could, I could not lift my end. This man was taller and stockier than the younger man. For a moment, the stretcher hung, Karim holding up one end, fortunately the end where the man's head rested, while my end, nearest the feet, swung unsteadily a few inches from the ground. A soldier moved to help me lift, and the second body was stored like the first.

$\backsim$

The days ground by; the killings and arrests continued. One early morning, waiting to go out on an ambulance run, I found, scattered across a parking lot, the distinctive uniforms of Palestinian police—rag dolls minus their stuffing—along with boots, tins of food, forks, tin cups, and plates. The men, who had been sleeping in their cars, were all gone—arrested, we learned.

Another morning, I came upon soldiers making their noisy way through the otherwise deserted center of Ramallah, with a flock of foreign journalists following them through streets clogged with tangles of downed electrical wire and glittering with glass from the broken windows.

The journalists, intent on filming the soldiers as they shot open padlocks on metal store doors and fired into offices in the upper stories of buildings, irritably tried to shoo me out of the way when I tried to interfere. It was not the only time our interests differed, the journalists trying to photograph something the soldiers were doing and I trying to stop it.

On its front page, the Palestinian daily newspaper *Al Ayam* featured a series of photographs taken by Agence France-Presse at the Al Ram checkpoint between Ramallah and Jerusalem. The first several pictures depicted a young man being detained at the checkpoint by Israeli soldiers. In another, they had forced him to his knees. In a third, he was prone and facedown on the ground, with most of his clothes stripped off. In the last photograph, the young man was lying facedown without his clothes, hands behind his back, no weapons or explosives having been found, blood flowing from his head onto the asphalt. Shot at point-blank range, he was dead.

Meanwhile, in a large concrete building of offices, all closed, and family apartment units, still inhabited, volunteers worked throughout the nights and days in the Ramallah hub of the UPMRC. Women living in the building supplied the office with enormous trays and cauldrons of hot food they cooked for us in the adjoining apartments. Buoyed by the presence and energy of one another, Palestinian and foreign volunteers babbled in various languages and cheerfully made up packages of food and drugs or stacked boxes of bandages. Then, in ones and twos on foot, or in little teams riding in one of our few ambulances, we'd all scurry silently through Ramallah's neighborhoods, avoiding soldiers and tanks, delivering our supplies to hungry families and employees trapped in homes and banks and stores. In the larger landscape, we were almost invisible, like ants, and, like ants, well organized and purposeful.

∾

On April 1, Israeli troops moved into Bethlehem, Qalqilya, and Tulkarem. I learned from a woman I spoke to on the phone from Tulkarem that the wounded were lying in the streets where they had fallen, as Israelis prevented ambulances from entering the area. It was not the first time that the Israeli military had entered Palestinian areas, but the scope and scale and intensity of the invasions were greater than they had been at any time I had been living in Palestine. According to the BBC English radio, fifty tanks had surrounded Tulkarem, then entered the refugee camps. Soldiers occupied four or five apartment buildings, trapping the residents inside, and then shot from the buildings, using the families as human shields against possible retaliatory fire.

The next day, Israeli forces attacked the Preventive Security headquarters in Beitunia, near Ramallah. When the curfew in Ramallah was lifted for a few hours, a group of doctors dug a mass grave in the parking lot of a hospital and buried twenty-five of the bodies that had been retrieved over the past four days, as an F-16 roared overhead.

On April 3, Israeli troops occupied Beit Sahour, took

over the Bethlehem municipality, and invaded Jenin and Salfit.

On April 4, the Israeli military invaded the lovely city of Nablus and encircled three adjacent refugee camps, including Balata, the largest refugee camp in the West Bank. Fighters tried to defend the city, and were killed, along with unarmed men, women, and children. Over the next days, some of Palestine's most beautiful architectural heritage was destroyed, including in the Old City, famous for its architecture, its sweets, and its factories that made the olive oil soap used throughout Palestine.

A few internationals began to head out of Ramallah to see if they could be of any use in the cities in the north.

26: JENIN REFUGEE CAMP

Jenin (pronounced *Je-neen*) shares the same Arabic root as the following English words: *cover, hide, conceal; descend, fall; demon; garden, paradise; obsession, madness, insanity, rage, fury; rapture; protection, shelter, shield.*

Shortly after the attack on Nablus, we heard that the refugee camp even farther north, in Jenin, had been bombed. Israel had claimed that the camp "served as a launch site for numerous terrorist attacks against both Israeli civilians and Israeli towns and villages in the area."

But the roads were closed to ordinary traffic; I would never be allowed through the checkpoints.

It was my good luck at that time to run into Amira Haas. With her press credentials, and as a Jewish Israeli, Amira, I knew, would be able to travel the roads inside Israel and to reach at least the outskirts of the refugee camp.

Amira told me that no one but the Israeli military was being allowed into or out of the refugee camp itself, but she agreed to let me ride with her as far as she could go. We talked on the way, and I tried to learn the answer to a question that has always interested me about those who don't act like everyone else: At what point had she become a queen, instead of a worker bee?

She surprised me by declaring herself "a complete conformist." Her father, from Romania, and her mother, from Yugoslavia, via the German concentration camp Bergen-Belsen, met in the Communist Party when they immigrated to Israel in 1949. As they moved about Israel doing work for the party, they always took Amira with them. When they first arrived in Israel, her parents, like other newcomers, were offered a house from which Palestinians had been expelled. But Amira's mother said, "We ourselves are refugees. How can we take the home of someone who is a refugee like us?" Although they knew nothing of the history of the Palestinian people, Amira's parents lived by the communist dictum "from each, according to his ability; to each, according to his need."

In Amira's eyes, therefore, she was just a well-brought-up child. She was impatient with other journalists who wanted to interview her. Irritably, she would ask them, "Why do you interview me when there are 3.4 million Palestinians and all of them are heroes? This is the first time I have lived through something like this—and voluntarily—while Palestinians have been forced to endure this treatment every day of their lives."

We spent the night along the way in the home of Amira's Palestinian photographer. Next day, the three of us drove as near as we could get to the camp, stopping at a village some miles outside, where soldiers were preventing cars from driving farther. On the edge of the village we found a big crowd of mostly foreign journalists, all sitting on a veranda overlooking a valley. Through that valley and some miles on down the road, I was told, lay Jenin. A couple of soldiers were stationed at the top of a steep hill above the valley.

I was still wearing the white vest with the striking red and yellow logo of the Union of Palestinian Medical Relief Committees (UPMRC), so I looked like a medic, rather than a journalist or photographer. I carried no camera. I hesitated a few moments at the top of the hill, then started down alone on foot, hoping I wouldn't be shot in the back as I descended into the valley. Amazingly, I was allowed to go. Across the valley I came to the next village, where more journalists, as well as nurses and doctors, were also waiting to be allowed into the camp. In the meantime they were interviewing or providing medical care for Palestinian men whom the Israelis had taken from the camp, interrogated, and released.

But I was anxious to reach the camp and figured that since I was on my own, rather than a journalist or part of some official delegation, I might have a chance of getting in. I'd walk until I was stopped. And so, through the brilliant morning, I walked past bright green fields studded with yellow flowers, and through silent villages with nothing in sight except a stationary tank or two. Leery, I ignored them. Though once, coming upon a tank parked in the middle of a crossroads, a soldier's head startled me by popping out of a hole in the top of the tank, and I asked it the way to Jenin. The head dropped down into the tank a moment, then reappeared with more of the soldier attached, including a pair of hands holding a map. The soldier consulted it, pointed straight down the road I was on, and I walked on by.

I arrived in Jenin Refugee Camp on the afternoon of April 14, eleven days after the Israelis had invaded. The Israeli military was still not letting the UN and the Red Cross or any of the other local or international relief or human rights organizations enter the camp. The usual camp characteristics, the dust, the crowding, were present. But the lower portion of the camp, at the bottom of the hill on which most of the camp is built, was completely empty. Not a human being was to be seen or heard, not in the streets, not in a single doorway. Not one face appeared in a window. No car, no cart moved. People in Wadi Burqeen, one of the villages I'd passed through on my way to Jenin, had told me that residents of the lower camp, near its outer edges, had fled or been forced out when soldiers first entered the camp.

In the unnatural stillness, however, I found myself making use of another sense on which most of us depend. This was the sense of smell, and what I smelled was death.

The stench is unmistakable. Even encountering it for the first time, no one needs to be told what it is: every human pore, every hair follicle strains away from the smell. When I walked into the camp, the reek rode on the still, dusty air, snaked out of open doorways, rose from rubble

and dirt and from water running in the streets. The awful smell and lifelessness made the camp seem a place of plague.

Each doorway in this part of the camp opened on the same scene of destruction. Every human artifact had been willfully wrecked or destroyed—mirrors, bathroom fixtures, kitchen cabinets. Televisions lay smashed; drawers and cupboards were broken; salt, beans, lentils, rice lay scattered amid shards of glass from smashed containers; metal, cloth, plastic, tin—everything spilled out onto the floor. Bedding was thrown about in disarray.

There were still tanks in the camp, and a few soldiers, whom I tried to avoid. Several saw me, but they let me stay, perhaps because they had ended their military action and also because I was obviously not Palestinian and had entered unseen, wearing a medic's vest, by a less-traveled dirt road, without a camera or vehicle. And they may have let me stay also because I was female and alone. They told me not to enter any of the houses; I could be blown up, they said, by explosives Palestinians had left behind. *Not likely*, I muttered under my breath. *Clearly you've been in each house ransacking.*

The smell of death also gave question to the story: clearly, some camp residents had been killed in these houses and their bodies had since been moved. But where?

Cover, hide, conceal; descend, fall . . .

The curfew continued unbroken for days more after I arrived. The first Palestinians I glimpsed were hiding high up the steep hillside on which the camp is partly built. A group of people of different ages, a family, probably, was sitting inside what was left of their house. Most of the walls lay in ruins around them, and part of the roof of the house had been blasted off, part caved in. The Palestinians and I were equally taken aback by the sight of one another. For a moment, I stared at them and they stared at me. Then I waved, and gestured round the back of the ruined building: Was that the way in? They nodded, their arms describing the same semicircle mine had made. I headed round the back, and out of sight.

Before I could get to them, another family appeared at another "window" in a blown-open wall close to where I was standing. They waved to me and gestured urgently. Picking my way through the shards of peach-colored half-moon tiles littering the alley, I came first to a larger opening blasted in the wall, this hole wide enough to serve as a door. I stepped inside. The dark center of the house had become a broken concrete cave where the family, like every other family in the camp, was living without electricity or gas, subsisting on dwindling quantities of uncooked food and water.

We greeted one another with smiles, hugs, and exclamations of wonder and surprise. Bright eyes looked into my own; wide smiles met mine, little hands reached for my larger ones. There were twenty-five of them in the house, a young man explained; mostly women and children, as I could see, but a few young men too, still in danger of being killed or taken by the soldiers.

In this immediate neighborhood I found some two

hundred more camp residents, all trapped, living in wrecked or ruined houses, hungry and thirsty, still fearing for their lives. On the small pad of paper I offered, one man wrote his name and the name of the quarter, ad-Dammaj, which sounded fitting, so that I could find them again and bring the precious supplies. When I asked them if they had water, they said no but still tried vigorously to refuse the bottle I had with me, while offering, again and again, with typical Arab hospitality, to make me coffee. I don't see how they could have made it if I had accepted. It was a measure of how little they had that I was not offered a choice—coffee, tea, cold drink—and served one or another, or even all three, even if I said no. The ritual politeness remained in place; only the drinks were missing.

∽

None of the people I met those first hours and days in the refugee camp in Jenin acted hopeless or defeated. In the camp, the human spirit, which can be so stunted, stood straight and tall, amid death and ruined lives. People generated love and the will to endure, and I skated on those forces amid the gradually unfolding pain. If Palestinians' hearts had not shown themselves so large, mine now would be less sad.

From that quarter high on the hilltop, I began my descent, until I came, unsuspecting, into the most ruined area of the camp. This ten percent of the Jenin Refugee Camp was a total disaster. Great slabs of concrete slanted upward from the rubble, their broken ends spewing spears of truncated rebar. Entire houses had been sheared open, leaving the insides of homes revealed like sets upon a stage. Most houses had been completely demolished. The nature and extent of the devastation reminded me of photographs I'd seen of European cities after World War II. The great void had been deliberately made by an Israeli soldier who later told Amira Haas that he had operated a bulldozer drunk the whole time, intending to carve out "a football field in the middle of the camp." He had done that and more.

Here, too, there was silence, except for the cries of chickens still trapped in their wire cages. I hoped the animals would provide sustenance if and when their owners returned.

Down the winding roads, here and there, a human being—a woman or a child—emerged cautiously from a house.

"Do you want to see the bodies?" each one asked, then led me into the cracked shell of a house, up broken concrete stairs, into a room emptied of everything but concrete rubble fallen on—on what?—a corpse, its flesh burnt black, no longer male or female, its skeleton head sticking out from the debris, eye sockets facing the ceiling. Up more stairs.

"Where is the other body?" the woman asked herself aloud, certain she'd seen it in this house before. Then: "Oh!" and she led me back up to a room next to the first, and there lay another corpse, scorched to the bone, the stench of burned flesh powerful as the image seared into my mind's eye.

I saw six Palestinian bodies that first day, two burned beyond recognition, the rest at least partly clothed, some broken and bloody. Open wounds swarmed with white, wriggling maggots and with flies. All of them stank with the smell of decomposing flesh. The scene most favored by the Israeli press, I saw later, was a man burned black, skeleton mouth grinning, his head capped with some kind of helmet, the only piece of soldierly or protective gear I saw on a Palestinian the entire time I was there.

If I had come for injured people, I had come too late: the injured had joined the dead.

"What do you need?" I asked.

Milk for babies, water, and food, in that order, came the replies. Then medicine, and an item that surprised me: disposable diapers, always referred to by the brand name Pampers, which I hadn't known were available in Palestine.

Down through the ruined camp I made my way that first afternoon, until a young man appeared from around a corner and led me to the man I asked for, Muhammad Abu Al Haijeh, in charge of the UPMRC for the camp. I found him, along with his mother, his wife, Tahani, and his neighbors, in a neighbor's house. His own house had been occupied by Israelis who rendered it unfit for use.

Warmly greeted, I learned I was in Harat as-Sumraa', Neighborhood of the Blacks; and in fact it might have been a corner of Upper Egypt or Sudan, so dark were the skins of many residents there. Two familiar cultures, Arab and African, double welcome.

Great care would be needed, I was told, because

Israeli soldiers were still in the camp, and still shooting; and although the military assumed they had arrested or killed all the young men in the camp, inadvertently I might lead them to someone they could arrest or kill. For safety's sake, each person acted as one short link in a chain that led me by only a few houses before passing me on to my next guide. In this way I was handed through the narrow streets, house to house, usually by children—smaller targets— until, in the care of two girls, aged fourteen and fifteen, I reached the nearby town of Jenin. Daylight was almost gone, and so we slept that night on the floor of a school with Palestinians who had escaped from the camp. Not until the next morning was I able to return the two girls I'd stolen to an anxious aunt and mother. From then on until the camp was opened, I went alone through the curfew, carrying only what I could carry on foot, from the UPMRC storehouse in the city through empty streets to the camp.

By this time Muhammad and Tahani had moved back into their house, swept up most of the glass and broken plaster, and scraped and scrubbed the human excrement from the sitting-room shelves and carpets where Israeli soldiers had deposited it. For the next two months, their home served as a distribution point for food and medicine and, when camp residents were allowed to leave their homes, as a temporary medical clinic. But for the time being, people remained trapped in their homes or in the ruins, or under their demolished homes.

As I walked about, those who dared called to me, or moved about quietly so I could see that they were there.

In many buildings, some of which had been blasted open on two sides so soldiers could move from house to house without being seen by people outside, I could see women and children hiding and looking up at me—fifty in one house, a dozen in another, sixteen here, unknown numbers there. We smiled and waved. I handed bottles of water and cans of babies' milk through broken walls.

When I reached the ground story of a house, older children often leaned down to receive the items and pass them to children on other rooftops; in this way, they distributed supplies to houses I could not reach. The concrete stairway leading to one house had been hit or bulldozed so that the stairs slanted backward, and you had to haul yourself up by the partially anchored iron stair rail to enter. In another house, where I found several women and at least a dozen children huddled, one woman showed me a child with a bad skin rash, and I raided the camp's already Israeli-ravaged pharmacy for medicine. While I was there, I gathered up handfuls of candy to bring the little ones. But some of the children cried and ran and hid their faces in their mothers' skirts when they saw me. I looked too much like the Israelis they'd seen invade the camp. Despite the goodies and their parents' reassurances, I remained an object of terror for one or two of the smallest.

Weeks later, I learned there were others who saw me from the first day but did not let me know they were hiding because they knew that wherever I went, soldiers could follow. Hungry and thirsty though they were, the young men still living knew better than to take that chance.

A few days after I arrived, Brian, a young American I'd met when he was working for an NGO in the West Bank, was able to enter the camp, along with a few other foreigners. At about the same time, the army allowed the Palestinian Red Crescent Society and the International Committee of the Red Cross into the camp as well. I came upon the ICRC white jeep, marked with the Red Cross insignia, stopped on its way into the camp, the driver talking to a contingent of soldiers. The soldiers had seen me coming and going in the camp for days, and one of them motioned me over to the car.

"Show them where there are living people," an officer commanded me.

"Of course," I said, "but not if any of your soldiers come along."

But that arrangement was not acceptable to the soldiers, and so the Red Cross jeep, along with its military escort, went on into the camp without me. That night, up on the hillside, in the direction they had gone, came sounds of Israeli gunfire.

∽

Finally, one day soon after, the people of the camp were allowed out of their homes for the first time since the camp had been invaded eleven days before. That day, for the first time, they saw the enormity of the destruction.

The first day camp residents were allowed out for a few hours, it was their new "football field" that they saw, the huge empty space where their homes had been. They learned that the devastation reached farther than they could see. Those who had been separated from their relatives or friends began looking for them, first among the living, then in the debris of houses.

That was the day Palestinian bulldozers were allowed into the camp, and while the camp residents scraped into the rubble with their bare hands, bulldozers began digging where houses had been destroyed. The terrible grind of the big machines as they started forward, backed up, and moved forward again, big shovels filling up mighty buckets with earth and broken concrete, sounded in our ears all day. From time to time, one or more dead bodies would be discovered, and a cry would go up as people ran to see who had been found.

All across the devastated landscape, men, women, and children were digging. One woman plucked black and white photographs from the rubble, turned them in her hands right side up, looked at the faces of people she loved. A woman near her unearthed a bloody pillow. But where was the body that had bled onto it? A child picked a schoolbook out of the sand, a notebook, a small backpack. Everyone was searching through rubble, picking through whatever meager possessions they could find, the air filled with the grating noise and the odor of decomposing bodies. It was heartbreaking.

As I stood, useless, with all this going on around me, I felt as if I were two beings simultaneously. I was both a Palestinian and an Israeli soldier, or US government and arms supplier, whose resources had made this possible.

We all had lost. We all *were* lost. I felt the awful place inside me from which the terrible actions might have sprung. I cried until a woman digging nearby pointed to her cheeks and mine, just as the Egyptian woman had the first day I'd been in Cairo years before. "Don't cry!" she urged. "You'll get a headache."

It was with an enlarged sense of my own humanity—and of my own inhumanity—that I ended that day.

∽

When I was in the camp and later, Palestinians always asked about Jenin: How many people had been killed? There was no way to know. The first day I entered the camp, I saw six bodies. The second day I saw seven. Sometimes I was led by smell. The third day I saw four bodies and came upon a chicken pecking at a severed foot sticking out of sandy rubble. Several yards away, I saw another foot unattached to a body. The ankles of both feet wore shreds of blue-and-green-striped sock, but the feet were at impossible angles to one another and an impossible distance apart. Stupidly, I stood there staring, unable to calculate if one was a right foot, the other a left—whether the two feet belonged to the same person. As the days went on, bodies appeared more piecemeal.

Once, on one of the streets that Israeli bulldozers had enlarged to allow easy passage for tanks and more bulldozers, I found an odd, gray, sack-like thing. Except for the smell, I would not have guessed it had ever been alive. What was this thing, elephantine in texture as well as color? It was nothing that I knew. Later, Dr. Muhammad Abu Ghali, director of Jenin Hospital, located on the edge of the camp, identified it as tanked-over human remains. A tank had passed enough times over what had once been a human body to reduce it to a kind of gritty sack of crushed bone and muscle.

Soon after my arrival in the camp, residents in a certain area told me that a neighbor had called them several times on his mobile phone, saying he was buried in the bathroom under the ruins of his house. The last call had come two days before, and although the neighbors had tried many times since to call the man, he had not answered. Neighbors speculated that he might still be alive, unable to communicate because the battery on his mobile phone had died.

I went to look for him. I found where the house had stood, and even found the top portion of what were unmistakably bathroom tiles sticking up out of the rubble. A teenage girl from the camp whose name was Amal (meaning "hope") appeared at my side as I began digging.

"A man is here! A man is here!" she kept saying, as we clawed at the earth with our hands, calling the man's name. We got some distance down into the area where he must have been buried, but each time we stopped to listen, we heard only silence. Only when the stench of decomposing flesh swarmed up to choke us did we give up our search.

Amal accompanied me for days after as I went on my rounds throughout the camp. She was fourteen years old. Slight in build, serious, stern, she was the first of the camp residents to join the volunteers, and among the most courageous and dedicated of any I knew.

∽

After the Israeli military left the camp, those who had taken refuge in neighbors' houses or in the hospital at the edge of the camp went back to their homes and exchanged stories of what they had endured. The family I had been staying with had returned to find that the soldiers who had occupied the house had deposited feces on the carpet in the main room. Entire families told of soldiers' forbidding them from accessing a bathroom. Those who lived in houses that had been built close together returned home to find gaping holes blasted in the outer walls of the houses, enabling the soldiers to pass from house to house without showing themselves. All these stories and more were told to journalists and internationals who came into the camp.

Later, at night, though, in the privacy of family, something curious would happen. This time the events would be bandied about as objects of humor, everyone howling with laughter at the very incidents they had described with such seriousness earlier in the day. At first I was taken aback: how could they be laughing at their own pain and humiliation? But soon enough I was doing the same—tipping the scenarios upside down, caricaturing the real events, and laughing myself breathless with all the rest. A person must go far into an unpleasant place to reach the point where humor renders the memory bearable.

∽

After the Red Cross and UN met many of the emergency needs of those still living in the camp, Brian and I began to interview camp residents about what they had experienced during the invasions. We would give our report to Palestinian NGOs, so that what had happened in the camp could be more widely known. Our methods were rigorous. No detail was allowed to pass unchecked, unchallenged. If it turned out that the person who was speaking had not seen or experienced the event him- or herself, we tried to find someone who could verify it firsthand. If we couldn't find anyone, we struck it from our record. One of us took notes while the other one interviewed, and after a time we obtained a video camera to record every person who spoke to us.

Witnesses were not hard to find. Medical relief workers testified that they were shot at when they tried to enter the camp in answer to residents' calls for help. Ambulances were shot at, and several were disabled or destroyed. Camp residents cited instance after instance of family and neighbors bleeding to death after being injured by gunshot, missile, or tank shell, or after having their houses bulldozed on top of them. They told us that people had been shot or their houses bombed if they so much as made a sound or showed their heads in windows or doorways. No noise was allowed; neighbors in one house could not call to those in another, and no one was allowed to move in the streets or on a rooftop.

From person after person, we heard testimonials of entire families or individuals being forced to act as human shields. Families had been herded into a single room of a house or apartment while soldiers took over the rest of the building and, from inside, fired at those outside. We were told that soldiers also took individual civilians, male or female, old or young, door-to-door throughout the camp, making them batter open the iron gates or stand beside the soldiers while they burst open a gate or a door with an explosive device. After the door was opened, the Palestinian was forced to enter the house in front of the soldiers, so that he or she would be the one to receive the blast of any explosives planted or bullets fired by Palestinians inside. One man described, voice and manner expressionless, how a soldier, on a whim, had killed his unarmed son.

"He shot him, with many bullets, and my son fell. And I fell beside him, so that the soldiers would think I had been shot also. I lay with his blood flowing down the sloping concrete toward me, until I was lying in a great mess of it."

We stood over the little concrete gutter in which his son's blood had collected.

"And there I stayed, for five hours, so the soldiers would think I was dead while they hung around the house."

The man's daughter-in-law, the wife of the man who had been killed, had been standing just on the other side of the door to the inner courtyard, where soldiers had locked up the women and children. Hearing the shots, she guessed that her husband, and maybe her father-in-law, too, had been killed, but was unable to go to them. She spoke of this calmly, her lovely face serene.

How could she speak with such gentleness, without apparent grief? How could her father-in-law speak without emotion? I hoped these early tellings could be in some way useful to those who talked to us. What was clear was that these tellers, who had endured so much, had built a protective shield around themselves, which the words they spoke could not penetrate. I know I did the same.

Another woman we interviewed told us that she, her mother, and her sister, all adults, were in their house when they heard a soldier call from outside the courtyard, "Come out and open the gate!"

The women did not answer, but the soldier called again, threatening to blow up the house if someone did not come.

So the older sister, in her thirties, left the house and walked along the short outdoor corridor, while her mother and sister watched from a window. Just as the woman reached the gate, there was a terrible explosion, and she was hit by a blast in the face. The younger sister showed us: on the wall were still bloody pieces of matter—the woman's eyes and cheek. Her teeth, she told us, had fallen to the ground.

War, we think, and we imagine something abstract. A just reason. Governments. Armies. But here, there was just one army. Didn't war take two? So why these stories we were told? Why did one soldier walk atop a corpse, laughing? Why did another walk on the shoulder of the man he had just shot, when he could have walked around? Why did a third soldier put his gun to the head of a two-year-old and ask him if he was ready to die? Why did someone drive a tank back and forth across a dead body until it became a slab of raw meat? And why did another soldier point his weapon at the developmentally challenged boy accompanying his grandmother to the hospital and blow him to kingdom come?

One man described how, after putting the family into one room, soldiers refused his aged grandmother permission to use the bathroom, so that she defecated on herself in front of everyone. Why had the soldier prevented her son, who moved to help her, from taking her aside and wiping her clean?

The horror was in the details.

Demon; obsession, madness, insanity, rage, fury . . .

I tried to tell people what I saw they still had left. I told them they had big, generous hearts, strong spirits, that they understood injustice and her opposite, and that these were greater gifts than all the material commodities the world could offer. Presumptuous of me, when they had lost so much. But they nodded—they knew.

As the camp gradually became more porous to outsiders, individuals and small groups arrived from France, Italy, the US, Holland, Spain, to volunteer their help. I turned to these foreigners for help in hauling food and water. But one day, as I wandered about searching for a non-Palestinian face, a mountain of children called to me from the highest point in the shattered landscape. Up on top of the very point of a tilted concrete slab, with their posters and Palestinian flags, they waved and called:

"Chips! Chips!"—their version of my name. They liked saying it; after all, it's not every day that a child gets the chance to call a grown-up a fried potato, as in "fish and chips." I waved back and called hello; then, after a second's scrutiny for strength and height, called to them again.

"Want to come with me to get water?" I shouted across the distance, as no self-respecting Palestinian adult would do. Fortunately for me, the children were just the right ages—seven, eight, nine, I guessed—for a venture of such dubious appeal.

"Yes!" came the cry, and the multicolored mountain unwound and began squirming erratically toward me. We headed toward one of the two places where I knew water could be found—down the hill, outside the camp, in a building in Jenin where the UN had stored bottles of water and a lot of powdered baby milk until it could distribute them.

∽

After the initial numbness of grief, and of amazement at the miracle of their collective survival, came anger. Tempers grew short. Angry words were exchanged here and there. There was grumbling at the shortage and slow delivery of food and water; and one young man killed another, it was said, in a fight over food. Those who heard of the killing shook their heads in sadness. Even the little ones sometimes fought.

A couple of times, when I found young boys arguing, I urged them to stop.

"This would be useful for Israelis, if Palestinians fought each other, if you were divided. But you belong together, and together you will be strong."

And—ever amazing me, from the West—the boys would listen to an adult, even one from outside their culture, and, for the moment at least, let their anger go.

Meanwhile, children, many without shoes or books or notebooks, all of which had been burned or buried under the ruins of their homes, were returning to school—in double shifts, due to the destruction of schools by the Israeli soldiers.

"What did you learn?" I asked of the three girls of ten or twelve who stopped by to visit me each morning after the early shift. That day, they'd brought me a rose.

"Did you learn anything today?"

"Oh yes!" they assured me eagerly. They had learned how to recognize some of the unexploded ordnance still lying around in the camp, capable of blowing off a hand or a leg or putting out an eye. In the first weeks after the camp had opened up, we heard several explosions each day, as a child was injured, blown apart, or badly burned by these unexploded bombs, parts of missiles, or grenades.

Meanwhile, all those who were living in the camp before the invasion were grieving, not only individual losses, but the destruction of their community, an entity in its own right. The refugees had to a large extent built their camp and managed it. There was a strong sense of community, which had been expressed in clean, orderly streets and a helping hand, which made the people proud.

Now this too had been torn. Some 4,000 people had been forced to leave the camp: many homes were unlivable, and buildings not completely demolished were about to be. By the time I left the camp, about a month after I had arrived, most of the homeless, now refugees twice over, had gathered their few remaining possessions and left to stay with relatives or friends outside the camp. They'd ridden away in borrowed trucks piled high with bedding, kitchen pots, bits of clothing, a refrigerator that was not too badly damaged, a wardrobe made of packed sawdust covered with a thin veneer chipping off due to water damage and decay. Those who still had jobs and were able to work returned to their jobs. Those who remained grieved not only the loss of their neighbors and friends, but the loss of what they had shared together. Although originally from Haifa, many residents of Jenin Refugee Camp had grown to love their home and the lovely fertile fields and orchards, famous throughout Palestine, which surround the dwellings.

Garden, paradise, protection, shelter, shield . . .

For weeks, anyone who looked up, just about any time of day, to the upper stories of the houses still precariously standing, would see people sitting on chairs in rooms open to the air. Framed by jagged wall edges and in full view because the entire front of the building had been blasted off, the figures looked like actors on an elevated, far-off stage, engaged in a performance.

In the camp, I had found all the meanings of the word "Jenin" except *rapture*.

◡◠

Brian and I left Jenin Refugee Camp when we were exhausted and had run out of people to interview. For a month, we had been sleeping on the living room floor in Muhammad and Tahani's house. It was time we left them to themselves. Ramallah was still being invaded, and although there the tasks were now shared by more people and were well organized by the UPMRC, people's needs were much the same.

But I wasn't the same. Now I was furious—at everyone—for no reason having to do with them. No longer on ambulance duty, I borrowed a baby carriage and delivered food around town to everyone I could find who needed it, including men who remained trapped inside the Arab Bank and various restaurants. I scowled at photographers who took my picture. I snapped at my fellow volunteers and even, for a reason I no longer remember, shouted once at members of the very family to whom I was bringing food.

That summer, there were no classes at the university. Paid workers, along with volunteers, cleaned the streets; people began to repair or rebuild their homes and stores and offices; and Palestinians throughout the West Bank and Gaza dealt with the trauma they had experienced in any way they could. Surviving sons and fathers were returned to their families, many wounded, mutilated, in shock like everyone else; mothers and sisters began to reshape their lives to include nursing and caring for those they loved who had been damaged in various ways, many of them permanently. Foreign NGOs sent therapists and set up clinics, but the Western way of speaking to strangers and professionals has not been the Palestinian way. Besides, some of us wondered, if a central aim of therapy is to help a person to adjust to and accept the world as it is, what would be the merit in helping someone to adjust to a life like this? Whatever healing took place, it seemed to those of us from outside the culture, took place in family and community.

Back in the US for a couple of months, Brian and I spoke in California, where I had lived, in Colorado, where Brian had family, and in Arizona, where I did. We spoke everywhere we were invited to speak on radio and television, to journalists, churches, and community organizations, telling what we had seen. At summer's end, we returned to Palestine.

Epilogue: After Jenin

For a long time after the spring of 2002, my mind categorized everything that happened as either before the invasions or after the invasions, and, in the case of those of us who had been in Jenin, as before or after Jenin. For a long time, too, walking through Ramallah or Al-Bireh, spotting a brick walk newly laid or the side of a house restored, I saw each time in my mind's eye the thing undone, bricks all smashed and scattered, the wall caved in, as if in the future lay only more destruction.

In my own home, things had changed as well. Ohaila had moved out, and another woman came to take her place. Eventually Fadwa returned from England, but she went to work at Al-Quds University in Jerusalem, where she founded a women's studies program, and she never returned to Al-Bireh to live. New housemates came and went, mostly foreigners, and for a long time I missed the first two friends with whom I'd shared a home. Outwardly, life began to resemble what it had been before the invasions. The intifada continued in its tepid way.

Meanwhile, a number of Palestinians I knew who were of middle age were dying. Taisir Hammad, who had welcomed me so warmly into the Department of Languages and Translation, and Izzat al-Ghazzawi, a renowned Palestinian author who had also taught in the department, both died of heart attacks. Nawal's husband died, and Moussa's brother, and Rema's only nephew. Palestine lost three of her most respected figures—Faisal Husseini in 2001, followed by Edward Said and Ibrahim Abu-Lughod in 2003. Since I've left Palestine, Lamis has lost her mother and Muna her son-in-law, a much-loved Palestinian musician.

I lived in Palestine for six more years after the invasions of 2002. During that time and ever since, Israel has continued to construct the apartheid wall, annexing to Israel another 9.5 percent of West Bank land, including Israeli settlements, aquifers, and fertile land.

In 2003, the US invaded Iraq again, initiating the Second Gulf War. The following year, President Arafat died. In 2005, Israel "disengaged" from Gaza, removing Jewish settlements, but continued to shut off Gaza from the rest of Palestine and the rest of the world. In 2006, Hamas won an election that gave the party a majority in the Palestinian Legislative Council and formed a new government. Displeased at the election result, the US and other Western countries cut off aid to Palestine. The following year, PNA head Mahmoud Abbas dissolved the government led by Hamas, and Hamas took over governance of the Gaza Strip. Gaza, still cut off from the rest of Palestine and the world, has become poorer and poorer. In 2008, in response to rockets sent into Israel from Gaza, Israel carried out a major attack on Gaza. Israel has attacked Gaza every year since then. The deadliest attack came in 2014, lasting fifty days and resulting in the deaths of more than 2,000 Palestinians, including more than 500 children, and wounding thousands more.

Each year, Jenin Refugee Camp commemorates the invasion of spring 2002 with a day of remembrance. Two years after the invasion, when I first could bear to, I went. Some new houses had been built, and they were nice. But the drunken soldier's "football field," now cleared of fallen houses and rubble, remained an open wound in the center of the camp. Before the ceremony began I walked into the empty space and sat down. A light wind blew back the cries I had heard when I was there.

By then many people who had fled the camp during the invasion had returned, and a group of children I didn't know, maybe six or seven years old, came down the hill when they saw me. I felt too sad to call to them. A few threw exploratory stones at me. I didn't scold them; I got up and walked away. I couldn't blame them. Had I been in their place, I might have done the same.

In July 2008, I left Palestine. Palestinians still demonstrate against the Israeli military occupation of their lands. In the West Bank, entire villages have held demonstrations every week for years. Foreigners and Israelis sometimes join them, and minor adjustments in the route of the wall have been made; but no one has been able to stop its progress. Palestinians continue to be killed and injured by Israelis as they participate in peaceful demonstrations. Israel continues to build settlements across the West Bank.

Gaza remains a prison, sealed off from the rest of the world. Israel doesn't allow enough food or clean water into Gaza, nor does it provide new hospitals or schools, and Gazans cannot leave to find or provide them on their own. When enterprising Gazans dug tunnels in the dirt in an effort to bring what they need from Egypt, Israel bombed the tunnels. The lovely airport in Gaza was bombed and rendered useless soon after it was built; and fishing boats are only allowed to travel three to six nautical miles from shore. Israel continues to demolish homes and other buildings. It continues to bomb and bulldoze the agricultural land on which Gazans try to grow their food. Exports are damaged or held so that Gaza is unable to trade with the outside world.

It always surprised me when, each time Israel finished a period bombing and invading Gaza or the West Bank, friends in the USA and Europe would write to me: "Well, things are okay now in Palestine, I'm glad to see."

"Things" are never "okay" in Palestine.

ᔑ

My heart does not heal from the time in Jenin, or in all of Palestine. As I write, there is upheaval, caused by both outside forces and inside differences, throughout the Arab world and in the broader Middle East as well—in Egypt, Tunisia, Syria, Iraq, Lebanon, Libya, Bahrain, Yemen, Afghanistan . . . Israel, supported by the US, still makes war on Palestinians, the US makes war across the region, and both countries threaten Iran as well. But the laughter, the kindness, and the enduring spirit of the Arab people I know remind me each day that through any loss, any oppression, it's possible to continue living and remain the best of what is human.

I lived continuously in the Middle East for more than sixteen years. Since then, I have traveled in Europe, Africa, Central America, and Asia, and found much to appreciate in all these places. The world is beautiful, filled with kind and generous people, unique customs, lovely works of art. But everywhere I go—Granada, Mombasa, Zanzibar, Kuala Lumpur—I find myself seeking out signs of Arab and Muslim life. Always I am drawn to what for me is most truly "home."

I always listen for the call to prayer.

AUTHOR'S NOTE

Although this is one person's experience, occurring in a specific period of time, everything I have described is happening today. The situation in Palestine doesn't change—except to become more excruciating for the people living there and all who care about them. In Palestine, you never hear people say, "Well, at least things can't get worse." Only the details differ, day to day, year to year, generation to generation.

Acknowledgments

I thank the people of Egypt, Syria, and Palestine, who opened their hearts to me and gave me of themselves and their civilizations. Without your welcome, I would be a poorer person indeed.

Special thanks go to Abdelhalim Ibrahim Abdelhalim, his sister Nahid, his brother Muhammad, and the rest of your family; to Hassan Fathy; to Hassan Ali Ibrahim and his sons, Mustafa and Mahmoud, and all your family; to Muna Giacaman and Lamis Abu Nahleh and your families; to Sharif and Pat Kana'ana, Fadwa, Ohaila, Moussa and Yusef; and to Abu Khaled and Taisir, who brightened every visit to the center of Ramallah; to my colleagues at Birzeit University; and to all the other thousands of people whose names I know and whose names I do not know, who welcomed me into your worlds and made yours part of mine.

Heartfelt thanks go to my brother Will, for tipping me over the brink into writing; to Sally Floyd, without whom this book would not be in print; and to Sally and her partner, Carole, who nurtured me through the years of my comings and goings. To my high school teachers, Betty Reardon, who offered us the world, and George Mayer, who taught me to describe it, I offer a lifetime of gratitude. Thanks also to Anne Menna, Jan, Terry, and everyone else who encouraged me over the years and helped make it possible for me to do this work. Sincere thanks also to my editors, Kate Ankofski, Annie Tucker and Alan Rinzler.

And, in no way the least, to my beloved Pat, whose love sustains me through it all.

WORKS CITED

de Lubicz, Isha Schwaller. *Her-Bak "Chick-Pea": The Living Face of Ancient Egypt.* Translated from the French by Charles Edgar Sprague and illustrated by Lucie Lamy. New York: Inner Traditions International, Ltd., 1978.

Eberhardt, Isabelle. *The Oblivion Seekers and Other Writings.* Translated from the French by Paul Bowles. San Francisco: City Lights Books, 1978.

Fathy, Hassan. *Architecture for the Poor: An Experiment in Rural Egypt.* Chicago: The University of Chicago Press, 1973.

Galwash, Dr. Ahmad A. *The Religion of Islam* Vol. II. The Supreme Council for Islamic Affairs, Studies in Islam Series. Cairo: SOP Press, 1966.

Kritzeck, James, Ed. *Modern Islamic Literature from 1800 to the Present.* NY: New American Library, 1970.

Russell, John. "The Enduring Fascination of Ancient Egypt." *New York Times Magazine*, Dec. 17, 1978.

Shah, Idries. *Wisdom of the Idiots.* NY: Dutton, 1979.